# THE
# WIDE, WIDE
# WORLD
# OF
# TEXAS
# COOKING

# THE
# WIDE, WIDE
# WORLD
# OF
# TEXAS
# COOKING

★

## Morton Gill Clark

❧

BONANZA BOOKS · NEW YORK

# Acknowledgments

Various people have contributed much toward the writing of this book not only with recipes but with suggestions, advice and sometimes criticism. Without them, as a matter of fact, there would have been no book. So here and now I thank them. First, Mrs. Jack Owens (Dorothy Sue McCauley) of Burleson, Texas, who collected scores of recipes for me from her friends, relatives and sometimes even strangers. In addition she sent me reams of Texas lore, ancedotes, and gustatory gossip. She sent me typical Texas home menus of the past and present. And she spent hours in second-hand book stores in Dallas and Fort Worth, digging out old books about Texas which had in them first-hand accounts of old-time barbecues, celebrations and early ranch and farming life. She gets extra thanks. And thanks, too, go to her brother Billy Ray McCauley, once of Hillsboro and Dallas, who prodded me into writing this book. And then I am grateful to Mrs. Weldon Brewer of Austin, Mrs. Joan Walker Iams of New York (once of Lampassos), Miss Emily Coleman now of Greenfield, Massachusetts, and Mrs. Ed Nemecek of West, Texas. Without them the book would have been thin indeed.

# Contents

# ONE

## *INTRODUCTION*

THIS book obviously has to do with Texas cooking and its size, quite as obviously, shows that the wide world of this region's cooking has been reduced to a mere essence. This may well be to the good. With limited space at one's disposal and so broad a subject to deal with, one must cull with double care to include only those recipes that are pure Texan—*puro Tejano*. But what is "pure Texan"?

Many Texans no doubt will challenge the right of a non-Texan to say what is and what is not a truly Texas dish. With cookery as with other matters, however, an outsider often gets a clearer view of the situation than one immediately and emotionally involved. And Texans are emotionally involved with everything that pertains to Texas, even when they have lived away from their native state for years. The outsider, by examining and comparing many recipes, soon spots those that are characteristic. Seasonings and methods make a pattern. But oddly enough, many of the characteristic recipes are not those most highly touted by housewives and cooks. Housewives recommend as a rule their special dishes that are made for special occasions—party fare; or they suggest those designed to show their sophistication and worldly experience, recipes picked up in the course of foreign travel or from some visiting celebrity. The characteristic dishes of a milieu are ones that housewives often take for granted, family dishes perhaps. They are mentioned casually if at all, so commonplace do they seem. And for the same reason housewives say nothing of the very things that give their meals a unique character. Texans, for instance, rarely mention the oceans of iced tea served at their tables. Oceans. You are left to discover for yourself that soup is something of a rarity at Texas tables. You have to discover that many of the dishes called "salads" in Texas are actually desserts (some are frozen creams) while the others appear either as a first course or as a main-course accompaniment, virtually never as a "salad course" following meat. And you must discover, too, that though broiled and grilled and barbecued meats are given the most lip service in Texas, the big, hearty, rib-sticking, "made" dishes are the backbone of the cuisine and are served daily in households of all kinds all over the state. It is in just such dishes, in fact, that the character of Texas cooking becomes most clearly evident—flavorful dishes with lots of gravy (Texans are as strong for gravy as they are for iced tea); lots of spring onions, lots of cheese; corn, cornmeal, green peppers, chili peppers, tomatoes; chicken, shrimp, pork, beef. And it is in the way these particular dishes are served—with what and when—that you get the character of Texas meals—friendly, informal meals with an old-fashioned abundance. There is in these dishes and in Texas meals a strong reflection of Texas itself and of the Texans who love it.

Who are the Texans? The typical Texan (of the mind's eye, at least) is a big man (never a woman) in Stetson and boots, open-handed to a fault, rich beyond measure, and given somewhat to boasting of his own and his state's resources. He speaks in hyperbole and superlatives; things in Texas, as he sees them, are the biggest and best in the world. But this is not really an imaginary figure and his statements are really not too much exaggerated. Texans ARE big and many of them are unbelievably rich and all are generous. If they talk in superlatives, it is because they have nothing around them that is not of outsize proportions. And if all is not indeed the best possible, most is very good and little, comparatively, is positively bad. Even those Texans who do not have ten or fifteen oil wells going for them or fleets of shrimp boats or a hundred thousand acres of rangeland, seem to have

4

more of everything than those similarly situated elsewhere. And this is what you find at the Texas table—more of everything.

Texans are predominantly of Anglo-Saxon origin, of course (as also are most Texas dishes, by way of the ante-bellum South: Spoon Bread, for instance, Grits, Sweet-potato Pone). But though other ethnic groups may have produced fewer Texans in point of number, they have contributed culturally disproportionately much. And as the Texas Anglo-Saxons through contact with these cultural gifts have become more wholly Texan because of them, as though a new and separate ethnic group, so the Texas table has become wholly Texan, too, its characteristic meals showing a peculiarly Texan kind of independence and its once-English dishes, changed by foreign touches, often recognizable as English only because of English names.

Chief among the non-Anglo-Saxon groups in Texas are those of Mexican and Spanish descent. Mexican dishes, virtually identical to those used five hundred years ago by the Aztecs, make for a second culinary language in every Texas home. Their special seasonings have come to be THE seasonings of Texas dishes. And among the Spanish touches important to the present-day cuisine are the generous use of fresh parsley an an ingredient and the service of salad as a first course. You also find salad served thus in California.

And then there are Texans of Polish origin (Panna Maria is the oldest Polish community in North America; Polish Sauerkraut Salads are served all over Texas). There are many Texans of Bohemian or Czechoslovakian origin, too (*Kolaches* are a favorite Texas pastry). At Dannevang many Texans still speak Danish; Serbin was settled a hundred years ago by Wends from Saxony; Elroy, near Austin, and Clairmont were both settled by Swedes. And while the Creoles from Louisiana were settling along the Texas Gulf Coast (Galveston gumbos are as good as the best of New Orleans), the two thousand odd Alsatian French brought to Texas by Henri Castro before 1847 were making of Castroville a

5

thoroughly Alsatian town, even architecturally (the *Sucru Garni* of Castroville today was once the *Choucroute Garni* of Strasbourg).

And last but not least of the settlers to leave their mark on Texas, Texans and the Texas table were the Germans brought over by Prince Karl of Solms-Braunfels to build lives in the country around what became New Braunfels. Because of their strong antislavery feelings, the Germans lived in almost complete isolation from other Texans (eating almost precisely the same kind of food as the Pennsylvania Dutch) and so their culture remained more foreign than others to a later date. German was spoken almost entirely in the German communities until the First World War. But the German dishes, at a comparatively early date, moved on to other Texas tables—the sweet-sour pickles, the sweet-sour sauces, dumplings.

The typical Texan, then, big though he is, is not wholly Anglo-Saxon by any means, even though his blood may be predominantly so. He, like his table, is strongly marked by foreign influences. So strongly, in fact, that in other parts of the United States he often seems a foreigner. His expansive way of life and his expansive manner aid and abet this impression. This way of his, present-day riches notwithstanding, stems from the Texas way of life of a hundred years ago, the life of the plains. Space and expansiveness are in Texas blood, no matter what one's ethnic heritage. Space is Texas.

The size of Texas is incomprehensible to anyone who has not traveled through it. Its size was the very thing that, in the earliest days of its modern history, made it unmanageable for Spain. The Spanish missions even as late as mid-eighteenth century were less than drops in the bucket. The Spanish settlement at Nacogdoches that marked the eastern border of the vast territory had but fifty houses and three hundred odd settlers to stand against the French when Louisiana was ceded back to France by Spain in 1800—and few more than that to stand against the *Americanos* in 1803. This

6

at the gate of a world of size and kind unknown, stretching away limitlessly south and west.

From the Sabine River on the east, Texas today stretches through eleven degrees of latitude to a bend in the Rio Grande, just west of El Paso—so named by Don Juan de Oñate on the fourth of May, 1598, a generation before the Pilgrims' landing. From Oklahoma, Texas stretches south through the Panhandle, through thirteen degrees of longitude, to the mouth of the Rio Grande. Brownsville, at the southernmost tip of the state, lies eight hundred and one miles from the tip of the Panhandle, almost as far away as New York is from Florida. Texarkana on the eastern boundary is closer to Chicago than it is to El Paso. The state contains 267,339 square miles, being four times as large as all New England put together.

People living elsewhere in the United States think of ten miles as being quite a distance, but to Texans the vast world of their state is their neighborhood. They move through it and across it and around it as though the hundreds of miles were no more than a step next door. In the early days when households were few and far apart, hospitality was essential to life; doors were always open, food was made available to all. And this is essentially the same in Texas today; food is a part of welcome. It is interesting, in this connection, that the state was named for the Tejas Indians, leaders of the Hasinai Confederacy, when the Mission San Fernando de los Tejas was founded in 1690. *Tejas,* in the Indian tongue, means "friendship."

Within the bounds of Texas there are twelve distinct geological sub-regions, each with its own special riches. And across the face of the state, the names of cities, towns and hamlets add their riches, reminders of Texas' past and people, keeping the history of the state alive as almost nowhere else in the Union. And Texas people take great pride in this; like their meals and their dishes, the names are distinctively Texan. There are Indian names, for instance . . . Nacogdoches and Natchitoches. The names of

7

early explorers are kept alive . . . Galveston, for example, was named for Hernando de Galvez. Then there are soldiers' names as in Fort Worth; General William J. Worth commanded the United States Forces in San Antonio when the town was founded June 6, 1849. And the names of Texas heroes—Austin, Houston. Along with these, there are names that have a kind of human touch—Big Tussle; and names that remind of human foibles—Mineola, so called for Minnie and Ola, dear, dear friends of one Texas and Pacific Railroad official.

Texas, for the most part, is farmland and grazing land. Texas meals, for the most part, have a kind of rural simplicity about them, big as they usually are and lavish though they may be—but more often in quantity than in trimmings. In the large urban areas in the last quarter century, the cuisine has become more sophisticated, of course, due to more and easier foreign travel and culinary interchange—a different matter altogether from the old-time interchange. And in many homes you find more and more the influence of Miss Helen Corbitt, a culinary magician who has made of the Zodiac Room at Neiman-Marcus' Dallas emporium a kind of Texas shrine. But in most Texas homes, the table is much as it was fifty years ago. It is homey in a Texas way. (Texas housewives actually cook! They bake; they put up pickles and preserves!) And the supply of food set forth at meals three times a day seems as inexhaustible as the open spaces of the Rolling Plains—which, if less open than a hundred years ago, are still vast and impressive. (The rural population of Texas is somewhat less than twenty-five persons to the square mile whereas New Jersey, for comparison, has some eight hundred!)

Take breakfast, for instance. Breakfast in Texas is never a sliver of dry toast and black coffee. Breakfast is a meal. You have fruit, fruit juice, or "stewed" fruit (which in Texas does not necessarily mean *canned* fruit); you have hot biscuits or muffins with a quantity of butter and jam, preserves or honey. (Texans are great ones for honey and always have been; the Indians of the region, before the white man came, used it as their only sweetener.) You

8

have meat for breakfast in Texas, too, as well as eggs and often fried potatoes. And this is not just a solitary slice of bacon but ham cut in what elsewhere would be called steaks, fried and served with Raised Gravy (the Red Gravy of the South). Often there may be pork chops for breakfast—these with White Gravy (not to be confused with White Sauce). Or there might be sausage with White Gravy. Or Roast Beef Hash with a bit of *jalapeño* pepper in it. Or Fried Steak or *Grillades* or Chicken-fried Steak. Or venison. And as though this were not enough, you have hot cakes, too, or fried mush or grits with syrup or honey (and lots more butter and more jam or preserves)—and coffee. In some Texas households breakfasts may even include dessert.

Come the middle of the day, there is either lunch (no snack in Texas) or dinner. And the midday dinner is found not only in rural households, as you might expect, but in many city ones as well. In one city household the midday dinner follows such a menu as this: Fried Chicken, Cream Gravy, Fruit Salad, Hot Biscuits, Buttered Rice, Green Beans, Leaf Lettuce with Sliced Tomatoes and dessert. In another household, you find Baked Short Ribs, Cornbread, Cole Slaw with Cooked Dressing, Mustard Greens, Baked Fresh Corn and Pecan Pie. In yet another, Barbecued Spareribs (oven-cooked), Fresh Black-eyed Peas, Fried Okra, Cornbread, Sauerkraut Salad, Fresh Peace Ice Cream.

Come night, the third meal of the day is geared to whether the midday meal has been lunch or dinner—but anyway, it is also usually a full-scale meal, though sometimes (and this is the exception that proves the gustatory rule in Texas) this may be a snack. A bowl of sweet milk with fresh cornbread crumbled in it is a favorite Texas supper dish; the late Sam Rayburn called this "Crumbin'."

And then between meals in Texas there is virtually always cake on hand for those who want it; no state in the Union has as much cake as Texas. Or there are sweet breads, or nut breads, or fruit breads, to take the place of cake.

If you say (as you may) that you see no foreign touches here and that these menus look much like any of the late nineteenth century in rural America, I can only answer that the touches are not as evident in menus as they are in actual dishes and that these menus, like the majority in Texas, do indeed recall the nineteenth century. But whereas most nineteenth-century menus in other sections of rural America made use of local produce (as they had to), only in Texas did you find—as you still find today—such foods as black-eyed peas, for instance, used not only for family meals, and by the poorest families, but for party meals as well— and by the richest families. Only in Texas do you find at the same table reflections and culinary evidence of all the state's many ethnic groups—sometimes, and happily, all at once.

Only in Texas do you find that one of its ethnic groups has so influenced the basically Anglo-Saxon cuisine that it seems no longer foreign but indigenous. I speak, of course, of the Texas Mexicans whose culinary ways, mentioned before, have given a second language to every Texas kitchen and whose seasonings— *comino* (cumin), chili powder, chili peppers—have come to be used as standard seasonings for all kinds of dishes. As a result, these seasonings are what the non-Texan traveling through the state comes to think of as the Texas taste. And even those dishes which do not have any of these particular seasonings in them he finds have a kindred savor—which stems, of course, from the expansive Texas spirit that loves much of a muchness in anything.

Texas food is good primarily because Texans like to eat. Liking to eat, they demand food that pleases them. And they get the food that pleases them not only on holidays and at parties but three times daily seven days a week. The recipes that follow are all for this kind of Texas food—*puro Tejano*. I hope you will find them as good as I do.

# TWO

# SOME GENERAL INFORMATION

Tables of Equivalents
and an Explanation of the
Mexican Words Used
in Texas Cookery

THE flour used in all the recipes of this book is all-purpose flour unless otherwise specified.

Cream, when mentioned without other qualification in recipes, means light cream; heavy cream, when required, will be so indicated.

Many recipes in this book (and throughout Texas) call for evaporated milk. I suggest you use it when it is called for. It has special cooking qualities. Many others call for sweetened condensed milk and this you *must* use to get proper results. While it may seem superfluous to warn cooks about the difference between condensed and evaporated milk, I do so anyway. Where cooks are in the habit of using only fresh milk, mistakes can happen.

In virtually all recipes I have stipulated precisely what cooking oil or shortening to use because the quality of the finished dishes can be affected by the type of oil or shortening. Many Texas recipes call for lard and some for bacon drippings; these fats, of course, add a flavor of their own. So does olive oil; so does peanut oil. And butter has been stipulated throughout in preference to margarine because it is superior to margarine in every respect. If cooks wish to use margarine instead of butter, however, they may do so at will except when baking pastry or cookies.

Ham, in all cases, unless otherwise specified means commercially processed, ready-to-eat ham of good flavor and texture. Country-cured ham, when required, has been designated as such. For real ham taste it has no equal, and its cooking qualities, especially where frying is concerned, are unique.

Many recipes in this book call for special ingredients which may not always be procurable in your local supermarket. All are available in specialty food stores that deal in Spanish-American foodstuffs. Such stores may be found in virtually all American cities today. If you cannot find such a store, the following ones will fill mail orders promptly:

La Luz del Dia, 610 North Spring Street
Los Angeles, Calif. 90012

Casa Moneo, 219 West 14th Street
New York, N.Y. 10011

Mi Rancho Market, 3365 20th Avenue
San Francisco, Calif. 94132

La Sevillana, 2469 18th St. NW
Washington, D.C. 20009

El Milagro Grocers, 1114 South Halsted
Chicago, Ill. 60607

S. S. Pierce Company, 133 Brookline Avenue
Boston, Mass. 02215

The number of servings has been given with virtually all the recipes in this book, but it should be remembered that this is an approximation only. What makes an ample portion for one individual may well be only a teaser for another. So I suggest that you, knowing as you do the appetites of those you will serve, check the quantity each dish provides. This can be done quickly by getting a rough total of the cups in each. Then determine whether a half cup, a whole cup, or whatever, of this mixture will suffice for each person. You may find that your estimate will vary considerably from mine.

In the course of cooking—and invariably at crucial moments— even the most experienced cooks forget things. To help in such emergencies, here are some tables of measures and equivalents.

14

## Liquid Measures

"A pinch," "dash" or "few grains" = less than ⅛ teaspoon
1 teaspoon = 60 drops = ⅓ tablespoon
1 dessert spoon = 2 teaspoons
1 tablespoon = 3 teaspoons = ½ liquid ounce
1 liquid ounce = 2 tablespoons = ⅛ cup
¼ cup = 4 tablespoons
⅓ cup = 5 tablespoons plus 1 teaspoon
1 gill = ½ cup = 8 tablespoons
⅔ cup = 10 tablespoons plus 2 teaspoons
¾ cup = 12 tablespoons
⅞ cup = 14 tablespoons
1 cup = 8 liquid ounces = 16 tablespoons
1 pint = 2 cups = 16 liquid ounces = 32 tablespoons
1 quart = 2 pints = ¼ gallon = 4 cups = 32 liquid ounces
1 gallon = 4 quarts = 8 pints

## Dry Measures

1 dry quart = 2 dry pints
1 peck = 8 dry quarts
1 bushel = 4 pecks

## Avoirdupois Weight

1 avoirdupois ounce = 28.35 grams
1 pound = 16 avoirdupois ounces = 453.6 grams
1 kilogram = 1,000 grams = 2.2 pounds

## Common Sizes of Cans

| Size of can | Approximate Net Weight* | Net Liquid Contents† | Approx. Cupfuls | Average No. Servings |
|---|---|---|---|---|
| 6 oz. | 6 oz. | 6 fluid oz. | ¾ | 2 small |
| 8 oz. | 8 oz. | 7¾ fluid oz. | 1 | 2 |
| No. 1 | 10½ oz. | 9½ fluid oz. | 1¼ | 2 to 3 |
| No. 300 | 15½ oz. | 13½ fluid oz. | 1¾ | 3 to 4 |
| No. 303 | 1 lb. | 15 fluid oz. | 2 | 4 |
| No. 2 | 1 lb. 4 oz. | 1 pint 2 fluid oz. | 2½ | 5 |
| No. 2½ | 1 lb. 13 oz. | 1 pint 10 fluid oz. | 3½ | 7 |
| 46 oz. *or* No. 3 cyl. | 3 lb. 3 oz. | 1 quart 14 fluid oz. | 5¾ | 11 to 12 |

* The net weights of various foods in the same size can vary with the density of the product. The weights cited are for foods of average density.
† The volume figures cited are average commercial fills.

## Oven Temperatures
(All Fahrenheit)

| | |
|---|---|
| Very slow | 250° F. |
| Slow | 300° F. |
| Moderately slow | 325° F. |
| Moderate | 350° F. |
| Moderately hot | 375° F. |
| Hot | 400° F. |
| Very Hot | 450° F. to 500° F. |
| Broiling | 500° F. and over |

Here for your convenience is a list of the Spanish and Mexican words that crop up most frequently in the course of Texas cooking.

| | |
|---|---|
| AGUACATE | Avocado |
| AJONJOLI | Sesame seeds |
| ANCHOS | Hot red chili peppers |
| ANIS | Anise |
| AZAFRAN | Saffron |
| CABRITO | Kid (goat) |
| CASUELA | Earthenware pot |
| CAMARONES | Shrimps |
| CARNE | Meat |
| CHILI | A pepper; a sauce, a highly seasoned meat dish |
| CHILITIPINS | Small round chili peppers |
| COMINO | Cumin seed |
| CULANTRO | Coriander |
| FRIJOLES | Pinto or red beans |
| HUEVOS | Eggs |
| JALAPENOS | Hot chili peppers |
| LAUREL | Bay leaf |
| MASA | Mexican cornmeal |
| METATE | A heavy pestle for grinding corn |
| MIEL | Mexican word for molasses; French for honey |
| MOLCAJETE | A round stone dish of Aztec origin, used for grinding |
| NIXTAMAL | A Mexican cornmeal to make *tortillas* |
| NOPALES, NOPALITOS | Prepared cactus leaves |
| OSTIONES | Oysters |
| PICANTE | Sharp, hot, highly seasoned |
| PIPIAN | Pumpkin seed |
| QUESO | Cheese |
| SALSA | Sauce |

| | |
|---|---|
| SERRANO | A hot green chili pepper |
| TAMALINA | A Mexican cornmeal used for making *tortillas* |
| TEJOLETE | A pestle, smaller than a METATE |
| TOSTADO | A crisp, fried *tortilla* |

# THREE

# *BEVERAGES*

I originally planned to put beverages at the end of this book, but I changed my mind after several Texans had glanced through the opening sections. "Where's the iced tea?" was their immediate question. "You can't have a book about Texas food without iced tea." So here are the beverages at the very beginning; and let me say quickly that iced tea is the universal drink in Texas. There's coffee, of course; oceans of strong, good, hot coffee, some of it heavily roasted like New Orleans coffee. And there's hot tea, too. But all the coffee and hot tea together are nothing compared to the quantity of iced tea Texans consume—sweet iced tea with lemon and sometimes spices, sometimes mint—really the best iced tea imaginable.

And though this is not a commercial, there is Dr. Pepper, too, and Kool-Aid. You read about Texas dinner parties in the homes of the Texas rich where the finest vintage wines are served. You read that ice-cold beer is the drink to accompany barbecue and chili dishes; and this is true, of course. Cold beer is delicious with both these hot, spicy creations. But what you find most people drinking, when they are not drinking iced tea, is either Dr. Pepper or Kool-Aid. And though I may be forever barred from re-entering the state for saying this, I will simply have to take my chances. And why shouldn't Texans drink Dr. Pepper and Kool-Aid if they want to? I do not find this any stranger, as an acquired taste, than sake or retsina or kava or, for that matter, Scotch whiskey. Be that as it may, here is a Texas recipe for iced tea.

## ★ Iced Mint Tea

| | |
|---|---|
| 1 cup bruised green mint leaves | 12 cups *boiling* water |
| 1 cup sugar | Lemon or orange slices (if desired) |
| 2 cups water | Fresh mint leaves |
| 6 tea bags (or 12 tsps. tea leaves) | |

Combine mint, sugar and 2 cups water in saucepan. Simmer 10 minutes. Set aside. Place tea bags in pottery bowl and pour on boiling water. Let stand until cool. Remove tea bags. Strain sugar syrup into cooled tea. Refrigerate. When cold, pour into tall glasses with chunks of ice or cubes. Garnish glasses with slices of lemon or orange and sprigs of fresh mint leaves. Makes about 18 glasses.

## ★ Coffeepot Coffee

Despite all the iced tea that Texans drink, the beverage that you visualize as *being* Texas is old-fashioned coffeepot coffee. It was the drink of welcome in the old days; it was nectar on the trail. And though it may not be quite as neat and easy as the percolator or drip-pot coffee of today, it surely had a better taste—or anyway seemed to have—and its marvelous aroma was (and is) incomparable. Here is how Texans made it.

Mix 1 cup freshly ground, freshly roasted coffee with 1 cup cold water and 1 crushed eggshell. Place over fire. Add 6 cups BOILING water. Bring to boil and boil 3 minutes. Add ½ cup cold water and remove from heat. Let stand 2 to 3 minutes to settle the grounds, then serve. Serves 4 to 6.

In the matter of spirits, Texans' first choice is bourbon whiskey, which they take in long or short drinks, on the rocks or with water, or with any of a wide variety of mixers. But fancy drinks and cocktails are comparatively seldom seen. Of the latter, one of the most popular is the Mexican Margarita—and deservedly so.

## ★ *Margaritas*

| | |
|---|---|
| 1 lime | 2 jiggers Cointreau or |
| Salt | Triple Sec |
| 2 jiggers tequila | Juice of 1 fresh lime |

Rub the rim of a chilled cocktail glass with a cut piece of lime. Turn glass upside down in saucer spread with salt. Turn upright again. Shake other ingredients well with cracked ice. Strain into glass. Serve immediately. Serves 2.

Milk Punch, more often than not in Texas, is merely whiskey and cold milk. Occasionally it's a fancy drink, however, as in the following:

## ★ *Milk Punch*

| | |
|---|---|
| 1 pt. vanilla ice cream | ¼ cup light rum |
| 1 cup half-and-half | 1 jigger (1½ ozs.) brandy |
| ½ cup bourbon | Nutmeg |

Combine all ingredients in blender and whirl for about 6 seconds or until blended. Pour into punch glasses, sprinkle each with nutmeg, serve immediately. Makes about 12 drinks.

Texas is not a great wine-drinking state; Texas food, for that matter, rarely asks for wine. Texas dishes, with their strong seasonings, take more kindly to cold beer or iced tea. But on special occasions you do sometimes find a wine punch such as the following:

## ★ *Claret Cup*

8 lemons
8 oranges
1 qt. grated fresh pineapple with juice
1 qt. rinsed, drained, hulled strawberries

2 tsps. grated nutmeg
2 tsps. whole cloves
4 bottles claret (red Bordeaux)
Extra strawberries for garnish

Squeeze lemons and oranges and strain the juice. Combine in a large "porcelain" kettle (enamel or such) with pineapple, berries and enough cold water to make 1½ gallons (6 quarts). Add spices and boil 5 minutes. Let stand half an hour. Strain into clean pot. Add wine. Heat almost to boil and serve hot, each cup or punch bowl garnished with extra berries. Sugar to taste may be added if desired. Makes about 2 gallons of punch.

# FOUR

## BREADS AND COFFEE CAKES

YEAST-risen white loaf bread has always
been called *Light Bread* in Texas, and so it is called by Texans
wherever they go in the world. The name, so far as Texas bread
is concerned, is no exaggeration. Texas bread is, indeed, about the
lightest bread you will find anywhere. In no other bread recipes
that I know of are such quantities of leaven called for. Here is a
typical Texas Light Bread recipe requiring, please note, *three*
envelopes of yeast for three average-size loaves.

★　*Texas Light Bread*

| | |
|---|---|
| 3 cups milk | 3 pkgs. dry yeast |
| 3 Tbs. sugar | 8 cups sifted flour |
| 3 Tbs. lard | Melted butter or lard for brushing |
| 1 Tb. salt | dough |

Scald milk and stir in sugar, lard and salt. Stir until lard is
melted. Let cool to lukewarm. Sprinkle in the yeast. Stir until
dissolved.

Now add 4 cups of the sifted flour. Beat until smooth. Add the
remaining 4 cups bit by bit, blending after each addition. The
dough should not be too stiff.

Turn out on a lightly floured board and knead until satin

27

smooth and elastic. Place ball of dough in a greased bowl. Brush top with melted butter or lard, cover and let rise in a warm place (about 80° F.) until doubled in bulk. This will take about 1½ hours. Punch down the dough and divide into three equal parts. Mold the flattened dough into three compact loaves. Place in greased 9 x 5-inch loaf pans. Cover and let rise again in a warm place until doubled, this time a little less than 1 hour. Bake at 400° F. for 50 minutes or until loaves pull away from the sides of the bread pans and have a hollow sound when tapped. Turn out on rack to cool. This dough may also be made into rolls after the first rising; or part may be bread, part rolls; or all the dough may be refrigerated until needed. When baking the rolls allow 20 to 25 minutes at 400° F. The loaves, once cooled, may be wrapped and frozen.

You find many buttermilk breads and biscuits everywhere in Texas, descendants no doubt of the sour-milk breads that were economic necessities in the early days.

★ *Buttermilk Light Bread*

| | |
|---|---|
| 1 envelope active dry yeast | 1½ tsps. salt |
| ¼ cup lukewarm water | 2 Tbs. lard |
| 1 cup buttermilk | 4 cups sifted flour |
| 2 Tbs. sugar | Extra shortening, melted |

Dissolve yeast in warm water. Combine buttermilk, sugar, salt and melted lard. Add dissolved yeast, then the flour. Mix until flour is moistened. Turn out on lightly floured board and knead until satiny and elastic. Place dough in greased bowl. Brush top with melted shortening. Cover and let rise in a warm place (about 80° F.) until doubled in bulk. This will take about 1½ to 1¾ hours. Punch dough down and knead lightly. Form into 2 loaves. Place in greased 5 x 8-inch loaf pans and let rise again until doubled (about 1 hour longer). Bake at 375° F. for about 50 minutes or until bread is done, at which point the crust will be well browned and the sides of each loaf will have pulled away from the pan. For further test, turn a loaf out of the pan and tap the bottom. If properly baked, it will have a hollow sound to it. Cool loaves on rack before slicing or wrapping. If desired, brush each loaf all over with softened butter while still hot. This will be completely absorbed by the bread and enrich its flavor. Makes 2 loaves.

In the old days in Texas, hot biscuits were one of the mainstays of diet. Not only at home but on the range or trail as well, biscuits of some kind appeared at every meal. The biscuits then were considerably larger as a rule than those served now (". . . big as a saucer," said one record), and thicker, too (". . . solid, fat fellows"), and once in a while hard enough to merit the name "Dobies," so called after the building bricks made of native clay along the Rio Grande. But most, big or small, were feather light; they had to be. Cooks in the Cow Country were judged good or bad by the quality of their biscuits before all else. Light biscuits were called "Doughgods." Here are a few of the many hundreds of Texas biscuit recipes in use today. Those calling for both yeast and baking powder are *puro Tejano*.

## ★ *Yeast Biscuits*

| | |
|---|---|
| 1 envelope active dry yeast | ½ tsp. salt |
| ¾ cup lukewarm water | 2 Tbs. sugar |
| 2 cups flour | 3 Tbs. melted butter |

Dissolve the yeast in warm water. Combine dry ingredients and sift together. Pour yeast and melted butter into flour mixture. Knead to a smooth dough. Roll out about ½ inch thick on a lightly floured board. Shape into biscuits about 1½ inches in diameter. Arrange on a lightly greased baking sheet and let rise in a warm place 30 minutes. Bake at 425° F. for about 12 minutes. Serve and butter while hot. Makes 12 to 18 biscuits.

Even lighter are these biscuits from Amarillo that are made with both yeast and baking powder. As they are definitely sweet biscuits, they are at their best at some informal meal such as a Sunday-night supper or a brunch.

★ *Amarillo Risen Biscuits*

| | |
|---|---|
| 1 pt. sweet milk | 3 cups flour |
| ½ cup butter or lard | ½ tsp. salt |
| ½ cup sugar | ½ tsp. soda |
| 1 envelope active dry yeast | ½ tsp. baking powder |

Scald milk and while it is still hot stir in the shortening and sugar. Cool to lukewarm. Add yeast and dissolve. Add 1½ cups flour and blend. Cover and let stand in a warm place 1½ hours. Combine remaining flour with other dry ingredients and sift into the risen dough. Blend. Turn out on a lightly floured board and roll to about ½-inch thickness. Cut out with 2-inch biscuit cutter. Place on a greased baking sheet, cover and let rise again for 1 hour. Bake at 425° F. for 12 minutes or until browned. Serve hot. Makes 18 to 24 biscuits.

The following biscuits may be frozen before baking and then baked without either thawing or rising. They are wonderful things to have on hand, hence the quantity!

★   *Butter Biscuits*

| | |
|---|---|
| 5 cups flour | 1 cup butter |
| 3 Tbs. sugar | 1 envelope active dry yeast |
| 1 Tb. baking powder | ¼ cup lukewarm water |
| 1 tsp. salt | 2 cups buttermilk |
| 1 tsp. soda | Melted butter (about ¾ cup) |

Combine the dry ingredients and sift together into a mixing bowl. Using 2 knives or a pastry blender, cut in the butter until the mixture is like coarse meal. Dissolve yeast in warm water. Add to dry ingredients with the buttermilk. Blend thoroughly. Turn out on lightly floured board and roll or pat to ¼-inch thickness. Cut out with round 2½-inch cookie cutter. Dip rounds of dough in melted butter, then fold in half. Freeze, well wrapped, in half-dozen lots, or bake on an ungreased cookie sheet at 400° F. for 15 minutes. The frozen biscuits, as I said above, may be baked straight from the freezer. Allow about 18–20 minutes if frozen. Makes about 5 dozen.

Sourdough Bread and Biscuits are as popular in Texas today as they were a hundred years ago, and are still made in almost the same way. The first step, of course, is to make a *starter*. This mixture of yeast, water and flour is what gives the bread its characteristic sour, yeasty taste. Once made, a *starter* can go on forever. In the old days it was carried along in jugs by the pioneers; it was taken along in the chuck wagon on cattle drives. All you need do to keep your starter going indefinitely is to replenish it each day with the same amount of flour and warm water that you take out. This will ferment and sour overnight. In the olden times, the starter was the only leavening used in this bread but nowadays some baking powder is sometimes added. Here is a recipe for Sourdough Biscuits:

★ *Sourdough Biscuits*

*The Starter:*

2 envelopes active dry yeast
2½ cups lukewarm water
Flour

Dissolve yeast in warm water. Add enough flour to this to give it the consistency of thick buttermilk. Place in some warm spot (about 75° to 80° F.) away from drafts. Let stand overnight. Once the starter has been made, keep it covered and refrigerated if not to be used for several days. When you measure out some for use from the refrigerated container, bring it to room temperature before mixing.

*The Biscuits:*

2 Tbs. butter or lard        1 Tb. sugar
1 cup starter                1 pinch salt
2 tsps. baking powder        Flour to make a stiff dough

Combine the measured ingredients, then add flour bit by bit to make the dough, which should be just stiffer than regular biscuit dough. Knead and shape into biscuits. Place biscuits in a well-greased pan or baking sheet and put them to rise in a warm place (about 85° F.) until doubled in size. Bake at 450° F. until browned (about 15 minutes). Makes about 3 dozen.

In many parts of the ante-bellum South, one of the most popular hot breads was a deep-fried, fritter-like biscuit. Here is a similar bread that is a Texas specialty today.

★ *Fried Dough*

Make a rich biscuit dough as on page 31. Pat out on lightly floured board into a rectangle ¼ inch thick. Cut in strips 2 inches long and 1 inch wide. Freeze several hours or overnight. Just before serving, drop "frozen" dough into deep hot fat (400° F.) and fry until puffed and golden brown. Drain on paper. Serve immediately with soup or as an appetizer with guacamole. Or, if you like, sprinkle the biscuits with sugar and cinnamon and serve them as dessert. The Spanish name for these is *Sopaipillas* and it is said that, as such, they were created in New Mexico.

Cornbread is made today in every Texas household just as it was a hundred years ago, and the battle is still being waged as to whether or not it should have any sugar in it and whether it is better made with sweet or sour milk. A survey made by the Home Economics Department of Texas A & M some time ago found that the most representative Texas Cornbread was made with either buttermilk or sour milk and no sugar whatever. But many an excellent Texas Cornbread is made quite the other way around. Here are recipes for either taste:

33

## ★ Cornbread

1½ cups cornmeal
½ cup flour
4 tsps. baking powder
1 tsp. salt
2 Tbs. sugar
1⅓ cups sweet milk

1 large egg, beaten
1 Tb. melted butter, lard, or drippings
Hot water as needed
Extra cornmeal

Combine the dry ingredients and sift together into a bowl. Beat milk and eggs together. Add to dry ingredients and blend. Stir in the butter or lard. As you stir, the batter will get thicker and thicker. Now, bit by bit, add hot water, blending after each addition, until you get a batter that will just drop from your wooden spoon in large plops. Grease a 9-inch iron skillet thoroughly but not to excess. Heat it almost to the smoking point. Sprinkle the skillet with some of the extra cornmeal. This will brown instantly. It should make an even gritty film over the skillet. Pour on the batter. Bake in preheated oven at 375°F. for about 30 minutes or until bread is golden brown. Serves 4 to 6.

## ★ Sour Milk (or Buttermilk) Cornbread

½ cup flour
2 cups cornmeal
1 tsp. baking powder
½ tsp. soda

1 tsp. salt
1 egg
2 cups sour milk (or buttermilk)
2 Tbs. drippings

Sift together the dry ingredients. Beat egg and beat again with sour milk. Add to dry ingredients and blend. Stir in drippings. Pour into hot greased 9 x 13-inch baking pan. Bake at 400°F. for

25 minutes. Serve hot, cut in squares with a quantity of butter.
Serves 6.

NOTE: This same batter may be baked at the same temperature in
hot greased corn-stick pans. Allow about 15 to 18 minutes.

Many Texas Cornbreads have cheese and/or whole-kernel corn
added to the batter, and some—like the one that follows—have
bits of chili pepper in addition.

### ★ *Jalapeño Buttermilk Cornbread*

| | |
|---|---|
| 1 cup cornmeal (water ground if available) | 1 medium onion, chopped |
| | 3 *jalapeño* chili peppers, chopped |
| ½ cup sifted flour | ¼ lb. grated Cheddar cheese |
| ½ tsp. baking soda | ½ cup olive oil |
| ½ tsp. sugar | 2 eggs, beaten |
| 1 cup cream-style canned corn | 1 cup buttermilk |

In a mixing bowl combine cornmeal, flour, baking soda, salt
and sugar. Stir in corn, onion, chilis and cheese. Combine oil with
eggs and buttermilk. Add to other mixture, and stir only until the
dry ingredients are moistened. Turn into a greased 8-inch skillet.
Bake at 450° F. for 20 to 25 minutes or until lightly browned. Cut
into wedges to serve. Serves 6 to 8.

The word *pone* in Texas, as in the South, has come to mean many
things, but its original meaning was "a small oval loaf." This was
always a simple affair of water-ground cornmeal.

## ★ Texas Pone

4 cups water-ground meal
1 tsp. salt
Boiling water

Combine meal and salt; dampen mixture with boiling water. Let stand. Add more boiling water as needed to make a stiff dough. Work by hand, then mold into oval pones about 8 inches long and 1 inch thick. Heat 16-inch iron skillet over moderate flame and add lard to a depth of about ⅛ inch. Add pones. Cook 1 minute; baste top of pone with hot lard from skillet. Slip pan into oven at 400° F. and bake until golden brown and crisp. Serve hot with a quantity of butter. Makes 6 to 8, depending on size.

Most Corn Sticks are baked in iron pans made especially for the purpose. These delectable ones are fried, however.

## ★ Fried Corn Sticks

1½ cups sifted cornmeal
½ tsp. sugar
1 tsp. salt
2 Tbs. cream

1 large egg
Butter and lard, half and half, as needed for frying

Combine dry ingredients and sift together into a bowl. Beat cream with egg and work into the cornmeal mixture. Little by little, pour in boiling water, blending after each addition, to get a stiff dough. By tablespoonfuls mold into small cylinders. Heat about ⅛-inch fat in 10-inch iron skillet. Add a few of the corn sticks at a time and fry over moderate heat until brown and crisp on all sides. Turn them gently so the crust remains intact. Keep hot in oven until all are done. Drain on paper if necessary. Makes about 20.

These crisp wafers are good with soups and salads, to serve with drinks before dinner, with cheese, or at any time. They tend to disappear as fast as you make them.

## ★ *Cornmeal Crisps*

1 cup boiling water
1 cup minus 2 Tbs. white water-ground cornmeal
3 Tbs. melted lard

½ tsp. salt
Celery seeds, poppy seeds, or sesame seeds

Pour boiling water over meal and, while hot, stir in lard and salt. Drop by teaspoonfuls onto a greased baking sheet. Flatten as thin as possible with a wet knife blade or spatula. Sprinkle with celery seeds, poppy seeds or sesame seeds. Bake at 400° F. for 15 minutes. Makes about 6 dozen.

Cornmeal and wheat flour are used together in many Texas breads. The following recipe is an old one, adapted from one made originally by the Zuni Indians. Whereas today we use some metal object like an ice pick to punch the finished bread dough full of holes before baking, the Indians in the old days used straws. The bread is excellent.

## ★ Mrs. Carroll's Zuni Bread

| | |
|---|---|
| 1 pkg. dry yeast | 2 cups cornmeal |
| ¼ cup warm water | 1¾ cups hot water |
| ¼ cup shortening | 4½ to 5 cups flour |
| ½ cup molasses | Butter |
| 2 tsps. salt | |

Dissolve yeast in warm water. Measure shortening, molasses, salt and cornmeal. Put into large mixing bowl. Add hot water and blend. Stir in 2 cups flour to make batter thick. Beat by hand until elastic—100 strokes. Add yeast and stir in another 2½ cups flour. Work in additional flour with fingers to make a dough that does not stick to fingers. Turn onto floured board and knead 2 minutes. Shape dough into ball and put into a greased bowl. Cover surface with butter (lightly), cover with towel and let rise in warm place (about 85° F.) until doubled in size or bulk (about 1½ hours). Punch down and shape into a round loaf about 2 inches thick. Place on greased baking sheet. Cover and let rise until puffed (about 1 hour). Prick full of holes with an ice pick. Bake at 400° F. 35 to 40 minutes. Makes 1 large loaf or 2 small.

Many small hot breads in Texas are made of a combination of meal and wheat flour, too.

## ★ Cornmeal Rolls

| | |
|---|---|
| 1 envelope active dry yeast (or 1 cake) | ¼ cup lard |
| | 1 cup cornmeal |
| ¾ cup lukewarm water | 3½ to 4 cups sifted flour |
| ¾ cup milk | 1 Tb. melted lard, additional |
| ¼ cup sugar | Extra cornmeal |
| 2 tsps. salt | |

Dissolve yeast in warm water; set aside. Scald milk and cool to lukewarm. Combine with sugar, salt and lard. Stir until lard has melted. Combine with yeast. Sift cornmeal and 3½ cups flour together. Add to yeast mixture and knead to a smooth dough. Add the extra ½ cup flour if the dough seems too soft. Place dough in greased bowl, cover with a clean towel and let rise in a warm place (about 85° F.) until doubled in bulk. Punch down and shape into 18 rolls. Place in large baking pan and let rise until doubled again. Brush each with a little of the melted lard; sprinkle tops with a dusting of dry cornmeal. Bake at 425° F. for 15 minutes. Serve hot with a quantity of butter. Makes 18.

★ *Cornmeal Biscuits*

| | |
|---|---|
| 1½ cups cornmeal | 2 tsps. salt |
| 2½ cups sifted flour | ½ cup butter or lard |
| 6 tsps. baking powder | 1⅓ cups milk |

Combine meal, flour, baking powder and salt. Sift together. Using 2 knives or a pastry blender cut in the shortening until the mixture is pebbly. Add milk and stir just until all of the dry ingredients are moistened. Turn out on a lightly floured board and knead gently a few seconds. Roll or pat out to ½-inch thickness. Cut out with a 2-inch cutter. Place on a lightly greased baking sheet. Bake at 475° F. for about 10 minutes. Makes approximately 24 biscuits.

Sweet breads, and particularly those made with fruits and nuts in combination, are popular everywhere in Texas. They are served as a rule at breakfast or informal meals or between meals; some are of a richness that lets them pass easily as cakes. While most of these breads are of the quick-bread sort, made with baking powder instead of yeast, some—and particularly the breads of European extraction—use a yeast-leavened dough.

★ *Pecan-Banana Bread*

| | |
|---|---|
| 4 cups flour | 2 cups sugar |
| 2 cups chopped pecans | 4 eggs |
| 2 tsps. baking powder | 3 cups mashed ripe bananas |
| ½ tsp. salt | 2 tsps. vanilla |
| 1½ tsps. soda | 1 tsp. grated orange rind |
| 1 cup butter or lard | ½ cup buttermilk |

Sift flour and measure out ¼ cup. Dredge pecans with the ¼ cup flour and set aside. Add the baking powder, salt and soda to the remaining flour and sift again. Cream butter and sugar together. Beat in the eggs, one at a time. Beat in the mashed bananas, vanilla, orange rind and buttermilk. Combine with the dry ingredients and blend thoroughly. Stir in the floured nuts with any flour remaining in dish. Pour into 2 greased and floured 9 x 5-inch loaf pans. Bake at 350° F. for 1 hour. Turn out on a rack to cool. Wrap in wax paper when cold and let stand 24 hours before slicing. This is delicious sliced, toasted and lavishly buttered. It is also good sliced, buttered and sprinkled with cinnamon-sugar, then browned under the broiler. It is good any way!

The citrus groves of the Valley (which in Texas always means the Rio Grande Valley) are among the nation's largest. It is not surprising, therefore, that oranges, lemons and grapefruit all play prominent roles in the state's cuisine. What Texas has, Texas uses—and with pride. Here is an Orange-Pecan Bread:

★ *Orange-Pecan Bread*

*For the Syrup:*

Rinds of 4 oranges        1 cup sugar
1 tsp. soda        ¾ cup water

*For the Bread:*

2 Tbs. butter        3¼ cups sifted flour
¾ cup sugar        1 Tb. baking powder
2 eggs, beaten        1 pinch salt
1 cup milk        1 cup finely chopped pecans

For the orange syrup, scrape all the white undercoat from the rinds of 4 oranges. Put rinds and soda in pot with boiling water to cover. Boil 5 minutes. Drain. Grind rinds and return to pot with 1 cup of sugar and ¾ cup water. Cook over moderate heat until very thick. Cool.

For the bread, cream butter with ¾ cup sugar. Beat in beaten eggs, then milk. Combine flour, baking powder and salt. Sift together. Work dry ingredients gradually into egg mixture. Stir in pecans and the orange syrup. Pour batter into 2 greased 5 x 8-inch loaf pans. Bake at 350° F. for 1 hour or until done. Cool 15 minutes in pans, then turn out on rack to cool completely before slicing. The bread is better for being left 24 hours before using. Makes 2 loaves.

Here, by way of comparison, is a rather plain pecan bread, but it is no less good for being so.

★  *Mrs. Jablonowski's Nut Bread*

| | |
|---|---|
| 2 eggs | ½ tsp. salt |
| 2 cups sugar | 1 tsp. baking powder |
| 2 cups buttermilk | 2 tsps. soda |
| 4 cups flour | 1½ cups finely chopped pecans |

Beat the eggs, then beat in the sugar; then the buttermilk. Combine flour, salt, baking powder and soda. Sift together. Stir the dry ingredients into the egg mixture. Add the pecans. Line 2 greased 5 x 8-inch loaf pans with wax paper. Pour in batter. Bake at 350° F. for 1 hour. Cool 20 minutes in pans when done, then turn out on rack to cool completely. Do not slice until cold. The bread is better if it stands 24 hours before serving. Wrap in wax paper to store.

The wide use of prunes for breads and pastries in Texas reflects the taste of the state's Central Europeans.

★  *Polish Prune Bread*

| | |
|---|---|
| ¼ cup butter | 1 Tb. baking powder |
| ½ cup sugar | ½ tsp. salt |
| 1 egg | ¾ cup prune juice |
| 1 cup cooked, drained, pitted, chopped prunes | 2 tsps. grated lemon rind |
| | ½ cup finely chopped pecans |
| 2 cups flour | |

Cream butter and sugar together thoroughly, then beat in the egg and the prunes. Combine flour with baking powder and salt;

sift together. Add dry ingredients and the prune juice alternately to the egg mixture, beating well after each addition. Stir in the lemon rind and the finely chopped pecans. Pour into a greased 9 x 5-inch loaf pan. Bake at 350° F. for about 60 minutes or until the bread is done. Cool 10 minutes in pan before turning out on rack to cool completely. When cold, wrap in wax paper. Refrigerate 24 hours before slicing. Marvelous toasted. Good with cream cheese and peach preserves.

While the New Englanders who flocked to Texas in the mid-nineteenth century may have taken their rather plain New England Brown Bread recipes with them, this particular Brown Bread shows little evidence of Puritan frugality.

## ★ *Brown Bread*

| | |
|---|---|
| 1 cup raisins | 3 eggs |
| 1 cup pitted dates, cut up | 2 tsps. vanilla |
| 1 cup molasses | 1 cup finely chopped pecans |
| 2 cups water | 5⅓ cups sifted flour |
| 2 Tbs. lard or butter | 1 tsp. salt |
| 1 cup brown sugar | 4 tsps. soda |
| ½ cup white sugar | |

Combine raisins, dates, molasses and water in a saucepan. Bring to a boil. Remove from heat. Cream shortening with the brown and white sugars. Beat in the eggs, one at a time. Add vanilla and chopped nuts. Stir into date mixture. Combine the dry ingredients and sift together. Add to egg-date mixture and blend. Beat several minutes. Pour batter into 6 greased #2 tin cans (with one end cut away), filling each almost half full. Bake at 325° F. for 1 hour.

Cool in the cans. Remove from cans by cutting away remaining end with a can opener. Bread may be sliced when cold, but it is better if left 24 hours. If desired, loaves may be wrapped and frozen. Makes 6 loaves.

Pumpkin Breads were made all through the ante-bellum South, but few were as rich as this one.

★   *Pumpkin Bread*

| | |
|---|---|
| 3½ cups sifted flour | 1 cup chopped pecans |
| 2 tsps. soda | 1 cup tasteless cooking oil |
| 1½ tsps. salt | 4 eggs |
| 1 tsp. ground cinnamon | ⅔ cup water |
| 1 tsp. ground nutmeg | 1-lb. can pumpkin |
| 3 cups sugar | |

Sift all the dry ingredients together into a mixing bowl. One by one, stir in the remaining ingredients, blending until just mixed. Pour into 2 greased 9 x 5-inch loaf pans. Bake at 350° F. for 1 hour. Remove from oven and let cool in pans 10 minutes. Turn out and let cool completely on racks before slicing. This bread is delicious toasted.

Though called *muffins,* the following hot bread may be served quite as well as cake.

★ *Ginger Muffins*

| | |
|---|---|
| 4 cups sifted flour | 1 cup sugar |
| 2 tsps. soda | 4 eggs |
| 1 tsp. baking powder | 1 cup molasses |
| 2 tsps. ground ginger | 1 cup sour cream |
| ¼ tsp. ground allspice | ½ cup chopped pecans |
| ¼ tsp. ground cinnamon | ½ cup white raisins |
| 1 cup butter | |

   Combine the 6 dry ingredients and sift together. Cream butter with sugar. Beat eggs into the butter mixture, one at a time. Add molasses and sour cream. Stir in the sifted dry ingredients. Fold in nuts and raisins. If desired this batter (all or in part) may be stored, covered, in the refrigerator for as long as three weeks. Fill greased cups of muffin pans ⅔ full of batter. Bake at 375° F. for about 15 minutes or until done. Makes 3 dozen muffins.

The following few recipes are indeed for cakes, but these, in Texas, are often served like sweet fruit breads. Though calorically disastrous, they are at their best with rich, cold, sweet milk between meals.

★ *Sour Cream Coffee Cake*

*For the Cake:*

| | |
|---|---|
| ⅜ lb. butter (1½ sticks) | 1 tsp. soda |
| 1⅓ cups sugar | 1½ tsps. baking powder |
| 3 eggs | ¼ tsp. salt |
| 1½ tsps. vanilla | 1 cup sour cream |
| 3 cups flour | |

*For the Filling:*

¾ cup brown sugar                    ¾ cup finely chopped pecans

*For the Syrup:*

1½ cups powdered sugar              1 tsp. vanilla
¼ cup lemon juice

Cream butter and sugar together until light and fluffy. Beat in the eggs, one at a time. Add vanilla. Combine the dry ingredients and sift together. Add dry ingredients and sour cream alternately to the egg mixture, beating after each addition. Pour ⅓ of batter into a greased tube pan.

Combine the brown sugar and chopped pecans. Sprinkle half this mixture evenly over batter in pan. Add half the remaining batter, pouring it in gently and evenly. Sprinkle with remaining nuts and brown sugar. Add remaining batter. Jiggle pan to set the batter. Bake at 350° F. for 1 hour.

While cake is baking make the syrup. Mix powdered sugar with lemon juice and vanilla. Add water by the teaspoonful to bring to a just barely liquid consistency. When cake is done, turn it out on a large plate. While it is still hot, spread it with the lemon-sugar syrup. Cool before serving. Serves 8 to 12.

★ *Mrs. Spitzenberger's Apple-Oatmeal Strudel*

1 #2 can sliced apple-pie apples     ½ tsp. soda
¾ cup sugar                          1 cup brown sugar, firmly packed
1 tsp. ground cinnamon               1 cup oatmeal
1 cup flour                          ¼ lb. butter, melted and cooled
½ tsp. baking powder                 Heavy cream

46

Combine apples, sugar and cinnamon; spread in a 13 x 9-inch greased baking pan. Sift together the flour, baking powder, soda, and brown sugar. Combine with oatmeal; blend. Sprinkle this evenly over apple mixture. Over the oatmeal mixture dribble the melted butter. Bake at 350° F. for 40 to 50 minutes or until done. Serve hot or cold in squares. If served hot, accompany with ice-cold heavy cream. Serves 8 to 12.

★ *Apple Kuchen*

| | |
|---|---|
| 1 pkg. active dry yeast | 1 tsp. salt |
| 1 Tb. lukewarm water | 1 tsp. vanilla |
| 1½ cups milk | ¾ tsp. ground cinnamon |
| ¾ cup lard | 5 medium-size tart apples, pared |
| 2 eggs, lightly beaten | and cored and sliced very thin |
| 1¼ cups sugar | 2 Tbs. butter, melted |
| 4 cups sifted flour | |

Dissolve the yeast in warm water; scald the milk and melt the lard in hot milk. Let cool to lukewarm. Combine with yeast. Add beaten eggs, ½ cup of the sugar, all the flour, salt and vanilla. Mix thoroughly. Let rise at room temperature 3 hours or in refrigerator overnight. (This is excellent for a Sunday brunch.) Spread dough in a greased, shallow, 10½ x 15½-inch baking pan. Let rise 1 hour. Punch down to ½ inch. (The dough will seem very moist.) Mix cinnamon with remaining ¾ cup sugar. Toss half this mixture with apple slices in large bowl. Arrange slices overlapping in lengthwise rows on top of the dough. Dribble with melted butter. Sprinkle with all remaining cinnamon mixture. Bake at 350° F. for 40 minutes. Serve hot or cold. Makes 2 dozen good-size squares. Serves 10 or more.

Short'nin' Bread has always been a great Southern favorite and it is no less so today in Texas.

## ★   Short'nin' Bread

| | |
|---|---|
| 4 cups sifted flour | 1 pinch salt |
| 1 cup light brown sugar | 1 lb. butter |

Combine flour, sugar and salt. Blend. Cut in the butter as you would for pastry (using two knives or pastry blender) until the mixture is pebbly. Press it together gently. Turn out on lightly floured board and pat out to ½-inch thickness. Cut into shapes as desired. Bake on an ungreased baking sheet at 350° F. for 20 minutes or until golden brown. Serve hot with preserves and butter. Serves 6 to 8.

## ★   Cinnamon Toast

Toast bread lightly on one side. Spread untoasted side liberally with butter; sprinkle buttered surface with a mixture of ground cinnamon and sugar. Place slices sugar-side up on baking sheet. Place on top shelf of oven at 450° F. and leave until sugar has melted. Serve immediately.

# FIVE

# *PANCAKES AND SUCH*

AS I mentioned in the introduction, breakfast in Texas is a big, old-fashioned country breakfast, as a rule. Along with the eggs and meat and gravy—and maybe potatoes—and hot biscuits—you may have hot cakes, too. These will be served with either maple syrup or Texas cane syrup or a home-made syrup such as this:

★ *Home-made Syrup*

Cover bottom of an iron skillet ½ inch deep with granulated sugar. Place over slow fire. When the sugar starts to melt and shows the first signs of smoking, add boiling water slowly just to cover. Simmer until very thick. Serve hot.

Honey is also frequently served with hot cakes in Texas. Honey, in fact, has been a basic Texas standby since the earliest days of settlement—and even before. The extent of the wild-bee swarms in the early days can be judged by the fact that the Indians watched the movement of the swarms to gauge the white man's encroachment, the hives of the wild swarms being always at least fifty miles in advance of the farthest point of settlement.

For the Hot Cakes, themselves, you find hundreds of recipes in Texas. Here are a few of the best of them:

51

## ★ Buttermilk Hot Cakes

6 eggs, separated
1 tsp. soda
2 cups buttermilk
½ cup cream

3 cups flour
1 Tb. baking powder
1 Tb. melted butter

Beat egg yolks until light. Dissolve soda in buttermilk. Beat buttermilk and cream with egg yolks. Sift flour with baking powder. Stir flour mixture into yolk mixture until smooth. Stir in butter. Beat egg whites until stiff and fold gently into batter. Drop batter by tablespoons onto hot, greased iron griddle or skillet. Cook cakes until lightly browned on both sides. Turn only once. Serve very hot with butter and syrup. Makes about 5 dozen little hot cakes.

## ★ Flannel Cakes

2 cups milk
2 tsps. butter
2 eggs, beaten

3 cups sifted flour
½ tsp. salt
1 scant tsp. dry yeast

Heat milk almost to the boil in a saucepan. Add butter. Reduce heat to low. Keep milk hot until butter has melted. Remove from heat and cool to lukewarm. Add eggs, flour and salt. Blend thoroughly. Stir in yeast. Pour into bowl, cover and let stand in a warm place about 3 hours. Then cook on a greased griddle by the spoonful like any pancakes. Serve with honey, maple syrup or cane syrup. Serves 6.

★  *Cream Pancakes*

| | |
|---|---|
| 2 large eggs | 1 cup cold water |
| 1 tsp. salt | ½ cup cream |
| 1 Tb. sugar | ¾ cup sifted flour |

Beat eggs until thick and lemon-colored, then beat in salt and sugar. Add water, cream and flour alternately to egg mixture, beating after each addition. Let stand 30 minutes, then beat again before making pancakes. Fry by spoonfuls on a hot, greased griddle. Butter as soon as cooked and roll. Serve with additional butter and maple sugar. The longer the batter stands and the more it is beaten, the better and lighter these delicious cakes will be. Makes 10 pancakes.

Fried Mush is a wonderful creation and it should have the popularity everywhere that it has (and deserves) in the South and in Texas. It is served most often as a breakfast dish, of course, but it is also excellent as an accompaniment to Fried Chicken. And plain, boiled Cornmeal Mush (from which the Fried Mush is made) is one of the world's truly great hot cereals.

★  *Cornmeal Mush* and *Fried Mush*

| | |
|---|---|
| 3 cups hot water | 2 Tbs. butter |
| 1 cup water-ground cornmeal | Cream |
| 1 tsp. salt | Brown sugar |

Put 3 cups water in top of double boiler and bring to a boil over direct heat. Add cornmeal gradually, then salt. Place over hot water. Cook gently until thickened, stirring frequently, for 20 minutes. Stir in butter. Serve hot with cream and brown sugar as a hot cereal or spread ½-inch thick on a buttered platter and chill. When cold, cut into squares or diamonds and fry quickly until brown on both sides. Serve Fried Mush with fried ham or pork of any kind or Fried Chicken or sausage. Recipe makes 4 cups Mush. Serves 4 if fried.

Though served somewhat less extensively than in the Deep South, Grits are nonetheless a favorite food in Texas. And as with Cornmeal Mush, they may appear either plain boiled or chilled, then fried. But if plain boiled, Grits are more a vegetable than cereal.

## ★ To Cook Grits:

Place 4 cups water and 1 tsp. salt in the top of a double boiler. Bring this to a full boil over direct heat. Very slowly, without stopping the boil, scatter in 1 cup hominy grits. Continue to cook over direct heat about 2 minutes longer. Place pan over hot water. Stir gently; cover and cook until done . . . 10 to 20 minutes. If the grits seem too dry, add the least bit of boiling water . . . but not too much. Do NOT overcook. Just before serving, if desired, stir in a heaping tablespoonful of butter. Serve (with additional butter) with ham, sausage or bacon and eggs. Fried Grits should be served with ham, sausage, bacon, pork, Fried Chicken or Fried Fish. Recipe makes about 4½ cups grits. If fried this will serve 4.

# SIX

## BASIC TEXAS-MEXICAN DISHES AND SAUCES

❧❧❧

IN any consideration of the gustatory scene in Texas, you must first look at those dishes, sauces and specialties of the region that are thought of as Mexican in origin. That they are all favorite and standard foods of the Mexicans in Texas, there can be no doubt (just as there is no doubt about their being favorite foods of the non-Mexicans in Texas). And that they have been so for generations, there is no question whatever. But most of these dishes, though using ingredients that have been Mexican standbys for centuries, are truly Texas dishes . . . and their importance gastronomically is not only for their own good sakes but because the flavor combinations that make them what they are—their spices and herbs and other seasonings—have come to be used in a host of dishes that are not thought of as Mexican at all. This combination has come to be the flavor of Texas, you might say.

And though many tables may boast the finest of dishes from the currently popular international cuisine (which is predominantly French) and may have their subtle international seasonings and tastes, and many other tables may boast of dishes copied from those that have given the Zodiac Room of Neiman-Marcus in Dallas its justified fame (mere thought of the Zodiac Room counts 1,000 calories), *most* tables in Texas again and again come up with this especially Texas flavor—it is of chili pepper and *comino* and *cilantro* (perhaps), with tomato and lard and chopped raw onion—and cheese—and corn. Find a Texan away from Texas any length of time and what is he longing to eat? Not filet mignon with Béarnaise sauce, not lobster à l'Americaine, but Tex-Mex dishes . . . or anyway dishes with a Tex-Mex taste, such as *enchiladas, frijoles refritos, tacos,* lettuce and sliced tomato with grated cheese, *Guacamole, Tortillas,* sauce picante. He may think of them as somehow intermingled with rather old-fashioned American dishes (of English extraction) with a German or Czechoslovakian or Polish dish thrown in for good measure. But he thinks of them.

In this section I have gathered together some of the basic Tex-Mex dishes, sauces and specialties that appear regularly in the general Texas cuisine. I venture to say that while there may be homes in Texas where none of these dishes has appeared, there is no home where their influence has not been felt from the culinary standpoint. First let's look at Chili; chili and *tortillas* are absolute essentials.

# CHILI

The word *chili* as used in the course of this book will of necessity refer to several different things and hence may lead to confusion unless some thought is given to its meaning on each appearance. Chili is a dish, of course, as in "a bowl of chili"; and when it is a dish without other qualification, it is of meat—generally chopped or ground beef but sometimes beef and pork in combination and sometimes beef and venison. Each household in Texas has its own favorite Chili recipe, many of which have been handed down through several generations. It may be served by itself, as a meat sauce, as a filling for rolled *tortillas,* or as a casserole ingredient. It is always "hot" in the peppery sense and sometimes very hot indeed. It usually contains both cumin (*comino*) and garlic and often has oregano and bay leaf as well. Its characteristic red color comes from tomatoes.

58

*Chili* may be made with beans in addition to the meat and it then becomes *Chili con Frijoles,* the frijoles being either pinto beans (garbanzos) or red beans which are *not* the same as kidney beans. Plain Chili Beans, however, as you will discover on page 254, may be simply beans highly seasoned with chili powder, and without any meat whatsoever. *Chili con Carne* by rights should be a plain meat chili, but it is not; it, too, has beans. *Chili* with or without beans, when served by itself, appears in a bowl with plain soda crackers or saltines on the side and a sour (not dill) pickle.

*Chili* primarily is a hot pepper of any of a number of kinds (pages 17–18). This, of course, not only gives the dish its name but its peppery hot character, too. One can only discover how hot chilis are by buying different ones to compare them. Some can burn your tongue out, some make you weep, others in comparison (but not actually) are mild. The chopped green chilis put up in cans are of the latter sort; *jalapeños, serranos* and the red *anchos* are hot.

*Chili* also often refers to a kind of sauce; in this book, in fact, it must refer to two very different kinds of sauces. There is, of course, the spicy (but not hot) chili sauce—predominantly of tomato—that you find in grocery stores all over the country. This is used extensively in Texas, both home-made and commercial. But Texas also has a hot, hot chili sauce made of puréed red chili peppers, salt and vinegar. And to confuse matters even more, Texas recipes often call for special sauces which use chili peppers in considerable quantity and hence are called chili sauces—the *Salsa Colorado de Chili* on page 60, for instance—but they are less hot than the *hot* chili sauces. . . . Confusing? Here are two of the hot ones.

## ★ *Salsa de Chili*

| | |
|---|---|
| 3 Tbs. lard | ½ tsp. oregano |
| 2 cloves garlic, crushed | 1 tsp. salt |
| 1 medium-size onion, chopped very fine | 1 cup *pasta de chili* (see below) |
| | 1½ cups water |

Heat lard in a heavy skillet. Add garlic and onion; sauté gently until golden. Add oregano, salt and *pasta de chili* (chili paste); blend. Add water. Bring to a boil, reduce heat to low and simmer 20 minutes. Press all through a fine sieve. Serve hot or cold. If to be kept any length of time, store covered in refrigerator. Makes about 2¼ cups sauce.

## ★ *Pasta de Chili*

Real *pasta de chili* is composed simply of the puréed pulp of red *ancho* chilis. One full-grown *chili ancho* yields as a rule about 1 tablespoon of paste, so for a full cup of paste you should allow about 15 of them. Remove the thin skin of the chili, as directed below, then cut the chili in half, scrape out and discard the seeds. What remains is the pulp to be puréed. A brief scalding with boiling water will make this an easier procedure.

If real chili paste is not available and cannot be made, a passable (but less flavorsome) paste can be made of chili powder. Use as needed in the following proportions: 4 tablespoons chili powder, 1 teaspoon flour and just enough water to make the paste. Blend.

*To Peel Fresh Chilis:*
Place chilis in a heavy iron skillet. Put into *very* hot oven and

leave just until outer skin scorches. Remove from oven immediately. Place chilis in damp towel. Fold towel over chilis and rub gently until skins slip off.

For an even simpler—and hotter—Chili Sauce you can prepare the following:

★ *Hot Chili Sauce*

Remove the seeds from little red chili peppers and scald the pulp with boiling water. Let stand a few minutes, then drain. Mash the chilis in a bowl. Add salt to taste and 1 crushed clove garlic (or less, depending on the quantity of chilis). Add vinegar, blending as you go, until the sauce comes to the desired consistency—one that will "shake from a bottle." Pass the sauce through a fine sieve and bottle. Keep covered until needed.

*Chili,* the dish, is a fixture at Texas-Mexican meals, for it is the central dish, as it were, of the entire Texas-Mexican cuisine. Its uses are varied; prepared in precisely the same way, it may be either a dish by itself, a sauce or filling. It may be used as a casserole ingredient—in a Tamale Pie, for instance. Then, too, true to the Texas tradition, it may appear at table with such un-Mexican foods as Fried Potatoes.

# ★ *Chili*

| | |
|---|---|
| 3 lbs. coarsely ground lean beef | 2 qts. water |
| ½ cup finely chopped beef suet | 3 cups chopped, peeled tomatoes or |
| 1 cup chopped onion | drained canned ones |
| 2 cloves garlic, minced | 2 Tbs. flour |
| 4 Tbs. chili powder | 2 Tbs. cold water |
| 1 Tb. ground cumin | 2 Tbs. cornmeal |
| ½ tsp. ground oregano | Grated cheese |
| 1 Tb. salt | Chopped raw onion |

Brown the beef in suet fat with onion and garlic, using a heavy pot large enough for all the ingredients. Break the meat up with a fork as it cooks. Add chili powder, cumin, oregano, salt and water. Cover and cook over low heat 1 hour. Add tomatoes and cook uncovered 30 minutes. Mix flour with cold water. Stir into the chili. Sprinkle cornmeal over surface and blend. Cooking, stirring frequently, until thickened. Serve with pinto beans or with *tortillas* or *Tostados* (page 65) or *fritos*. Pass grated cheese and chopped raw onions separately. Serves 10 to 12. This can be made the day before and reheated if desired. Leftover chili can be frozen.

So many Texas recipes in the past few years have been given as favorites of President and Mrs. Johnson that I hesitate to add another. Suffice it to say that this excellent Chili bears the name of the lazy river that flows through the LBJ Ranch and is good enough to be a favorite of anyone.

## ★ Pedernales Chili

| | |
|---|---|
| 4 lbs. ground lean beef | 2 Tbs. (rounded) chili powder |
| 1 large onion, chopped | 2 cans Ro-tel tomatoes,* #2 size |
| 2 cloves garlic, minced | 2 cups hot water |
| 1 tsp. ground oregano | Salt to taste |
| 1 tsp. cumin seed | |

Sear meat in heavy iron skillet. Add onion and garlic. Cook 4 to 5 minutes. Stir frequently. Add remaining ingredients. Blend. Bring to boil. Reduce heat to low. Simmer 1 hour. As the chili cooks, skim off fat. This may be served as soon as done, but it is better if set aside (or kept overnight) and reheated. Serves 12.

As I mentioned before, plain chili recipes are almost invariably made of meat alone; but Chili con Carne (actually meaning chili with meat) seems always to indicate the presence of beans, as in the following:

## ★ Chili con Carne

| | |
|---|---|
| 1 large onion, chopped | ½ tsp. celery salt |
| 2 cloves garlic, minced | ¼ tsp. cayenne |
| 3 Tbs. olive oil | 1 tsp. ground *comino* |
| 1 lb. chopped lean beef | 1 small bay leaf |
| 1 #2 can tomatoes | 1½ tsps. salt to taste |
| 1 green pepper, seeded and chopped | 6 cups water |
| | 2 cups cooked *frijoles* |

* As these are usually only available in Texas and the Southwest, you should substitute whatever canned tomatoes you like. If plain canned tomatoes are used, add 1 extra tablespoon chili powder.

In a heavy pot over moderate heat sauté onion and garlic in olive oil until golden. Add beef and brown thoroughly. Add all remaining ingredients except *frijoles*. Add 6 cups water. Bring to boil, reduce heat and simmer until sauce is of desired thickness (about 3 hours). Remove bay leaf. The chili may now be removed from the fire and reheated when needed or cooled and refrigerated overnight. Before serving, reheat gently with the *frijoles*. Serves 4 to 6.

# TORTILLAS

*Tortillas* are thin pancakes of a special sort, made by a special process from a special kind of cornmeal ground from a Mexican corn called *nixtamal,* which has been in continuous cultivation for this use since Aztec days. The *nixtamal,* as in the making of samp in this country, is first slowly cooked in a lye or wood-ash solution to bleach and soften it and loosen the coarse hulls. The corn may then be ground wet and subsequently dried to a meal called *masa,* or it may be dried and then ground to a meal called *tamalina.* Most Mexican families process their own corn and hand-grind it, wet or dry, on a stone by means of a heavy pestle-like object called a *metate.* There is, however, one firm in San Antonio that makes *tamalina* commercially and the Quaker Oats Company puts out a *masa* (Masa Marina); one or another of these is usually available in stores that deal in Spanish-American foodstuff.

*Tortillas* of different sizes (5 to 8 inches in diameter) and of excellent quality are available in cans in stores and supermarkets the country over. There is little to be gained, therefore, by giving a detailed description of how Mexican women have made them

64

for centuries. Suffice it to say that once the *masa* has been properly moistened, they take up a small ball of dough in one hand and then, with incredible dexterity and speed, slap it back and forth from hand to hand in midair, getting the cake thinner and thinner as it grows wider and wider until at last it is the desired size.

Once made, the *tortillas* are briefly cooked on a griddle, not to brown them or make them crisp but merely to take the rawness from the corn. At this stage, when they are tender and pliable, they are called *suaves* or *blanditas*. They are ready for use in any of the wide variety of Mexican dishes that require them specifically, all closely related to the *taco* and the *enchilada*. They may also be eaten like a bread, or they may serve as a kind of eating utensil (many Mexican Indians have no other), or they may be stored for later use.

All *tortillas* tend to toughen as they cool. They will become tender again, however, if brushed with or dipped in hot oil. Thus they may be used like fresh *tortillas*. Or they may be fried in hot oil to a medium crispness and then if folded in half will form a kind of loose envelope for a filling. Often *tortillas* are cut into quarters and fried until really crisp—to become *tostados*. These serve as vehicles for dips such as *guacamole* (actually a sauce or main dish accompaniment) or they may be covered with cheese and a bit of *jalapeño* chili and broiled to become *nachos*. Hot appetizers or tidbits in Mexico and such tidbits in general among the Texas Mexicans are called *antojitos*.

Though *tortillas* are most widely used in Texas in the more or less standard Texas-Mexican dishes, they have also come to be used in purely Texas dishes, and casseroles of Mexican flavor. These I have included in other sections of the book as main meat ingredients have indicated. See, for instance, the *Chilaquilles* (page 123), primarily cheese, and the Green Chili-pork Casserole (page 220).

For those who wish to make their own *tortillas*—an easy

enough process unless you wish to be a purist about it—here are two simple recipes, one using *masa,* the other the *tamalina.*

## Tortillas de Masa

Measure 2 cups Masa Marina into a bowl and slowly work in 1⅓ cups warm (not hot) water to make a thick paste. Proceed as directed below for the *Tortillas de Tamalina.*

## ★   Tortillas de Tamalina

Packaged, ready-to-use *tamalina* is sold in most stores dealing in Spanish-American foods and in some general markets in Texas and the Southwest. To make these *tortillas,* add ¼ teaspoon salt for each cup *tamalina* and just enough lukewarm water to make a soft cornbread dough. Roll by hand into small balls. Press these individually between two sheets of wax paper. Roll out until very thin. Remove top sheet of paper. Lifting by means of under sheet and a spatula, carefully invert onto a hot, lightly greased griddle or iron skillet. Gently pull off second sheet of paper, now on top. Cook 2 to 3 minutes, turn carefully and cook other side 2 minutes longer. Serve like any *tortilla.*

*Enchiladas* are rolled, filled *tortillas,* usually baked briefly with a characteristic sauce and invariably served with more sauce, grated cheese and chopped raw onion. Their fillings may be fancy, but

66

more often than not they are plain. Sometimes they simply have a mixture of grated cheese and chopped raw onion that will also serve as topping when they go to table. Here is a typical *Enchilada* recipe:

★ *Basic Enchiladas*

| | |
|---|---|
| 12 *tortillas* | 1 cup shredded Cheddar cheese |
| ¼ cup olive oil | 1 lb. (2 cups plus) chili (page 62) |
| 1 cup finely chopped onion | |

Grease *tortillas* on both sides with oil. Combine onion and cheese and place a generous spoonful of the mixture on each *tortilla* (here you must use your own judgment as to how much filling to use). Roll and place side by side in a greased, shallow baking dish from which they can be served. Add a skimming of water, just enough to make steam (about 3 tablespoons). Cover and cook over low heat 10 minutes. Remove from heat. Cover with chili (heated thoroughly) . . . the chili on page 62, for instance. Top with additional onion if desired and more grated cheese. Serve with *Frijoles Refritos* (page 252), *Tacos* (page 70), *Guacamole* (page 102), soft *tortillas,* sliced ripe tomatoes with lettuce and grated cheese, and for dessert either Orange *Biscochitas* (page 330) or *Pralines* (page 359).

NOTE: A simple meat filling for *enchiladas* may be made by browning 1 cup chopped, lean, cooked beef, pork or chicken in 2 to 3 tablespoons lard with ¼ cup chopped onion. Then add 1½ cups of the *Enchilada* Sauce (page 68) and simmer 20 minutes or until the mixture is of the desired consistency. Use 2 to 3 tablespoons of this meat filling for each *enchilada*.

*Chili,* when available, may be used as the sauce for *Enchiladas,* but more often they have a special sauce such as the following; which also is used for *Tacos* (page 70):

★ *Enchilada* or *Taco Sauce*

1 medium-size onion, chopped
1 Tb. lard
2 cups canned tomatoes
½ cup water
1 tsp. salt

1 clove garlic, mashed
½ tsp. paprika
1 *Jalapeño* pepper, ground or chopped very fine

Brown onion in lard over moderate heat. Add all the remaining ingredients and blend. Cook 20 minutes, stirring frequently. Press through a sieve or store covered in refrigerator as is. Makes about 1¾ cups sauce.

Of a fancier sort are these delicious *Enchiladas* which make for a company dish. The menu for a Texas-Mexican company meal, incidentally, is essentially the same as that for a family meal. And the same general principle holds true for barbecue meals, family or company. The dependable sameness is, in fact, one of the things that Texans like about them; quality stands as the mark of distinction, not difference. At all events, make these Green *Enchiladas* for your enjoyment:

★  *Enchiladas Verdes (Green Enchiladas)*

*For the Sauce:*

1 can peeled green chilis*
1 medium-size, seeded sweet green pepper
3 cans tomatillos* (10-oz. size)
1 medium-size onion, peeled
1 clove garlic, minced

¾ cup solid-pack canned tomatoes
¼ cup olive oil
Salt to taste
*Salsa Jalapeño** (or any other canned green chili relish) to taste
½ cup minced fresh parsley

*For the Filling:*

2 lbs. lean boneless pork, diced (use shoulder if available)
2 cloves garlic, minced
¼ cup water
2 tsps. salt
1 medium-size onion, chopped

¾ cup solid-pack canned tomatoes (additional)
12 tortillas*
Oil for frying
3 Tbs. grated sharp cheese

Remove seeds from the chili peppers; cut the chilis and the sweet pepper into strips or chunks. Drain one can of the *tomatillos.* Combine the drained and the undrained *tomatillos,* the chili peppers, sweet pepper, onion, garlic and tomatoes in a blender (using only a third of each ingredient at one time). Blend to a rather coarse consistency. If you have no blender, put the ingredients through your food grinder. Heat the olive oil in a heavy saucepan. Add the blended or ground mixture and salt to taste. Stir in the *Salsa Jalapeño* to taste and the parsley. Set aside.

For the filling, put pork, garlic, water and salt in a heavy skillet; cover and simmer 30 to 40 minutes. Uncover and let the water cook away. When the pork starts to brown, stir it fre-

* Many of these items are now available in supermarkets, but if not, they are always available in stores dealing in Mexican or Spanish foods or by mail (see page 14).

quently. Add onion and tomato. Cook over low heat until all the liquid has again cooked away. Keep warm until needed.

Now dip the *tortillas* in the sauce to coat them evenly all over. Heat the oil in a large skillet. Fry the *tortillas* lightly on each side. Remove from pan. Place a spoonful of the filling on each. Roll up. Place seam-side down in a shallow Pyrex baking dish. Cover all with the remaining green sauce. Sprinkle with cheese. Keep warm in the oven until needed. Serves 6.

# TACOS

*Tacos,* like *enchiladas,* are made of *tortillas* with a meat or chili filling, but unlike *enchiladas, tacos* are not rolled; they are merely folded in half without creasing. The folded *tortillas* are baked to a crispness before any filling is added. Finished *tacos* are always served with shredded lettuce, chopped raw onion and chopped, peeled, ripe tomatoes. These same ingredients, it should be noted, sometimes serve also as filling.

 *Tacos*

| | |
|---|---|
| ½ cup chopped onion | 1 generous dash Tabasco |
| 2 cloves garlic, minced | 12 *tortillas* |
| ⅓ cup lard | ½ cup lard, melted |
| 2 lbs. ground lean beef | 2 to 3 cups very finely shredded and |
| 2 Tbs. chili powder | chopped lettuce |
| 3 Tbs. tomato catsup | 3 ripe tomatoes, peeled and |
| 1 tsp. *comino* seed | chopped |
| Salt and pepper to taste | ½ cup grated sharp cheese, optional |

70

In a heavy skillet, sauté the onion and garlic in lard over moderate heat until golden. Add beef, chili powder, catsup and *comino* seed. Cook 5 minutes, crumbling the meat as it browns. Add salt and pepper to taste. Add Tabasco. Cook 20 minutes over lowest heat, stirring from time to time. If the meat gets too dry, add a little more catsup and/or a bit of hot water.

While the meat is cooking, brush the *tortillas* on both sides with melted lard. Fold them over in half without creasing or breaking them; the fold should be somewhat rounded. Arrange on a baking sheet and toast 15 minutes at 400° F. Brush the outside again with lard if needed. When done to a surface crispness, remove from oven. To serve fill each with a portion of the meat mixture, some shredded lettuce and chopped tomato. Arrange on heated platter and serve immediately. For additional oniony flavor, if you like it, stir an additional ¼ cup of finely chopped onion into the meat mixture about 2 minutes before serving. And, if you like, stir in ½ cup grated sharp cheese. Serves 6.

## ★ Chicken Tacos Filling for 12 Tortillas

1 medium onion, chopped fine
2 Tbs. lard or drippings
1 cup tomato juice
2 Tbs. canned chopped green chilis
1 cup slivered, cooked, boned chicken
⅛ tsp. thyme
½ tsp. salt, or to taste
12 *tortillas*
Lard for frying
Shredded lettuce
1 cup or more grated cheese

Sauté onion in lard or drippings in a heavy skillet over moderate heat until just golden. Add tomato juice and green chilis; blend. Cook 3 to 4 minutes. Add chicken, thyme and salt. Cook gently until almost all the liquid has cooked away. Brush *tortillas* with lard as described above. Fold and bake as directed. Fill with chicken mixture; add lettuce and sprinkle with cheese. Serve immediately.

# TAMALES

*Hot Tamales* are not difficult to make, but the process has several steps which make it seemingly complicated. The outside wrapper of each *tamale* is a prepared corn husk. You can find these husks, packaged, at most stores that deal in Spanish-American foods. But if they are not available, fresh corn husks, free of silk, will do. Or you can use 7-inch squares of cooking parchment. Corn husks, however, add a great deal of flavor to *tamales*.

Then, too, you should use *tamalina* if possible (page 66). Lacking this, white, water-ground cornmeal will do. But note this difference in procedure for the different meals: in mixing *tamalina* to a paste you use *warm* water as in the *Tortilla* recipe (page 66). With regular cornmeal you always use *boiling* water unless otherwise noted.

Here is your recipe for *tamales!*

## ★ *Hot Tamales*

36 corn husks (see above)
2 lbs. lean pork, cut into cubes
Salt
½ tsp. cracked pepper
½ tsp. dried red-pepper flakes
4 Tbs. chili powder
4 Tbs. paprika
2 tsps. oregano
2 tsps. *comino* seed
½ tsp. cayenne

3 to 5 cloves garlic (as desired) minced
Additional salt and pepper
3½ cups *tamalina or* 3 cups white cornmeal
1 cup lard, softened at room temperature
1 Tb. salt
Chicken or beef broth as needed
2 tsps. chili powder

Put corn husks in bowl; cover with boiling water and let stand 1 hour.

In a heavy pot combine pork, salt to taste, cracked pepper, and red-pepper flakes with water to cover. Bring to boil; reduce heat to low and simmer 45 minutes. Drain, reserving the liquid. Put pork through meat grinder.

In a bowl blend the ground meat with chili powder, paprika, oregano, *comino,* cayenne, garlic and 1 cup of the reserved liquid. Add salt and black pepper to taste. Set aside until needed. (This pork mixture may be prepared ahead of time. Covered, it will keep at least a week in refrigerator. Also note that blended with mayonnaise this makes an excellent appetizer spread!)

Now put *tamalina* or cornmeal in a separate bowl and cut in the softened lard, using two knives or pastry blender. Add salt. Measure the remaining reserved broth from the pork and add chicken or beef broth to it to make 3 cups. Stir in the chili powder or more to taste. If *tamalina* is used, just warm this liquid; if cornmeal is used, bring it to a boil. Add liquid to meal mixture gradually to make a thick paste. Do *not* let it get runny.

Drain corn husks. In the center of each husk spread a square of paste about ⅛ inch thick, leaving 1½ inches uncovered at each end and at least 1 inch uncovered on the sides. Roll a rounded tablespoon of the pork mixture into a thin cylinder as long as a side of the square of cornmeal paste and lay this (lengthwise with the husk) in the center of the square. Roll the husk from the sides rather loosely so the cornmeal paste encloses the pork. Tie the ends of the husk about ¾ inch from the end of the paste filling with threads that you can tear lengthwise from an extra corn husk. (If you don't care about the looks of the *tamales* and are not a purist, use plain thread.) Place the *tamales* on a rack over hot water in a large heavy pot, cover the pot tightly and let them steam, with the water at a boil, for 1 hour. Add more boiling water, if necessary. Serve hot with lemon wedges, Tabasco and a bowl of *Taco* Sauce (page 68).

An odd thing about the Texas cuisine is that many of the

Mexican dishes included in it regularly are not thought of as having really become Texan. The *mole* dishes are among these, for no matter how often they appear at Texas tables, and no matter whether or not they are made by Texas recipes, they are thought of as Mexican.

*Mole* dishes take their name from their sauce whose ingredients may either be added separately or combined in a prepared, highly seasoned paste, home-made or canned.

In Mexico, the *mole* dishes frequently, and in Texas sometimes, contain chocolate. Chocolate in Mexico, of course, has been used since Aztec days as a meat and poultry seasoning and as a thickener for sauces as well as for drinks and sweets. A small bit of it does surprising things to various dishes, not making them especially chocolaty as you might suppose but giving a special richness. It acts as a catalyst to other seasonings and flavors. Mention of *mole* in most parts of the United States has come to be thought of as always inferring the presence of chocolate. Such, however, is not the case. And here is a recipe for plain *Mole* Paste to prove the point. The *mole* dishes are given elsewhere as indicated by their main meat or poultry ingredients. They are, for the most part, informal dishes and, hence, are excellent for buffets.

Jars or cans of ready-made *mole* paste are available in many food specialty stores, especially those dealing in Spanish-American foods. Should you wish to make your own, here is the way to do so.

## ★   *Mole Paste*

2 tsps. sesame seeds (*ajonjoli*)
¼ tsp. *comino* seeds
4 whole almonds
2 whole cloves
1-inch stick cinnamon

1½ tsps. salt
¼ tsp. black pepper
⅛ tsp. nutmeg
*Pasta de chili* to taste (page 60)

Place seeds in an iron skillet and toast them over moderate heat, shaking the pan to and fro, until golden brown. Combine seeds, almonds, cloves and cinnamon in an electric blender and pulverize or put through the finest blade of your grinder. Add salt, pepper and nutmeg. Add *pasta de chili,* bit by bit, to taste. Store covered until needed.

Most *mole* dishes call for either turkey or chicken. Here is a slightly different one, however, which requires chicken livers. Delectable.

★    *Chicken Liver Mole*

| | |
|---|---|
| 1 lb. chicken livers | 2 cups well-seasoned chicken stock |
| Salt and pepper | or broth |
| Flour | 4 Tbs. *mole* paste |
| ¼ cup butter | 3 cups cooked rice |

Cut chicken livers into equal-size pieces; sprinkle with salt and pepper, dredge with flour and shake off any excess. Heat butter in a heavy skillet and sauté the livers gently just until the last trace of pink has gone from them. Remove them from the pan and reserve. Add 1 tablespoon flour to the butter in the skillet. Blend and let brown. Add 1½ cups of the stock and cook, stirring constantly, until thickened. Stir in *mole* powder that has been mixed with the remaining broth. Reduce heat to low and simmer about half an hour. Add livers and heat. Arrange hot, cooked rice on a platter and pour the *mole* sauce over all. Serves 6.

NOTE: As all *mole* sauces thicken considerably as they cook, and even more if they are cooled and then reheated, the amount of broth used in this recipe may have to be increased.

Many Mexican (or Mexican-inspired) sauces are used in Texas for thoroughly American dishes as well as for those of the Texas-Mexican cuisine. You frequently find them with chicken, beef, pork and shellfish. Their constant and universal use within the state probably accounts for the fact that Texas does not use as many French sauces as are found elsewhere. They are also used at times as ingredients in dishes. But since they are basically as Mexican as the two Chili sauces given on pages 60 and 61, I include them here rather than later with the Texas-American sauces.

*Gaucamole,* as just about everyone in this country has learned, is a delectable creation made predominantly of mashed or puréed avocado. As it is most frequently used as an appetizer dip, I have included it among similar recipes (see page 102). But mention is made of it here, for with Tex-Mex dishes it is also used as a kind of sauce. Almost identical ingredients give us another popular sauce, the *Salsa de Aguacate,* that is used in Texas not only with the Mexican dishes but with vegetables, too, and as a relish with meats of all kinds.

★   *Salsa de Aguacate*

| | |
|---|---|
| 2 medium-size ripe avocados | 1 small can chopped green chilis, |
| 2 Tbs. strained fresh lime juice | drained |
| 1½ Tbs. finely chopped onion | 1 tsp. salt |
| 1 small clove garlic, mashed | 1 medium-size peeled ripe tomato, chopped |

Halve the avocados, peel and discard seeds. Mash the avocado meat to a paste with the lime juice. Stir in remaining ingredients and refrigerate, covered, until needed. If a more liquid sauce is desired, blend the liquid from the canned green chilis with the avocados before adding the other ingredients. Makes about 2 cups sauce.

*Chilis serranos* are *really* hot, so go warily when using them unless you have had experience with them before and enjoy their fire. They also have a distinctive flavor hidden in their heat and provide one of the best Hot Sauces for meats, poultry, barbecue, *tacos* or eggs.

## ★   Salsa de Chili Serrano

| | |
|---|---|
| 1 tsp. crushed coriander (*cilantro*) seeds | 1 small onion, chopped |
| 3 Tbs. hot water | 1 clove garlic |
| 2 cups solid-pack tomatoes | 2 *chilis serranos* (canned) or more to taste |

Soak the crushed coriander seeds in hot water for 5 minutes; strain, reserving the water. Discard seeds. Combine the reserved water with all other ingredients in an electric blender and whirl until puréed. If you have no blender, put all together through the fine blade of a food grinder. Use as is or simmer gently 5 minutes and serve hot. Makes about 2 cups of sauce.

*Tomatillos,* which may be found canned in all markets that sell Mexican food stuffs, have a very special flavor that is closely akin to that of green tomatoes. They make a sauce that is excellent with beef, pork or chicken and, of course, many of the Mexican dishes that use cornmeal in one way or another. Here is a *Salsa de Tomatillo.*

★ *Salsa de Tomatillo*

| | |
|---|---|
| 1 small onion, chopped | 2 cloves garlic, minced very fine **or** |
| 2 Tbs. olive oil | mashed |
| 4 10-oz. cans *tomatillos* (green | ½ tsp. sugar |
| tomatoes) | Salt to taste |
| 2 3½-oz. cans chopped green chilis | |

In a heavy saucepan, sauté the onion in oil until transparent. Do not brown. Add the liquid from the canned *tomatillos* and chilis. Cook 2 minutes. Add all the remaining ingredients. Simmer 20 minutes, stirring frequently. If desired, thicken with 1 teaspoon cornstarch moistened with 1 tablespoon water. Cook, stirring frequently, 5 minutes longer. Makes about 1 quart of sauce.

There are in Texas many recipes for *Salsa Verde,* but though all are for a green sauce, their flavors and degrees of heat may vary considerably.

★ *Salsa Verde #1*

| | |
|---|---|
| 6 Tbs. olive oil | 3 cans *tomatillos* (green tomatoes) |
| 2 medium onions, chopped | (8-ozs. each) |
| 1 tsp. minced garlic | ½ cup minced fresh parsley |
| ½ cup toasted pumpkin seeds | 6 to 8 canned hot green chili peppers, |
| ¼ cup toasted sesame seeds | seeded |
| | Salt |

In a heavy saucepan, heat the oil; add onion and garlic. Cook gently until onion is transparent. Do not brown. Add the pumpkin seeds and sesame seeds. Cook 4 minutes. Drain half the liquid from *tomatillos* and discard. Add *tomatillos* and remaining liquid to pan. Add also the parsley and hot green chili peppers.

Bring mixture to boil. Reduce heat to medium and cook 5 minutes. Put sauce through food mill or grinder or purée in an electric blender. Add salt to taste. Store, covered, in refrigerator until needed. Serve with *tortillas, enchiladas,* fish, seafood. If a thicker sauce is desired, reheat with a little butter and flour rubbed together. Use 1 tablespoon each as a starter. Makes about 3 cups sauce.

★ *Salsa Verde #2*

4 green chili peppers
1 Tb. (rounded) minced onion
1 Tb. (heaping) minced fresh
  parsley

4 large green tomatoes, chopped
½ cup lard
Salt and pepper to taste

Combine the green chilis, onion, parsley and tomatoes with cold water just to cover. Bring to boil over moderate heat; reduce heat to low and cook until tomatoes are tender. Add water when needed, but only a little. When done, press through a collander or coarse sieve. Heat lard in a skillet. Add tomato mixture. Cook over low heat 15 minutes, stirring frequently. Add salt and pepper to taste. Store, covered, in a glass jar until needed. Makes about 1½ cups.

This cold creation, though called a sauce, is served more like a side dish at Texas-Mexican meals. It is also delicious with seafood.

## ★   Salsa Fria

| | |
|---|---|
| 4 medium-size tomatoes | ½ tsp. oregano, rubbed |
| 6 scallions, slivered | ¼ tsp. pepper |
| ½ small chili pepper, minced | 2 Tbs. red wine vinegar |
| 1 tsp. salt | |

Peel and chop the tomatoes. Add slivered scallions (with part of their green tops), minced chili pepper and salt. If the oregano is not fine, rub it between your finger tips. Add this, the pepper and vinegar. Blend. Chill 2 hours before serving. Makes about 2 cups sauce.

# SEVEN

# *BARBECUE AND BARBECUE SAUCES*

LIKE the Texas-Mexican dishes, *barbecue* makes for yet another culinary language in Texas, but the word itself has come to have many very different meanings to different people. Real barbecue, of course, is a matter of long, slow cooking done out of doors in either of two special ways. In one, the meat is pit-cooked and, being smothered, steams in its own rich juices. In the other, it is cooked over hot coals with constant basting and turning. The end result of both methods is meat of a very special quality, highly seasoned as a rule because of its special basting sauce or a dry seasoning rubbed on the meat prior to cooking. It is served with another special sauce, the *barbecue sauce,* whose characteristic spicy taste has come to be thought of as *the* taste of barbecue itself.

Unfortunately, any dish that has this taste has come to be called barbecue, too. And to confuse matters further, any dish cooked out of doors over any kind of fire has also come to be called barbecue. Most of these latter ones, wonderful though they often are, are simply broiled or grilled. Most of those which take the name because of taste are simply braised, or they may even be stewed. Real barbecue, of necessity, is always well done—but never dry; if cooked over slow-burning coals, the outside of the meat, when done, will be crusted with a marvelous char while the inside will be moist and succulent. Here, in this section, I will deal only with real barbecue. Other so-called barbecue recipes will appear throughout the text under the headings appropriate for their chief ingredient—beef, pork, chicken, whatever.

The origin of the word *barbecue* has much bearing on what true barbecue, the dish (if it can be called such), should be. The actual genesis of the word is anybody's guess, of course, for when and where it was first used has never been established. But the two chief schools of thought on the matter, one of which has the word deriving from the Spanish *barbacoa* (a grill-like arrangement of green sticks on which to cook meat over an open fire) and the other from the French *barbe-à-queue* (head-to-tail), both arrive at the same end: Barbecue in the old days was always a whole or half carcass (or several carcasses at once) and when the meat was not cooked in a pit (as it often was), it would indeed be cooked on a grill-like arrangement of green sticks which, to make them even more fire-resistant, were also first well soaked in water.

Barbecue in the old days was always food for a crowd—sometimes numbered in the thousands, often in the hundreds. The gathering itself came to be known as a barbecue, a very special occasion. Size is inherent in the whole idea of barbecue—which, of course, appeals to Texans. And it is doubly appealing because, cooked out of doors as it must be, it relates to the old days and the open range.

Barbecue cooked over hot coals is, of course, the only practical one for household purposes, whether for a crowd or not.

Very little in the way of equipment is needed to cook the meat to perfection. Actually elaborate outdoor fireplaces are not as efficient for barbecue as some simple draft-free firebox built on the bare ground. A fireplace chimney not only draws off the heat in its up-draft but also the smoke. And the draft, moreover, will cause the fire to flame.

Flames are ruinous to barbecue. To prevent flames, a pot of cold water with a whisk broom in it should always be kept close at hand while cooking. At any sign of flame from melting fat or such, water should be sprinkled from the broom onto the coals. Actually, flames or not (and especially for large cuts of meat), the

84

coals should be sprinkled several times during cooking as a matter of routine. The ensuing cloud of steam that envelops the meat acts as a tenderizer; it also briefly cooks the meat at a higher temperature, the normal heat of a barbecue fire being about 250° F.–275° F. at the level of the grill and the temperature of the steam being around 400° F.

The kind of fire you cook over is the most important factor of good barbecue. It must give a slow, steady heat throughout the required period of cooking time. To do this, the fire of briquets or charcoal must be started ahead of time (but never with kerosene; kerosene will taint your meat) so that you will have a bed of hot coals lightly coated with gray ash over which to start your meat. You must have enough coals to make the bed several inches longer and wider than the meat. From time to time, if necessary, additional coals may be added to the fire. These should be taken from a subsidiary fire kept burning nearby especially to furnish them. Moist chips of any wood except pine or cedar (beware of resin!) may be scattered over the coals now and then to furnish smoke. Moist chips, remember; dry ones will simply burst into flames.

The firebox itself, if built on bare ground, need consist only of four sheets of heavy metal stood upright in a rectangle and hooked or wired together at the corners. The height of the sides should be no more than thirty inches and no less than twenty. Over the top you can lay a square of ⅛-inch expanded metal grill covering the area of your rectangle. On this you arrange the meat to be barbecued, large or small cuts as desired, but always touching one another. If you leave spaces between the pieces of meat, they will act like flues and draw off the heat of your fire which should all be directed to the meat itself. You can overlap the pieces, if you like, but never separate them.

As a general rule, meats to be barbecued are rubbed on all sides with dry seasonings (premixed or not) before cooking. Then, during cooking, they are basted frequently with a special mopping sauce which, though seasoning the meat, serves primarily as a moistener. And of course the meats are turned at frequent intervals to brown and crisp them evenly on all sides as they gradually cook through to succulent moist tenderness. The combination of crisp, smoky crustiness and succulence is the chief characteristic of grill-cooked barbecue. The so-called barbecue sauce is never used during the cooking time unless for one last-minute basting. But it is always served with the meat at table; sometimes it is poured over the meat after it has been carved. The pronounced tomato-spice taste of this sauce, however, has come to be thought of as barbecue's chief feature—which it is not. But because of this any dish cooked with this sauce or a similar one has come to be called barbecue, too. It is not true barbecue.

At real barbecue meals, several different kinds of meat are often barbecued at once. You may have spareribs and short ribs and a brisket and/or steaks. You may have a boned rib roast. You may have half or quarter of a shoat. You may have ham or fresh ham or a haunch of venison, or maybe *cabrito*.

The general menu plan of a barbecue in Texas never varies, however; you will be served Ranch Beans or some similar dish, Potato Salad, sliced ripe tomatoes, sliced raw onion, Cole Slaw, pickles, relishes, Cornbread, hot rolls, hot biscuits, and pies; maybe Fried Pies. Non-Texans, because of the pepper-heat they associate with Texas-Mexican dishes, think of barbecue meals as being hot also, but such is not the case—at least not always the case. Barbecue is always spicy, but it is only sometimes hot. It is hearty food with a very typical Texas air about it. It tastes good anywhere, of course, but in Texas it tastes downright wonderful.

To proceed with a home barbecue, using whatever kind of fireplace or cooking arrangement you have:

1. Start fire of briquets or charcoal at least half an hour before you plan to start cooking. Do *not* use kerosene to light the fire. If you use any starter, use something made for the purpose, or lighter fluid.

86

2. The coals are ready for cooking when they are covered by a fine gray ash.

3. Never have meat closer to heat source than 8 inches; big cuts and virtually all pork should be farther away. Long, slow cooking with frequent basting and turning is the secret of good barbecues.

4. Never use a so-called barbecue sauce as the basting sauce. Its sugar content will cause it to burn. Even if it has no sugar, it will burn, for it is thick with onion and tomato, et cetera.

5. Do *not* let the cooking fire flame at any time. To avoid this, prevent drafts and dripping fat. Some of the latter is bound to get into the fire, so if the meat is excessively fat to start with, trim it. Bear in mind that the wonderful char of barbecue is not really a *burned* char. Burned meat has a bitter, unpleasant taste to it.

6. Spareribs, for barbecue, should be cut into slabs weighing no more than 2 pounds each.

7. Steaks, for barbecue, should be at least 1½ inches thick.

8. Other excellent cuts for barbecue are lamb shanks, beef short ribs, boned beef brisket, any cubed, boneless beef to be cooked on skewers, half a pig's carcass (80 pounds on the hoof is an excellent size for about 12 people).

9. Spit-roasting in many respects is more closely related to oven cooking than it is to real barbecue. If you have a rotisserie, follow the manufacturer's directions.


The following seasoning, made specially for spareribs, is excellent also with short ribs and chicken. Rub meat on all sides with the seasoning about 30 minutes before cooking.


★ *Dry Rib Seasoning*

| | |
|---|---|
| 6 Tbs. salt | 2 Tbs. monosodium glutamate |
| 6 Tbs. sugar | 2½ Tbs. black pepper |
| 1 Tb. dry lemon powder | 1 Tb. paprika |

Combine all ingredients and blend. Store in a tightly covered jar until needed. Makes 12 ounces.

Here is another dry seasoning with a very different flavor.

## ★ Dry Barbecue Mixture

¼ cup celery seed, bruised
¼ cup paprika (Spanish)
½ tsp. sesame seeds

6 dried chili *tipines* (small, round hot peppers)
1 Tb. chili powder
2 Tbs. salt

Combine ingredients and mix thoroughly. Sprinkle over meat on grill after it has begun to brown and its surface is moist enough to hold the mixture. Sprinkle a little at a time but repeatedly, at intervals, until surface of meat has a light but thorough coating. Excellent on spareribs. It may also be used on many oven-roasted meats. Try it on any pork roast. This is also fine sprinkled into the bone cavity of a boned shoulder of pork before roasting or braising.

All barbecue must be basted regularly during cooking, but the so-called barbecue sauce is never used for this purpose. Basting is done with a mopping sauce such as the following:

## ★ A Mopping Sauce for Barbecue

1 cup strong black coffee
½ cup Worcestershire sauce
1 cup tomato catsup
¼ cup butter

1 Tb. freshly ground black pepper
1 Tb. sugar
1 Tb. salt

88

Combine all ingredients and simmer 30 minutes. Stir frequently. Store in a tightly covered jar in refrigerator until needed. Heat gently before using. This is wonderful, too, for oven roasts of pork, et cetera.

Barbecue sauces, as I have mentioned before, are the special sauces with which barbecue (the meat) is served at table. Because of their distinctive and always somewhat similar flavor, many dishes of like taste are called barbecue, too, though they may actually bear no resemblance to the real thing.

★ *Barbecue Sauce #1*

| | |
|---|---|
| 1 cup chopped onion | 2 Tbs. chili sauce |
| ¼ cup butter | 1 Tb. lemon juice |
| 1 clove garlic, minced | ½ tsp. Tabasco sauce |
| 1 cup bouillon or chicken stock | 1 bay leaf |
| ¼ cup vinegar | ¼ tsp. ground cloves |
| ½ tsp. dry mustard | 2 Tbs. sugar |
| 4 tsps. Worcestershire sauce | 2 Tbs. flour |

In a heavy saucepan sauté the onion in butter over moderate heat until golden; do not brown. Add garlic and cook 2 minutes. Add all the remaining ingredients except flour and simmer 20 minutes. Moisten flour with a little cold water and stir into sauce. Cook, stirring constantly, until sauce is thickened. If a hotter sauce is desired, add more Tabasco. Makes 1½ cups.

NOTE: Although I have said that this sauce is never used as a basting sauce, it may be used once or twice at the very end of the barbecue cooking time to give the meat additional flavor. If used before meat is done, it will burn.

Surprisingly, the Barbecue Sauces used in Texas are not always hot sauces. Here is one from Hillsboro.

★ *Barbecue Sauce #2*

1 cup catsup or chili sauce
½ cup water
½ clove garlic, minced
1 medium onion, chopped fine
1 tsp. salt
½ tsp. pepper

1 Tb. paprika
1 Tb. brown sugar
⅓ cup strained fresh lemon juice
1 Tb. Worcestershire sauce
¼ cup (4 Tbs.) butter

Combine catsup and water in saucepan and bring to a boil. Add garlic, onion, salt, pepper, paprika and sugar. Blend. Cook 3 or 4 minutes over high heat. Remove from fire and stir in lemon juice, Worcestershire sauce and butter. Store covered in refrigerator until needed. Heat before using to blend butter. Use for pork, beef or venison. This is also excellent with or in meat loaves, meat balls and such.

By changing the proportions of barbecue-sauce ingredients, you can, with one basic recipe, arrive at a wide variety of sauces. Sometimes, as in the following, a barbecue sauce (and a good one, too) can be made predominantly of commercial sauces—in this case catsup and Worcestershire.

## ★ Barbecue Sauce #3

| | |
|---|---|
| ½ cup butter | 1 cup peanut oil |
| 1 large onion, grated | 1 bottle tomato catsup (12-oz. size) |
| 3 cloves garlic, minced | 1 small bottle Lea and Perrins |
| 3 Tbs. brown sugar | Worcestershire sauce |
| ¼ tsp. red pepper | Juice of 1 lemon, strained, or to taste |
| ½ tsp. dry mustard | Tabasco sauce to taste |

Melt butter in a saucepan over moderate heat; add onion and garlic. Cook until onion is a golden color. Add all the remaining ingredients and simmer 10 minutes. Let stand at least 30 minutes. This makes enough sauce for 6 chickens.

As I mentioned before, barbecue has become many different things to different people, and one of these things is a kind of highly seasoned stew. So popular is this dish in many parts of the South and certain sections of Texas that it is thought of as *the* barbecue. One recipe from Bynum, Texas, simply calls it *Barbecue.*

## ★ Barbecue

| | |
|---|---|
| 3 lbs. lean beef, cut in 3-inch chunks | 2 Tbs. Worcestershire sauce |
| 1 large onion, chopped | 1 tsp. garlic salt |
| 3 Tbs. bacon drippings | 1 tsp. red pepper |
| 2 Tbs. chili powder | 2 Tbs. vinegar |
| 1 cup catsup | 2 cups beef bouillon |

In an iron Dutch oven, brown beef and onions over high heat in the bacon drippings. Combine the remaining ingredients except bouillon. Pour over the meat. Add bouillon and blend. Cover tightly. Place in oven at 275° F. and cook 3 hours. Serve as is with rice and/or beans *or* (better) let stand in the refrigerator 24 hours, then reheat gently. Whether this is "barbecue" or not, it's very good!

# EIGHT

# *APPETIZERS*

# APPETIZERS in Texas

tend to be simple as a rule. You may be offered elaborate canapés, of course, but often what appears with pre-dinner drinks is a spread or dip (usually with a markedly Texas flavor) or tidbits (called *antojitos* by the Mexicans) such as *fritos* or *tostados*, perhaps. These also regularly serve as vehicles for the spreads or dips. Then, too, these crunchy, bite-size bits are often spread with cheese and broiled.

## APPETIZERS, HORS D'OEUVRES AND SUCH

Cheese is much in evidence everywhere in Texas appetizers—just as it is through all of Texas cookery. In fact, hot or cold, cheese is *the* favorite food for before-meal nibbling. If I had to pick one dish as representative of all Texas in this category I would choose *Chili con Queso*. There's not a housewife in the state that does not have her own special *Chili con Queso* recipe. *Chili con Queso* has a host of other uses in the Texas cuisine, to be sure: it appears as sauce, as filling, as an ingredient in "made" dishes, as topping. But most frequently it is served as an appetizer, hot in a bowl with *tostados* for dunking . . . or it may be served over crisp *tostados* on little individual plates.

In close second place to cheese as favorite appetizer food come shrimps. Shrimp dips are almost as ubiquitous as the *Chili con Queso*. Along the Gulf Coast and all the eastern part of the state, shrimps are eaten by the million. Brownsville thinks of itself as the shrimp capital of the world—and maybe it is. Anyway shrimps appear cooked, shelled, whole for dunking; or made into spreads, pastes, combinations with cheese, sauces; in pastries, biscuits and turnovers. And they not infrequently appear as first course at table.

Texas households, as a rule, do not go in for elaborate hors d'oeuvres served at table any more than they do for elaborate appetizers with cocktails. At the fanciest, most formal dinners you do occasionally find some small, hot, rich seafood dish as an opener—crabmeat au gratin, for instance—or you may have oysters in season, or shrimp, but usually dinners begin without prelude . . . though salad, contradictorily, may be eaten first. And at out-of-door meals and especially at barbecues, the first course (and a good, big, filling one at that) is served with drinks but hardly as appetizer. You may have spareribs, for instance, or charcoal grilled shrimp—with appropriate sauce or dip and with both meat (or shellfish) and sauce in quantity.

Here for your appraisal is a group of typical Texas appetizers.

Velveeta cheese is widely used in Texas for the melted cheese dishes with chilis. With seasonings of so strong a character, and where melting qualities are of paramount importance, it serves the purpose admirably and often actually better than a higher-priced natural cheese which, by itself *as* cheese, would be vastly superior.

★ *Chili con Queso #1*

| | |
|---|---|
| 1 large onion, chopped | 1 can chopped green chili peppers |
| 2 Tbs. butter | 1 lb. Velveeta cheese |
| 1 clove garlic | Salt to taste |
| 1½ cups canned tomatoes | Hot pepper sauce to taste |

In a heavy pan or skillet brown the onion slowly in butter with garlic. When the onion is just turning brown, add the tomatoes. Mash with a fork as the juice cooks away. When very thick, add chili peppers and cheese cut in small chunks. Cook over very low heat, stirring frequently, until all the cheese is melted. Add salt and hot pepper sauce to taste. Keep hot in chafing dish to use as dip for *tostados* or refrigerate covered until needed. If refrigerated, reheat gently before serving. This also may be used as a sauce over rare hamburgers or with hot dogs or as an ingredient in meat loaf. It is also wonderful stirred into Cream of Corn Soup. If you want a thicker mixture use more cheese. Makes about 4 cups.

★ *Chili con Queso #2*

| | |
|---|---|
| 3 large onions, chopped | 5 Tbs. Worcestershire sauce |
| 3 Tbs. butter | Tabasco sauce to taste |
| 4 cans chopped green chilis, 3½ oz. each | Salt, if needed |
| | Pepper |
| 3½ lbs. Velveeta cheese, diced | |

Sauté the chopped onions in butter until beginning to color. Add chilis and cook gently 4 minutes. Add cheese. Cook over lowest heat until cheese has all melted, stirring frequently. Add

Worcestershire, Tabasco, salt if needed, and pepper. If the cheese is too thick and starts to "string" during cooking, add a few tablespoonfuls of cold milk blended with 1 tablespoon flour. Serves 12.

## ★ *Cheese Ball*

| | |
|---|---|
| 1 lb. Cheddar cheese, rather soft and grated | ¼ cup scraped or grated onion |
| 1 lb. cream cheese | ½ tsp. celery salt |
| ¼ lb. Bleu or Roquefort cheese | ½ tsp. garlic salt |
| ¼ cup sour cream | 2 Tbs. brandy |
| 1 Tb. hot pepper sauce | 3 ozs. cream cheese |
| 1 Tb. prepared mustard | 2 Tbs. milk or cream |
| | ½ cup finely minced fresh parsley |

Work the cheeses together with the sour cream, seasonings and brandy until smooth and evenly blended. (The job will be easier if at first you work each cheese separately to a blendable consistency.) Form into a ball and chill. Work the additional cream cheese to a thick paste with the milk or cream. Spread this evenly over the cheese ball. Roll the frosted ball in minced parsley. Wrap loosely in wax paper and store in the refrigerator until needed. The flavor will be more mellow if the cheese ball is made several hours before serving.

For extra bite and an interesting flavor, blend the cream cheese and cream for frosting with 1 or 2 tablespoons chili powder. In lieu of the hot sauce in the ball itself, ¼ cup chopped green chilis may be added to the mixture.

★ *Mrs. Nemecek's Cheese Balls*

| | |
|---|---|
| 2 pkgs. cream cheese, 8-ozs. each | 2 cups chopped pecans |
| 4 cloves garlic, mashed | ½ tsp. salt to taste |
| 1 can evaporated milk, 5-oz. size (see note below) | 4 dashes Tabasco |
| | ¼ tsp. soda |
| 1 lb. grated natural Cheddar cheese | ½ tsp. paprika |
| ¾ cup chopped pitted ripe olives | |

Soften cream cheese and beat in garlic and evaporated milk. Add grated Cheddar and blend thoroughly. Add all remaining ingredients except paprika and work together until well mixed. Chill. Divide in 3 or 4 equal parts. Roll into balls and sprinkle with paprika. Wrap in foil and refrigerate until needed. These will keep very well for at least a week. They are better if aged a day before using.

NOTE: The use of evaporated milk in the above recipe is a typical Texas touch. Nowhere else that I know of do you find evaporated milk so often in recipes that would just as well use sweet milk or cream or even sour cream. In the early days in cow country fresh milk was a rarity in the ranch homes because virtually all of it, when available, was used for calves. And the only milk used in the households was canned of one sort or another. I assume that this habitual use of canned milk influenced the recipes that were handed down. And today, even in the recipes created by home economists for commercial use, you find canned milk regularly and bountifully in evidence.

Cheese-onion mixtures make excellent appetizers and many of these, made up on the spur of the moment, follow whim rather than specific format. Here are two recipes to use as points of departure:

## ★ *Liederkranz Spread*

Liederkranz and cream cheese . . . with onions: Blend a standard Liederkranz (rind and all) with 1 ounce cream cheese and enough cream to give a spreadable consistency. Sauté 1 cup finely chopped onion in 2 tablespoons butter until golden. Do *not* brown. Remove from heat and blend with ½ cup minced fresh parsley. Add this to the cheese mixture; blend. Pile in a bowl, sprinkle lightly with chili powder, serve with *tostados* or some such.

## ★ *Cream Cheese-Onion-Bacon Dip*

Work as much cream cheese as you need to spreadable consistency with sweet or sour cream. Season it to taste with a little garlic salt and some coarsely ground black pepper. Use plenty of pepper. Pile this in a serving dish. Sprinkle liberally with slivered scallions, including a bit of the green top, and crumbled crisp bacon. There should be enough of the scallion-bacon mixture on top so that some will go with every helping of the cheese. Serve with *tostados, fritos* or rye melba toast.

Canned chili is an excellent product and needs only a little doctoring for it to pass as home-made. Combined with Velveeta cheese it makes a fine dip for *tostados*.

★ *Hot Chili Dip*

2 cups chili (page 62, or canned,  1 #300 can tomatoes
   without beans)  2 Tbs. canned chopped green chilis,
½ lb. Velveeta cheese     drained

Combine chili and cut up cheese in saucepan and heat gently until cheese is melted; stir frequently. Add tomatoes to taste and the green chilis. Keep hot over hot water until needed. Serve in a bowl with *tostados*. Serves 8 to 10.

*Nachos,* among the most popular of Texas appetizers, are crisp *tostados* with cheese and a bit of *jalapeño,* broiled until browned and bubbly.

★ *Nachos*

12 *tortillas*  1 3½-oz. can *jalapeños,* drained
Oil for frying     and seeded
Sliced cheese (Cheddar or Velveeta)

Cut each *tortilla* in wedges of desired size to make *tostados* (see p. 65). Fry in oil over high heat until golden and just crisp. Drain on paper. Cut cheese into wedge-shaped pieces, each a little smaller than *tostados.* Place a wedge of cheese on each. Top each with a sliver or two of the *jalapeños.* Arrange on baking sheet. Slip under broiler and cook until cheese is bubbly. Serve immediately. Serves 8 to 12.

*Guacamole,* one of the best-known Texas-Mexican specialties, has many uses. It is primarily a side dish at Texas-Mexican meals, though at the same time its function is somewhat that of a sauce. At other kinds of meals it may appear either as hors d'oeuvre or salad. And it frequently appears as a dip with drinks before dinner. Lime juice, I think, is the secret of the best *guacamole,* but lemon juice will do when limes are lacking.

★ *Guacamole*

| | |
|---|---|
| 2 ripe avocados | 2 Tbs. chili sauce (the tomato kind) |
| 1 Tb. olive oil | Tabasco or other hot pepper sauce to |
| 1 Tb. lime juice, or to taste | taste |
| 1 Tb. scraped or grated onion | Salt to taste |

Peel avocados and remove (but reserve) stones. Mash the meat with oil and lime juice until absolutely smooth. Add more lime juice to taste if you like. Add seasonings and blend thoroughly. Place avocado stones in bowl touching the *guacamole* mixture and leave until ready to serve, keeping the bowl covered, and chilled if you like (I find the flavor better at room temperature). The avocado stones will keep the meat from discoloring as long as they are with it. Discard before serving, of course. Serve with *tostados* or such for a cocktail-hour snack; a whole bowlful should be served with any Tex-Mex dinner. Makes about 2½ cups.

★ *Stuffed Green Chilis*

| | |
|---|---|
| 6 medium-hot, large, canned green chilis | 1 cup sour cream |
| | Paprika |
| 4 cups *guacamole* (page 102) | |

Drain chilis, peel if necessary, slit and remove seeds. Fill with *guacamole;* chill. To serve, place a stuffed chili on each plate, top with sour cream and sprinkle with paprika. Serves 6.

Shrimp dips—and good ones, too—are about as common in Texas as *Chili con Queso.* Here is a typical one:

★ *Shrimp Dip*

| | |
|---|---|
| 1 hard-boiled egg yolk | 2 tsps. prepared horseradish |
| 1 clove garlic | (drained) |
| 1 lb. cooked shelled deveined | 2 tsps. Worcestershire sauce |
| shrimp, chopped | 1 Tb. vinegar |
| 2 tsps. prepared mustard | 2 heaping Tbs. minced fresh parsley |
| ¾ cup mayonnaise | Salt and pepper to taste |
| 1 tsp. paprika (heaping) | Dash of Tabasco |

Press egg yolk through a sieve. Mash garlic to a paste. Combine yolk and garlic with all the remaining ingredients. Blend. Refrigerate, covered, 12 hours before serving. When ready to use, if the dip seems too thick, thin it with a bit more mayonnaise or some heavy cream. Serves 12.

Pickled shrimp were popular in New Orleans in the early nineteenth century. They may have been brought to Texas by the Creoles.

## ★ *Pickled Shrimp*

2 Tbs. olive oil
1 lb. cooked shrimp, shelled and deveined
1 cup white wine vinegar
2 Tbs. water
1 medium-small onion cut in paper-thin slices

8 whole allspice
1 bay leaf
3 whole cloves
2 tsps. salt
1 tsp. sugar
1 dash (to taste) hot pepper sauce

Dribble the oil over the cleaned shrimp and blend. Combine remaining ingredients in an enamel pot, bring to a boil and then simmer 2 to 3 minutes. While hot, pour over the shrimp. Cool and refrigerate 24 hours before using. Serves 4 to 6.

These delectable Peanut Sticks are a Texan invention, more insidious than pretzels or potato chips. Make plenty of them if you make any!

## ★ *Peanut Sticks*

Cut crusts from thin-sliced white bread. Cut remaining bread slices each into five fingers. Put fingers in one large flat pan and crusts in another. Place both in oven at 200° F. and leave about 50 minutes, or until crisp. Roll crusts into even fine crumbs. Dip fingers gently into a mixture of equal parts peanut butter and peanut oil which has been seasoned to taste with salt. For best effect it should be just noticeably salty. Roll the dipped fingers in the fine crumbs to coat them evenly all over. Shake off any excess. Store in a box with wax paper between layers. These will keep for a week at least—if they are not all eaten immediately.

# NINE
# *SOUPS*

# TEXAS is not a great soup state. There are

households that serve soup regularly, of course; and where the tables have a non-Texas character, non-Texas soups appear frequently. But for the most part, the emphasis is on the main, more filling part of the meal which, if not always actually meat and potatoes, has a meat-and-potatoes, no-nonsense quality about it— or anyway so it is wherever men dine, whether or not women are present. Where women dine alone in Texas (which is usually at luncheon), you will find smaller, daintier, more typically feminine dishes. Where families dine together, with or without company, soup is generally considered something extra.

You do, however, find some big hearty meat-and-vegetable soups, which are in fact the main part of the meal. These, for the most part, are like country soups served anywhere in the United States. And along the coast, you also find many fish and seafood soups, bisques and stews, often with a markedly Creole taste to them. You find gumbos, too, which are wholly Creole. And in hot weather, cold soups. But as any collection of Texas recipes, published or private, will quickly inform you, Texas soups are really few and far between. And oddly enough outsiders visiting Texas rarely miss them. Here are a few of the few, however, to prove that those you do find are worth making anywhere!

The upper Gulf Coast of Texas, and in fact all the area north and east of Galveston with Beaumont at the center and Nacogdoches at about the northern extremity, is as much, if not more, an extension, gastronomically, of Creole Louisiana across the Sabine River than it is of the area to the south. Here you find many specialties that are identical to those of New Orleans. While the chili seasoning is present in many dishes, you find in many others the blend of spices and herbs that gives Creole cookery its characteristic taste. You also find many dishes made with a French precision, in carefully measured, timed steps, that gives them a sophistication seldom found in the popular Texas-Mexican dishes. This gumbo is typically Creole:

# ★ *A Red Shrimp Gumbo from Galveston*

¼ cup chopped onion
¼-inch thick ham slice cut in ½-inch squares
2 cloves garlic, minced
½ cup lard
2 Tbs. flour
2 lbs. fresh okra, stemmed and sliced

1½ cups canned tomatoes, partly drained
2 Tbs. chopped green pepper
1 Tb. chopped celery
2 bay leaves
¼ tsp. thyme
2 qts. hot water
Salt and cayenne to taste
2 lbs. shelled, deveined raw shrimp

In a heavy pot sauté the onion, ham and garlic in the lard over moderate heat until the onion is golden, stirring frequently. Add flour and blend. Cook until flour is browned. Add okra and cook, stirring from time to time; watch, for okra burns easily. When the okra has stopped "stringing" (which it will do shortly), add tomatoes, green pepper, celery, bay leaves, thyme and water. Blend. Cook 5 minutes over low heat. Add salt and cayenne to taste. Add shrimp. Simmer for 1 hour. Correct seasoning as needed. Serve in soup plates or bowls. Pass plain fluffy rice on the side so each diner may help himself. Serves 8 to 10.

Game birds of many kinds are plentiful in Texas. Here is a wonderful gumbo of wild duck.

★ *Wild Duck Gumbo*

2 Tbs. bacon drippings
1 wild duck
2 large onions, chopped
2 cloves garlic, minced
2 Tbs. flour
2 sweet green peppers, seeded and
  chopped

3 cups chopped celery
6 cups chicken stock or broth
Salt and pepper to taste
Dried red chili pepper to taste
¼ cup minced fresh parsley
1 Tb. gumbo filé
Cooked rice

In a deep heavy pot heat the bacon drippings and brown duck on all sides over moderate heat. Remove duck to plate. Add onion and garlic to drippings. Cook until golden. Add flour and blend. Cook until brown, stirring frequently. Add green pepper and celery. Cook 3 minutes. Add stock and blend. Return duck to pot; cover and simmer over low heat until bird is tender. Remove duck from pot again. Discarding skin and bone, dice all the meat (or slice it, if desired). Return meat to soup. Season to taste with salt, pepper and red pepper. Add the latter carefully, waiting a minute after each addition for the seasoning to take hold. Stir in parsley. Remove soup from heat and stir in gumbo filé. (This must never be added while the dish is still cooking.) Serve in deep soup bowl with a spoonful of cooked rice placed at the center of each. Serves 6.

Dried shrimp are widely used in parts of Texas and they impart to dishes an excellent, somehow Oriental flavor, even when used for thoroughly Texas recipes, as in this soup.

## ★ *Shrimp Soup*

| | |
|---|---|
| 1 medium-size onion, chopped | 1 cup dried shrimp |
| 1 clove garlic, minced | 2 whole cloves |
| 2 Tbs. butter | 4 cups sweet milk |
| 1 tomato, peeled and chopped | 1 cup water |
| 3 raw Irish potatoes, peeled and diced | Salt and pepper to taste |
| | Minced fresh parsley |

In a saucepan sauté the onion and garlic in butter until the onion is golden. Add tomato and cook 3 to 4 minutes. Add potatoes and cook another 3 to 4 minutes, stirring frequently. Add shrimp, cloves, milk and water. Reduce heat to low. Simmer gently until potatoes are tender. Add salt and pepper to taste. Serve with a sprinkling of minced fresh parsley. Serves 6.

Gulf oysters have a more metallic flavor than those of the Atlantic Coast and, in consequence, often appear in dishes with pronounced seasonings. Here, however, is an Oyster Bisque not unlike those made in Georgia and South Carolina in the nineteenth century.

## ★ *Oyster Bisque*

| | |
|---|---|
| 1 medium onion, chopped | 1 qt. rich milk |
| 2 stalks celery, chopped | 2 cups heavy cream |
| 2 Tbs. butter | 1 tsp. salt (or to taste) |
| 1 qt. oysters with their liquor | ½ tsp. white pepper |
| ½ cup butter | 3 Tbs. minced fresh parsley |
| ¼ cup flour | Additional minced fresh parsley |

In a saucepan gently sauté onion and celery in butter until tender. Do *not* brown them. Add oysters and their liquor. Simmer until oysters plump and their edges curl. Drain, reserving liquor. Put oysters and vegetables through a food mill or grinder. Set aside.

Melt ½ cup butter in saucepan or double boiler over low heat. Add flour and blend. Stir in milk. Cook, stirring constantly, until smooth and thickened. Stir in cream, ground oysters and 1 cup of the reserved oyster liquor. Heat thoroughly but do not boil. Add salt, pepper and parsley. Serve hot in cups with a sprinkling of additional minced parsley. Serves 6 to 8.

Cold soups are popular in the hot Texas summer, especially at women's luncheons. There is a great difference, in Texas, between women's and men's dishes. Men's soups, in Texas, are the big, filling ones.

## ★ *Cold Buttermilk Soup*

1 qt. buttermilk
1 tsp. salt
1 tsp. sugar
1 Tb. fresh dill weed (1 tsp. dried)
1 medium-size cucumber, peeled, seeded and diced

½ lb. cooked, shelled, deveined shrimp, chopped
Prepared mustard to taste
Parsley or additional dill

In the container of your electric blender combine 1 cup of the buttermilk with salt, sugar, dill, cucumber and shrimp. Blend until smooth. Pour into bowl, stir in remaining buttermilk and add mustard to taste. Cover and chill several hours. Serve very cold in cup with a sprinkling of parsley or additional dill. Serves 6.

Another cold soup popular everywhere in Texas is the Spanish (and Mexican) *Gaspacho*.

★ *Gazpacho*

5 very ripe tomatoes, peeled
1 cucumber, peeled and chopped
1 green pepper, seeded and chopped
1 onion, chopped
1 clove garlic, crushed
1 rounded Tb. minced fresh parsley

1¼ cups tomato juice
3 Tbs. olive oil
2 Tbs. wine vinegar or lemon juice (or half and half)
¼ tsp. paprika
Salt to taste

Seed and chop the tomatoes; set about ⅓ of them aside. Combine the remaining ones in blender container with cucumber, green pepper, onion, garlic and parsley. Blend until almost smooth. Stir in tomato juice, oil, vinegar, paprika and salt to taste. Add the remaining chopped tomatoes. Chill thoroughly. Serve in chilled soup bowls with an ice cube in each. Serves 6.

# TEN

## *EGG DISHES*

**THE** setting and the company in which any dish is served make a great difference in the way a dish appeals to any diner. The best eggs I ever ate, it seems to me, were some fried ones that I had one morning some years ago in Texas; they were old-fashioned (and maybe indigestible) fried eggs cooked and basted in drippings so that, when done, the yellow eyes had a pale film over them. The edge of each egg white had a fine brown lace around it. But the eggs were not rubbery; they were tender and of that wonderful flavor that only really nest-fresh eggs can have. They were served that morning by the platterful with fried ham and gravy and fried potatoes and hot biscuits. The Fried Eggs with Green Chilis that are served in Texas are wonderful, too.

★ *Eggs with Green Chilis*

| | |
|---|---|
| 2 rounded Tbs. canned chopped | 4 eggs |
| green chilis | Salt |
| 3 Tbs. butter | |

Sauté the chopped chilis in butter for 2 to 3 minutes over moderate heat. One by one, break eggs carefully into a saucer and slide into the hot butter. Fry over moderate heat until white is set. Baste with hot butter as they cook. The yellow of each egg should have an opaque glaze when done. Sprinkle with salt and serve immediately. Serves 2 to 4.

*Nopalitos* (or *nopales*) are the prepared leaves of certain cactus plants indigenous to Texas. Canned, they are sold in stores that deal in Mexican food specialties. They are used in sauces, salads and such egg dishes as the following:

## ★ *Lupalitas*

3 Tbs. lard
2 cloves garlic, minced
1 small onion, chopped
1 Tb. canned, chopped green
  chilis, drained

1 Tb. chili powder
4 eggs, beaten
Salt and pepper to taste
1 cup canned cubed *nopales*,
  drained

Heat lard in an 8-inch iron skillet over moderate flame and sauté garlic and onion until just beginning to take on color. Add green chilis and chili powder; blend. Beat eggs lightly and season to taste with salt and pepper. Pour into skillet and scramble over low heat, stirring and turning the eggs gently until almost set. Stir in the *nopales*. Heat through—by which time the eggs should just be done. Serve immediately. Serves 2 or 4.

Many other egg dishes in Texas have a pronounced Mexican taste. These are cooked with a *salsa verde*.

## ★ *Barelas Eggs*

6 large eggs
¾ cup Salsa Verde #2 (page 79)

Butter 6 custard cups. Carefully break an egg into each. Add 2 tablespoons *Salsa Verde* to each cup. Set cups in pan with 1 inch hot water. Bake at 350° F. until whites are set. Do *not* overcook.

Potato-egg dishes are popular in Germany and perhaps the German settlers around New Braunfels and Fredericksburg brought with them the recipes for such omelets as this:

## ★ *Bacon-and-Potato Omelet*

| | |
|---|---|
| 6 slices bacon, diced | ½ tsp. salt |
| 2 Tbs. finely chopped onion | ⅛ tsp. white pepper |
| 1 cup raw potato, grated | Generous dash Tabasco |
| 6 eggs | 2 Tbs. minced fresh parsley |

Fry bacon until crisp. Remove from pan. Drain off all but 2 tablespoons drippings. Add onion to drippings and sauté over low heat until tender. Add potatoes and cook until golden brown. Lift with spatula to keep from burning. Beat eggs with salt, pepper and Tabasco. Pour over the potatoes. Lift edges of omelet gently with spatula as it cooks. Tilt the pan slightly to let the soft part run under. When omelet is nearly firm throughout, sprinkle with crisp bacon and parsley. Fold omelet over on itself, slide onto a heated platter and serve immediately. Serves 6.

# ELEVEN

# *CHEESE DISHES*

SO many Texas dishes have cheese in or on or with them that it is sometimes difficult to decide which ones should be thought of as primarily of cheese. Here are a few such, however. And first and foremost is a dish that could also have been included with the Texas-Mexican dishes:

★  *Chilis Rellenos (Stuffed Peppers)*

12 canned *chilis poblanos*
¾ lb. *each* Monterey Jack and
    Cheddar cheese, both grated
 2 tsps. hot *jalapeño* sauce
Flour for dredging

4 eggs, separated
¼ cup flour, additional
Fat for frying
*Jalapeño* sauce

Make a cut down the side of each chili, but do not open the pepper full length. Using a teaspoon, scoop out seeds and pith and discard. Combine the two cheeses and mix with the *jalapeño* sauce. Fill peppers with the cheese mixture and press them gently into shape. Dredge each lightly with flour to coat evenly all over; shake off any excess. Beat the egg whites until stiff and gently mix in the ¼ cup flour. Beat the yolks lightly and blend these also into the whites. Dip floured peppers in this batter. Fry them in deep fat at 370° F. until golden brown. Serve with *jalapeño* sauce. Serves 6.

Texas "economy" dishes rarely if ever have an "economy" taste. This delicious loaf is typical:

★   *Cheese Rice Loaf with Chilis*

| | |
|---|---|
| ½ cup chopped onion | 1 cup milk |
| 3 Tbs. butter | 2 cups grated Cheddar cheese |
| 1 can chopped green chilis, drained | 3 eggs, beaten |
| ¼ cup sifted flour | 4 cups cooked rice |
| 1 tsp. salt | ¼ cup minced fresh parsley |
| ½ tsp. dry mustard | |

Sauté onion in butter until golden. Add chilis; blend. Stir in flour, salt, and mustard. Add milk. Cook over low heat, stirring constantly, until smooth and thickened. Add cheese and blend. Remove from heat. Stir in beaten eggs, rice and parsley. Pour into a greased loaf pan. Bake at 300° F. for 1 hour and 15 minutes or until firm. Turn out on heated platter to serve. Serves 6 to 8.

There is a vast group of dishes in Texas which, though surely of Mexican inspiration and certainly with Mexican names, are now thoroughly Texan and appear more often at family or even company meals than at Texas-Mexican ones. This is a marvelous creation!

## ★ *Chilaquilles*

2 medium-size onions, chopped
1 clove garlic, minced
2 Tbs. lard
2 cans tomatoes, #2 size
Salt and pepper to taste
1 can chopped green chilis, drained,
   3½-oz. size

12 *tortillas* cut in quarters
Fat for frying
  2 lbs. cheese (preferably Monterey
    Jack), grated
2 cups sour cream

Sauté onions and garlic in 2 tablespoons lard until golden. Add tomatoes and salt and pepper; simmer until thick, stirring frequently. Stir in chili peppers and set aside. Cut *tortillas* as directed and fry briefly in hot fat. Drain on paper. In a greased baking dish or casserole arrange the ingredients in alternate layers of *tortillas,* tomato-chili sauce, and grated cheese, until all are used. End with cheese on top. Bake at 350° F. until cheese is bubbly. Just before serving top with sour cream. Heat thoroughly but do not really cook. Serve immediately. Serves 8 to 10. Serve soft, heated *tortillas* on the side.

# TWELVE

## *FISH*

ALONG the Texas Gulf Coast, some of the world's finest fish make some of the best dishes that appear at Texas tables. Some of these show a strong Creole influence, but most have a Texas taste.

★ *Baked Fish*

| | |
|---|---|
| 1 whole fish, bass or similar (5 lbs.) | ⅓ cup butter |
| Flour | 3 cups canned tomatoes |
| Salt and pepper | 1 Tb. Worcestershire sauce |
| ½ cup chopped onion | 1 Tb. catsup |
| 1 cup chopped celery | 1 rounded tsp. chili powder |
| 1 clove garlic, minced | 2 Tbs. fresh lemon juice |
| ½ cup chopped, seeded green pepper | 1 bay leaf, crumbled very fine |
| | Cayenne or Tabasco to taste |

Dredge fish inside and out with flour and sprinkle with salt and pepper. Lay it in a greased baking dish. Set aside while you prepare the sauce.

Sauté onion, celery, green pepper and garlic in butter over moderate heat until onion is golden. Add remaining ingredients and simmer 20 minutes or until the vegetables are all tender. Press the mixture through a fine sieve and pour around the fish. Bake at 350° F. for 45 minutes, basting frequently after the first 15 minutes. Remove to a platter when done and spoon the remaining sauce over fish. Serves 6.

NOTE: Baked fish, cooked with a sauce similar to the above, is often called barbecued fish in Texas.

Fish fillets, both fresh and frozen, are used for a wide variety of dishes in Texas, some very plain, some very fancy. This dish from Galveston is reminiscent of many from New Orleans.

## ★ Red Snapper with Mustard Sauce

| | |
|---|---|
| 3 lbs. red snapper fillets (1½ lb. each if possible | 1 Tb. prepared mustard |
| Salt | 1 Tb. tarragon vinegar |
| 2 egg yolks | ½ cup butter |
| | Paprika |

Poach fish fillets in salted water until they flake easily when tested with a fork. Remove carefully to a platter. Keep hot until needed. In the top of a double boiler, over hot but not boiling water, cook the egg yolks, mustard, tarragon vinegar and butter together, stirring constantly, until smooth and thickened. Remove from heat and add salt to taste. Spread sauce over fish fillets. Sprinkle with paprika and serve immediately. Serves 3 to 4.

Many dishes are made with fish fillets and crabmeat in combination.

## ★ Flounder Fillets with Crabmeat Dressing

| | |
|---|---|
| 2 cloves garlic, minced very fine | 1 cup cornbread crumbs |
| 1 cup slivered green onions with part of their green tops | ½ tsp. salt, or more to taste |
| | ¼ tsp. pepper |
| ⅓ cup butter | 1 Tb. sherry |
| 1 hard-cooked egg, chopped | 8 flounder fillets of equal size |
| 1 lb. well-picked crabmeat | 3 strips bacon cut in 1-inch lengths |
| 1 cup milk | |

Sauté garlic and onions in butter over moderate heat until golden. Do not brown. Add egg, crabmeat, milk and crumbs. Blend. Season with salt, pepper and sherry. Place half the flounder fillets on the bottom of a buttered rectangular Pyrex baking dish. Spread evenly with the dressing. Top with remaining fillets. Dot with the lengths of bacon. Bake 30 minutes at 375° F. or until done. Serve from the baking dish. Serves 8.

What with the immense citrus groves of the Rio Grande Valley, it is hardly surprising that Texas has many dishes with a citrus taste. The garnish of spring onions in this one makes it doubly Texas.

## ★ Baked Fish Fillets with Lemon Butter

| | |
|---|---|
| ⅛ lb. butter (½ stick) | ¼ tsp. white pepper |
| 1 Tb. lemon juice | 4 fish fillets, about ½ lb. each |
| ½ tsp. salt | Minced spring onions and parsley |

Melt butter and blend with lemon juice, salt and pepper. Dip fillets in this lemon butter and lay in shallow baking pan or Pyrex dish. Bake at 325° F. about 30 minutes or until lightly browned. Baste with remaining lemon butter twice during cooking. Sprinkle with minced spring onions and parsley before serving. Serves 4.

Corn finds its way into all kinds of Texas dishes. (In the old days, sweetened corn puddings were served as desserts.) Here it is combined with salmon to make delectable fritter-like puffs.

## ★ Salmon-Corn Puffs with Parsley Sauce

| | |
|---|---|
| 2 eggs | ¼ tsp. pepper |
| ⅓ cup milk | ½ tsp. paprika |
| 2 Tbs. melted butter | 1 cup canned salmon (skin and |
| 1 cup flour | bones removed) |
| 1 tsp. baking powder | 1 cup cooked whole-kernel corn |
| ½ tsp. salt | Fat for frying |

Beat eggs and then beat again with milk. Add butter. Combine dry ingredients and sift together. Add to egg mixture and blend. Flake salmon. Add salmon and corn to batter. Drop by table-spoons, a few at a time, into deep fat at 375° F. Fry until golden brown on all sides. Skim out and drain on paper. Keep hot on baking sheet in oven at 250° F. until all are done. Serve with Parsley Sauce (page 236). Serves 6.

Frequently in Texas you will find preparations and/or sauces that have multiple uses. This sauce is made to be spread over fish fillets before baking or to be combined with flaked, cooked fish or shellfish to be baked in ramekins or shells.

## ★ *Imperial Sauce*

| | |
|---|---|
| 2 Tbs. finely minced onion | 2 Tbs. finely chopped mustard |
| ¼ cup finely chopped mushrooms | pickle |
| 2 Tbs. butter | ½ tsp. sugar |
| 1 cup rich cream sauce | 1 Tbs. chopped pimiento |
| 1 cup mayonnaise | ½ tsp. Worcestershire sauce |
| 1 tsp. lemon juice | |

Sauté onion and mushrooms in butter; combine with remaining ingredients. Spread on fish fillets and bake at 300° F. for 30 to 40 minutes. Makes 2½ cups.

Fresh-water fish abound in Texas lakes and rivers and find their way ultimately to Texas tables in all parts of the state. A favorite everywhere is catfish which, when fried, makes for wonderful eating.

## ★ *Fried Catfish*

| | |
|---|---|
| 1 lb. catfish fillets | 1 Tb. flour |
| Salt and pepper | Cornmeal |
| 1 Tb. water | Lard |
| 1 egg | |

Cut fillets into serving portions of uniform size as desired. Sprinkle with salt and pepper on both sides. Mix water, egg and flour together; beat thoroughly. Dip fillets in batter to coat all over. Dredge in cornmeal. Shake off any excess and let coated fillets rest 5 to 10 minutes on wax paper for the coating to set.

Heat lard to a depth of ¼ inch in a heavy 10-inch skillet. Fry a few fillets at a time over moderate heat, turning them once to brown evenly. Serve with Hush Puppies. Serves 4.

Hush puppies—actually fritters of a sort—were created in the South many years ago to serve with fried fish, the stories of how they were first made to quiet hungry, yapping hound-dogs notwithstanding. When well made, quickly fried and properly drained, they are a perfect fish accompaniment.

## ★ *Hush Puppies*

2 cups cornmeal (water-ground if available)
2 tsps. baking powder
½ tsp. salt

¼ cup grated or finely chopped onion
1½ cups sweet milk
Fat for frying

Combine meal, baking powder and salt. Add onion and milk. Blend thoroughly. Preheat deep fat (preferably lard) to 365° F. Dip a tablespoon first into the hot fat, then into the cornmeal mixture and shape each spoonful to make the Hush Puppies round. Drop one at a time into the hot fat. Do not crowd. Fry to a rich golden brown on all sides. Drain on paper. Serve immediately with the fried fish. Makes about 18.

NOTE: In the early days the Hush Puppies were always fried in the same fat that had been used for the fish and its fish flavor gave them an extra something. If you have fat left in the skillet from frying the fillets, strain it into the deep fat before frying the Hush Puppies.

# THIRTEEN

## *SHELLFISH*

# BROWNSVILLE,

at the mouth of the Rio Grande, regards itself as the "shrimp capital" of the world—and it well may be. It accounts annually for a well-nigh inconceivable mountain of shrimp, which are marketed fresh, frozen, canned and dried. Here is a typical Texas shrimp dish:

★ *Corpus Christi Shrimp Bake*

¾ lb. fresh mushrooms, sliced
1 cup chopped, seeded sweet green pepper
½ cup chopped celery
⅓ cup chopped pimiento
¾ cup butter

2 cups small, cooked, shelled shrimp
2 cups cooked rice
1 can tomatoes, drained, #2 size
1 can chopped green chilis, drained
1 Tb. chili powder
Salt to taste

In a large, heavy skillet sauté mushrooms, green pepper, celery and pimiento in ¼ cup of the butter until mushrooms are just barely cooked (about 5 minutes). Add remaining ingredients and blend. Pour into a greased 2-quart casserole. Melt the remaining ½ cup butter and dribble this over all. Bake at 300° F. for 1 hour. Serves 6 to 8.

New Orleans, itself, never created a better Shrimp Creole than this one:

★  *Houston Shrimp Creole*

| | |
|---|---|
| 2 medium-size onions, chopped | 1 small bay leaf, crumbled |
| 1 sweet green pepper, seeded and chopped | 1 Tb. minced celery leaves |
| | 2 Tbs. minced fresh parsley |
| ½ cup celery, chopped | ½ tsp. Tabasco |
| 4 Tbs. bacon drippings | 4 cups cooked, shelled, medium |
| 4 cups canned tomatoes | shrimp |
| 3 Tbs. tomato paste | Salt to taste |
| 3 Tbs. Worcestershire sauce | Cooked rice |

Sauté the onions, green pepper and celery in bacon drippings over moderate heat until onion begins to brown. Add tomatoes, tomato paste, seasonings and herbs and simmer until thick (about 40 minutes). Add shrimp and salt to taste. Cook gently 15 minutes longer. Serve over or with cooked rice. Serves 6 to 8.

Many shrimp and oyster dishes made along the Texas coast call for potatoes in a way that is reminiscent of New England chowders, though the Texas dishes are main course dishes as often as they are soups. The difference between them lies chiefly in the use of more or less liquid, more or fewer potatoes and/or shellfish. Here is a Shrimp Stew made with beer. The "crab boil" is a packaged herb and spice mix, widely marketed in Texas and often available in fish markets elsewhere.

136

## ★ Shrimp Stew

| | |
|---|---|
| 2 medium-size onions, chopped | Salt and pepper to taste |
| 5 cloves garlic, minced | 6 medium-size potatoes, peeled and |
| 1 3½ oz. can *jalapeños,* drained | cubed |
| and seeded | 1 large onion, chopped |
| ¼ cup "crab boil" | 1 lb. shelled, deveined, raw medium- |
| 1 qt. beer | size shrimp |
| ½ cup fresh lime juice | Fresh parsley or paprika |

In a heavy pot combine onions, garlic, *jalapeños,* "crab boil", beer and lime juice. Bring to boil; reduce heat and simmer 30 minutes. Strain and return to pot. If too much liquid has cooked away, add more beer or a little hot water. Add salt and pepper to taste. Add potatoes and the additional chopped onion; cook over moderate heat until potatoes are barely tender. Add shrimp and simmer 5 minutes or until shrimp are firm and pink. Do not overcook them. There should not be too much liquid left. Before serving sprinkle with paprika or minced fresh parsley. Serves 4 to 6.

Shrimp are ideal for the seasonings that Texans like best. This dish has almost all of them.

## ★ Spiced Shrimp Casserole

½ cup chopped onion
2 cloves garlic, minced
4 Tbs. butter
2 lbs. shelled, deveined, raw, medium-size shrimp
1 cup raw rice
1 can tomatoes, #303 size
1 small bay leaf, finely crumbled
2 cups chicken stock or broth

3 Tbs. minced fresh parsley
½ tsp. ground allspice
½ tsp. oregano
1 Tb. chili powder
1 Tb. salt (or less if the chicken broth is very salty)
1 generous dash hot pepper sauce
½ tsp. freshly ground black pepper
3 Tbs. extra butter

Lightly brown the onion and garlic in butter. Combine (scraping in all the melted butter) with all the remaining ingredients (except extra butter) in a buttered casserole or baking dish. Blend thoroughly. Cover tightly and bake at 350° F. for 1 hour and 30 minutes. Toss with a fork lightly at the end of 1 hour. Add a little more chicken stock (hot) if needed, but remember that this dish, when done, should be quite dry. Cover and finish cooking. Dot with 3 tablespoons butter and serve immediately. Serves 6.

Wild rice is widely used in Texas for party dishes. Many of these are made also with shrimp.

## ★ Shrimp with Wild Rice

1½ lbs. shelled, deveined raw medium-size shrimp
2 tsps. salt
1 clove garlic, halved
1 small bay leaf
2 celery leaves
¼ tsp. oregano

½ lb. fresh mushrooms
½ cup chopped onion
¼ lb. butter
1 8-10-oz. pkg. wild rice
¼ cup minced fresh parsley
Extra butter

138

Combine shrimp, salt, garlic, bay leaf, celery leaves and oregano in a saucepan with boiling water to cover. Simmer over low heat 8 minutes. Set aside until cool. Then remove shrimp; halve them lengthwise. Strain and reserve ½ cup of the liquid. Rinse mushrooms under cold water and drain. Slice caps. Reserve stems for some other use. Sauté sliced caps and chopped onion in butter until the onion is golden. Set aside. Cook the wild rice according to package directions, using the ½ cup reserved stock from the shrimp as a part of the liquid. When done, toss with the mushroom and onion and any butter remaining in the skillet. Toss again with the halved shrimp and minced parsley. Add dabs of extra butter and toss once more. Serve immediately or reheat at 350° F. Serves 6 to 8.

The following dish, though called a Jambalaya, is not really one despite the fact that it contains all the correct jambalaya ingredients. True jambalaya is cooked and served in the same dish. This dish is simply put together. It's delectable nonetheless.

★ *Shrimp Jambalaya*

2 lbs. shrimp, shelled and deveined
Salt
1 bay leaf
3 Tbs. bacon drippings
1 sweet green pepper, seeded and chopped
6 scallions, with part of their green tops, slivered
4 stalks celery, slivered
1 Tb. minced celery leaves

3 Tbs. flour
2 cups chicken stock or more as desired
Tabasco to taste
1½ cups diced lean cooked ham
1 cup diced cooked chicken
2 doz. oysters with their liquor
4 cups cooked rice
¼ cup minced fresh parsley

Place shrimp in pot with cold water to cover, salt to taste and bay leaf. Simmer until shrimp are firm and pink (about 5 minutes). Do not overcook. Let shrimp cool in liquid. Heat drippings in a large heavy skillet. Add green pepper, scallions and celery. Cook over low heat 5 minutes. Add celery leaves. Cook over low heat 5 minutes. Add celery leaves. Sprinkle all with flour. Blend and let flour brown slightly. Stir in chicken stock and cook 3 to 4 minutes, stirring constantly. Add ½ cup of the liquid the shrimp have cooled in. Add Tabasco and additional salt to taste. Stir in ham and chicken. Cook 5 minutes. Stir in oysters and their liquor. Cook until oysters are plump. Add shrimp, drained, and cooked rice. Blend. Cook until shrimp and rice are thoroughly heated. Turn out on a heated platter and sprinkle with parsley. Serves 6 to 8.

Shrimp Patties, made of either fresh or dried shrimp, are as popular in Texas as crab cakes are in Maryland. Here are some made of fresh shrimp.

## ★ Shrimp Patties

| | |
|---|---|
| 1 lb. shelled, deveined raw shrimp | 1 egg, lightly beaten |
| 1 large peeled raw potato | 1 medium sweet green pepper, |
| 1 medium-large onion, quartered | seeded and chopped very fine |
| 2 cloves garlic | ¼ cup fine cracker crumbs |
| ¾ tsp. salt | 2 Tbs. melted butter |
| ¼ tsp. pepper | Fat for frying |

Grind together the shrimp, potato, onion and garlic. Add salt and pepper. Blend. Add egg and blend. Stir in chopped green pepper and melted butter. Form into small patties not more than

½ inch thick. Dredge in cracker crumbs. Pat these on with the fingers so they adhere. Shake off any excess. Fry in deep fat at 370° F. until golden brown. Drain. Serve with sauce. Serves 4. Smaller, thinner patties may be served as appetizers with cocktails.

As you'd expect, shrimp salads of many kinds are made in all parts of Texas. Here is one made with macaroni.

★ *Shrimp and Macaroni Salad*

1 lb. cooked, shelled, deveined shrimp (medium-size)
1 lb. elbow or shell macaroni, cooked and drained
1 medium onion, chopped
1 small sweet green pepper, seeded and chopped
1 cup slivered celery
1 Tb. minced celery leaves
2 Tbs. minced fresh parsley
2 hard-cooked eggs, chopped
Salt and pepper to taste
1 cup mayonnaise
Lettuce
Additional minced fresh parsley

In a large bowl combine all the ingredients except mayonnaise and extra parsley. Toss with two forks to blend. Add mayonnaise and toss again. If the salad seems too dry, add cream spoonful by spoonful, tossing after each addition. Chill at least 3 hours before serving. Serve on a platter with lettuce and the extra parsley sprinkled over all. Serves 8.

Texas housewives have a passion for molded salads of all kinds. Many of them are actually desserts. Here is a Shrimp Mold with Olives, an excellent dish for luncheon or buffet.

## ★ *Shrimp Mold with Olives*

| | |
|---|---|
| 3 envelopes unflavored gelatin | 1½ lbs. cooked, shelled, deveined |
| 1 can tomato juice, 1 qt. 14 oz. size | shrimp, chopped |
| ¼ tsp. Tabasco | 1 cup chopped pimiento-stuffed |
| 1 tsp. chili powder | olives |
| 1 tsp. paprika | 1 cup very finely chopped celery |
| ½ cup strained fresh lime juice | 6 pimiento-stuffed olives, sliced |
| 8 ozs. cream cheese, softened | Watercress |
| ½ cup mayonnaise | Extra mayonnaise |

Moisten gelatin with 1 cup tomato juice. Combine with remaining tomato juice in saucepan. Bring to boil and remove from heat. Stir until gelatin is dissolved. Add Tabasco, chili powder, paprika and lime juice. Blend. Beat together the softened cream cheese and mayonnaise. Gradually beat in the tomato mixture. Cool, then chill until very thick but not set. Stir in chopped shrimp, chopped olives and celery. Turn into a 2½ quart mold that has been rinsed in cold water. Chill until set. Unmold on a cold serving dish. Arrange sliced olives on top. Fill center with a clump of watercress. Pass extra mayonnaise separately. Serves 8.

I mentioned in the introduction that in Texas you often find some very typically Texas dish (and a simple one at that) at the same table with elaborate ones. Coming now to crab meat I am reminded of one Texas buffet at which Crab Newberg appeared (not unhappily) with black-eyed peas and champagne. And of an informal dinner table where the following delectable Crab Soufflé appeared with *Chilis Rillenos*—not unhappily either.

## ★ Crab Soufflé

1½ cups rich White Sauce (page 232)
1¼ cups grated Gruyère or Swiss cheese
4 eggs, separated
3 cups well-picked crab meat
2 Tbs. minced fresh parsley
Salt and cayenne

Make White Sauce as directed on page 232 in top of double boiler; add cheese and stir until melted. Beat egg yolks lightly and stir into sauce. Remove from heat. Add crab meat and parsley. Season to taste with salt and cayenne. Beat egg whites until stiff and fold into crab-meat mixture. Pour into buttered 2-quart soufflé dish. Set in pan of hot water and bake at 325° F. for about 1 hour. Serve immediately. Serves 4 to 6.

## ★ Crab Casserole

2 cups cream
2 Tbs. melted butter
¾ cup mayonnaise
2 tsps. salt
2 Tbs. minced fresh parsley
1 lb. well-picked crab meat
2 cups fine soft breadcrumbs
4 hard-cooked eggs, chopped
1 Tb. chopped green onion with some of the green top
½ tsp. Tabasco
Extra butter

Combine cream, butter, mayonnaise and salt; blend. Cook over low heat, stirring constantly, for 5 minutes.

In a bowl combine parsley, crab meat and crumbs. Toss to blend. Add the hot cream mixture and blend. Stir in eggs, onion and Tabasco. Season to taste. Pour into a buttered 2-quart casserole. Bake at 350° F. for 20 minutes. Remove from oven. Dot with extra butter. Slip under the broiler for a minute to brown. Serves 6 to 8.

Wherever crab meat is used at all, it finds its way into rather special dishes . . . and in this respect, Texas is no different from the rest of the country.

## ★ *Crab Meat Salad*

| | |
|---|---|
| 2 cups well-picked crab meat | ¼ cup chopped walnuts |
| ¼ cup diced seeded cucumber | ½ cup mayonnaise |
| ¼ cup very finely slivered celery | Lettuce or watercress |

Combine all the ingredients except the lettuce in a bowl and toss to blend. Season to taste with a little salt and pepper. Cover and chill at least 1 hour before serving. To serve, turn out into a nest of lettuce or watercress on a platter or arrange on individual plates. Serves 6.

Though this is rather bland by Texas standards, it still manages to have a somewhat Texas taste to it.

## ★ *Green Peppers Stuffed with Crab Meat*

| | |
|---|---|
| 6 medium-size green peppers of equal size | 1 tsp. fresh lemon juice |
| 1 cup cream | 2 cups well-picked crab meat |
| 4 Tbs. butter | 1 cup cooked rice |
| 1 generous pinch nutmeg | 1 tsp. salt |
| 2 Tbs. cornstarch | 2 Tbs. minced fresh parsley |
| ¼ cup chicken stock | Paprika |

Cut a slice from stem end of each pepper and remove seeds and membranes. Parboil peppers for 5 minutes, skin, and let drain upside down.

Meanwhile combine cream and butter in saucepan and heat gently. Combine nutmeg and cornstarch with stock and lemon juice. Stir into cream and cook over low heat, still stirring, until thickened. Remove from heat and stir in crab meat, rice, salt and parsley. Fill peppers with the mixture. Sprinkle each with paprika. Stand peppers upright, supporting one another, in a greased baking dish. Bake at 350° F. for 20 minutes. Serves 6.

Texas Oysters Creole are more often than not pure Texas. These, though seasoned only with catsup and Worcestershire sauce, are wonderful!

★ *Texas Oysters Creole*

3 Tbs. butter  
1 cup chopped green onions with a few tops  
1 cup catsup  
½ cup Worcestershire sauce  
1 qt. oysters and their liquor  
½ cup minced fresh parsley  
Salt, if needed

In a heavy pan heat butter and sauté the onions until limp. Add catsup and Worcestershire sauce. Blend. When heated, add oysters and their liquor. Cook gently until the oysters are plump. Stir in parsley. Add salt if needed. Serve in bowls as a kind of soup or with rice as a main dish. Serves 6 to 8.

Green onion tops, celery leaves and parsley combine to give these oysters a very special character.

## ★ Texas Deviled Oysters

1 cup white part of scallions, chopped
½ cup celery, chopped
1 Tb. minced celery leaves
3 Tbs. olive oil
1 qt. oysters

1 cup green onion tops, minced
1 cup minced fresh parsley
½ cup soft breadcrumbs, toasted
Fine dry breadcrumbs
Butter

Sauté the chopped white onion parts, celery and celery leaves in olive oil over moderate heat until onion is golden. Drain oysters and add them to the onion tops, parsley and toasted crumbs. Toss to blend. Divide oysters and onion sauce among 6 to 8 greased ramekins or shells. Sprinkle with dry crumbs. Dot with butter. Bake at 375° F. for 10 minutes. Serve immediately.

Oyster Stew, in Texas, as with similar shrimp dishes, often has potatoes in it, thus being somewhat like a chowder. But as it is also highly spiced and has a quantity of green onions in it, along with celery leaves, it has a Creole taste. This combination, it seems to me, is very Texan. In this stew, the potatoes and other vegetables are puréed.

## ★ Oyster Stew

1 stalk celery, diced; leaves, minced
6 green onions with part of tops, sliced
4 large white potatoes, peeled and diced
2 medium-size white onions, chopped
2 Tbs. mixed pickling spices in a cheesecloth bag

4 cups water
¼ lb. butter
1 qt. rich milk or half and half
2 qts. oysters and their liquor
1 Tb. Worcestershire sauce
Salt and cayenne to taste

In a heavy pot combine vegetables with spices and water. Cover and simmer until all are very tender. Drain, reserving the liquid. Discard spices. Purée vegetables through sieve. Combine with reserved cooking water, butter and milk. Heat until butter has melted. Blend. Add oysters and their liquor. Cook gently until their edges ruffle and the oysters are plump. Season with Worcestershire sauce, salt and cayenne to taste. Serve immediately. Serves 12 to 16.

Oysters for frying in Texas are sometimes batter-coated, sometimes merely rolled in cornmeal. This sauce with its oniony flavor is delicious with either.

★  *Salsa Para Ostiones*

2 green onions slivered with a part of their green tops
2 cloves garlic, crushed
3 Tbs. olive oil
½ cup chopped, peeled, seeded tomato
⅓ cup minced fresh parsley
Salt and pepper to taste

Sauté onions and garlic in oil until golden. Do *not* brown. Add tomato and cook gently 3 minutes. Stir in parsley. Add salt and pepper to taste. Remove from heat. Serve warm with Fried Oysters.

# FOURTEEN

# *POULTRY*

IN the old days in rural communities everywhere, chickens were kept as much (if not more) for their eggs as for eating. Consequently there were many chicken dishes made of hens past their prime as layers. Such dishes were primarily matters of economy but, by good fortune, they happened to be excellent ones as well—some of the best chicken dishes, in fact, that have ever been made. Many of these are still in wide use in Texas together with new ones of a similar kind that by popular demand have been added to the culinary repertoire.

Hundreds of Texas dishes call for young birds, too. Roast chicken, stuffed or unstuffed or with the stuffing (dressing) baked separately, is a standard dish in every household—as is broiled chicken (cooked in the kitchen range or over charcoal out of doors). And Fried Chicken is as basic in Texas cookery as Chili.

But the chicken dishes that strike the non-Texan as most characteristic of the state are those that call for cooked chicken meat in considerable quantity—3 or 4 cups. Though today chicken parts are available everywhere, this was originally to be had only from a hen. In the following recipe, you will find the standard Texas cooking procedure for such a hen in the first half of the directions. Follow this if you are making Chicken Salad or a casserole or some similar dish, cutting the cooked chicken meat as required by the specific recipe. Hens over 5 pounds—though giving adequate meat once cooked to tenderness—are apt to be so fat that weight loss in cooking makes them less economical than a smaller bird.

## ★ A Baked Hen with Dressing

| | |
|---|---|
| A 5- to 6-lb. hen | ½ tsp. pepper |
| 1 medium-size onion, halved | ½ tsp. rubbed sage |
| 1 carrot, quartered | ¼ cup minced fresh parsley |
| 1 stalk celery with leaves | 3 Tbs. flour |
| 1 small bay leaf | 1 cup milk |
| 1 medium-size onion, chopped | 4 egg yolks |
| 6 cups soft breadcrumbs, toasted | Additional salt and pepper |
| 4 hard-cooked eggs, chopped | Fine buttered crumbs |
| 2 tsps. salt | |

Place hen in large pot with cold water to cover. Add onion, carrot, celery and bay leaf. Bring to boil, reduce heat to low and simmer until chicken is tender (about 1½ hours). Remove chicken to platter. Strain and reserve stock. Cut up all the chicken meat into even-size pieces, discarding skin and bone. Skim fat from stock as it rises to surface. Reserve 5 tablespoons fat for later use.

Using 2 tablespoons chicken fat, sauté the chopped onion until golden. Add the toasted breadcrumbs and toss together. Add the chopped eggs, 2 teaspoons salt, pepper, sage and parsley. Toss again. Remove from heat. Spread in an even layer in a greased 8 x 11 x 2-inch Pyrex baking dish. Cover with a layer of all the chicken meat.

In a double boiler, over hot water, blend flour with remaining 3 tablespoons chicken fat. Stir in 2 cups stock and 1 cup milk. Cook over low heat, stirring constantly, until smooth and thickened. Beat ¼ cup of the hot sauce with the 4 egg yolks, then pour all together into the sauce. Cook until thickened over lowest heat, still stirring. Add salt and pepper to taste. Pour over chicken. Let stand 3 to 4 minutes. Sprinkle top with buttered crumbs. Bake at 350° F. for 30 minutes. Serve from the baking dish. Serves 8.

Chicken Pie, such as the one given below, and Chicken and Dumplings, as in the recipe that follows it, are both popular dishes everywhere in Texas and are made today much as they were made a hundred years ago. Though often virtually identical insofar as ingredients are concerned, they may be quite different dishes once done. The Chicken and Dumplings can itself have different appearances, for while the dumplings are sometimes dropped on top of the chicken and gravy to be steamed, they are also often made of a rolled dough cut into strips and immersed in the gravy to be boiled. This was the way of the "pot pie" made in the nineteenth century.

★ *Chicken Pie*

*For the Chicken:*

| | |
|---|---|
| A 5- to 6-lb. hen | 1 bay leaf |
| 1 medium-size onion, quartered | Salt to taste |
| 1 stalk celery with a few leaves | 1 tsp. peppercorns |

Simmer hen with all ingredients in water to cover until tender. Remove from pot and cut up all the meat into good-size pieces, discarding skin and bone. Strain and reserve the stock. Skim off and reserve the chicken fat.

*For the Sauce:*

| | |
|---|---|
| 3 Tbs. butter | 5 cups reserved chicken stock |
| 3 Tbs. reserved chicken fat | 1 cup heavy cream |
| 6 Tbs. flour | Salt and pepper to taste |

In the top of a double boiler over hot water combine butter, chicken fat and flour. Stir until smooth. Add chicken stock. Cook, stirring constantly, until smooth and thickened. Add cream. Let cook gently 10 minutes, stirring from time to time. Add salt and pepper to taste.

### For the Crust:

| | |
|---|---|
| 2 cups flour | 3 Tbs. butter |
| 2 tsps. baking powder | 1 egg, beaten |
| ½ tsp. salt | 1 cup rich sweet milk |

Combine flour, baking powder and salt; sift together into a bowl. Cut in the butter. Add egg and blend. Add milk and mix thoroughly.

### For the Pie:

Arrange cut up chicken in a wide, rather shallow casserole or baking dish. Cover with sauce, which should be thoroughly hot at the time. Drop the crust by spoonfuls on top of the chicken and sauce to make an *almost* complete layer. Bits of sauce should be able to bubble up between the spoonfuls of batter. Bake at 350° F. for 30 minutes or until the crust is a golden brown. Serve from the casserole. Serves 6. If desired, either thyme or rubbed sage may be added to the crust mixture or, if you like, add a considerable amount of minced fresh parsley—say, ½ cup.

Chicken and Dumplings is as popular a dish today in Texas as it was in the nineteenth century—which means very popular indeed. There are many recipes for making it. This is from Burleson.

★ *Chicken and Dumplings*

| | |
|---|---|
| 1 large hen, about 5 lbs. | 1 Tb. melted butter |
| 1 onion, quartered | ½ cup milk |
| 1 bay leaf | ¼ cup softened butter (additional) |
| Salt and pepper to taste | ⅓ cup very finely minced celery |
| 2 cups sifted flour | leaves |
| ½ tsp. salt | ¼ tsp. freshly ground black pepper |
| 1 Tb. baking powder | 2 Tbs. butter (additional) |
| 1 egg, beaten lightly | |

Disjoint the hen as though it were a frying chicken. Place it in a large pot with the onion, bay leaf, water to cover by 2 inches and salt and pepper to taste. Bring to the boil; reduce heat immediately to low and simmer until the bird is tender. Remove chicken. Cut the meat from the bones in large pieces and reserve. Strain the broth and return 6 cups to the pot.

Now sift flour, ½ teaspoon salt and baking powder together into a bowl. Combine egg, melted butter and milk; beat together and add to dry ingredients. Work to a good doughlike consistency, turn out on a floured board and roll to somewhat less than ¼-inch thickness. Spread with softened butter; sprinkle with the celery leaves and pepper. Cut into strips 2 x 3 inches.

Bring broth to a good simmering heat; do *not* boil. Stir in 2 tablespoons flour rubbed with 2 tablespoons extra butter. Cook, stirring, until smooth and thickened. Add the dumplings a few at a time, sliding them down into the hot broth. Continue until all are in. Cover tightly and cook 20 minutes without lifting the lid. Arrange the cut-up chicken on a deep platter, spoon on the dumplings and cover with as much of the delectable sauce as you desire. Serves 6.

One of the most noteworthy features of the Texas cuisine is the special kind of Texas independence that makes a good dish of any kind a possibile and eminently acceptable dish for any occasion. So simple a dish as a Chicken Loaf may appear at family table and buffet alike.

★  *Chicken Loaf*

| | |
|---|---|
| A 5-lb. hen | 3 Tbs. very finely chopped celery |
| ¾ cup soft white breadcrumbs | 2 tsps. salt, or to taste |
| 3 large eggs, beaten | Pepper to taste |
| 3 Tbs. grated onion | Paprika or minced fresh parsley |

Simmer the hen until tender as directed on page 152. Remove from pot. (The remaining broth you can use for soup.) Take all the meat from the carcass, discarding skin and bone. Grind the meat and combine with the remaining ingredients. If the mixture seems too dry, moisten it with several tablespoons of the reserved broth. Blend thoroughly. Press into a large buttered loaf pan or ring. Set pan in a larger pan with 1 inch hot water. Bake at 325° F. for about 50 minutes or until well set. Turn out on a platter when done. Sprinkle with paprika or parsley and serve with a mushroom sauce. Serves 8.

Virtually all of the Texas-Mexican dishes usually made with beef or other meat are also frequently made with chicken.

---

### ★ *Chicken Tamale Casserole*

*For the Tamale Shell:*

3 large eggs, separated
½ lb. fresh *masa* (or water-ground cornmeal)
1 cup heavy cream (see below)

¼ cup softened butter
Salt to taste
1 tsp. baking powder

*For the Filling:*

4 Tbs. butter
1 medium onion, chopped
2 cups solid-pack tomatoes
1 3½-oz. can peeled chopped green chilis
3 cups cooked, cubed chicken
½ cup stuffed olives, drained and halved

½ cup raisins, plumped in hot water and drained
Salt to taste
2 tsps. chili powder
Grated sharp cheese (about 1 cup)

Beat egg whites until stiff and set aside. Blend *masa* or meal with cream. If the mixture seems too dry, as it may (different lots of cornmeal require different amounts of liquid), add a little milk. Beat in butter and salt. Stir in baking powder. Then fold in the stiffly beaten egg whites.

For the filling, melt butter in skillet and sauté the onion over gentle heat until golden. Add tomatoes and cook 5 minutes. Add chilis, chicken, olives, raisins, salt to taste and chili powder. Cook 2 or 3 minutes longer. If you like a more moist filling, add ½ cup tomato sauce and blend.

Now spread half the cornmeal mixture over the bottom of a greased 2-quart baking dish or casserole. Cover with the filling. Spread on the remaining cornmeal mixture. Bake at 350° F. for 45 minutes. Sprinkle with the cheese and bake 15 minutes longer. Serves 6.

The name *chalupas* is used in connection with a wide variety of Texas dishes. Sometimes they are appetizers, sometimes a main-course meat dish. But however they are made, *tortillas* are a major ingredient, sometimes fried to become *tostados,* sometimes plain. Here is a main-course *Chalupas* of ground beef, cheese and *tortillas.*

## ★ Chicken-Chili Chalupas

| | |
|---|---|
| 1 large onion, grated | Tabasco to taste |
| 1 clove garlic, mashed | A 4-lb. hen |
| 2 cups milk | Celery salt |
| 2 cups heavy cream | 1 lb. Cheddar cheese, grated |
| 2 tsps. salt | 24 *tortillas* |
| ¼ tsp. pepper | 3 Tbs. canned chopped green chili, |
| 1 Tb. Worcestershire sauce | or to taste |

In a bowl combine onion, garlic, milk, cream, salt, pepper, Worcestershire sauce and Tabasco. Set aside. Simmer chicken until tender in water to cover, seasoned to taste with celery salt. When chicken is done, remove from broth. (Save broth for some other use.) Remove meat from hen and cut in small strips. Combine chicken meat with ⅓ of the cheese. Put a heaping tablespoon of the mixture on each *tortilla* and roll up. Arrange a layer of *tortillas* in a buttered baking dish. Sprinkle with some of the remaining cheese and a bit of the chopped green chili. (I personally like a good deal of the chili.) Repeat layers of *tortillas,* cheese and chili until the dish is filled. (Reserve some of the cheese to make a topping later.) Now pour on all the milk-cream mixture. Cover dish and refrigerate overnight. Before cooking add more milk if needed—and it will be needed if all the first mixture has been absorbed. Top with reserved cheese. Bake at 350° F. for 40 to 50 minutes. Serves 8.

★ *Chicken Shortcake*

| | |
|---|---|
| 1 cup milk | 2 eggs, separated |
| 1 cup chicken broth | 2 tsps. baking powder |
| 1 cup cornmeal | 2 Tbs. butter |
| 1 tsp. salt | 1½ cups diced, cooked chicken |

In a saucepan, combine milk, chicken broth, cornmeal and salt. Cook, stirring almost constantly, 5 minutes. Remove from heat. Add beaten egg yolks, baking powder, butter and chicken. Beat the egg whites until stiff and fold them into the batter. Turn into a greased casserole or baking dish and bake at 425° F. for 40 minutes. Serve with Chicken Giblet Gravy (page 173). Serves 4 to 6.

Hot Chicken Salads—which are not really salads at all—are found in many sections of the Midwest and through all of Texas. By some other name they might be more acceptable in other parts of the country, but they could not be better eating.

★ *Hot Chicken Salad*

| | |
|---|---|
| 2½ cups cooked diced chicken | 1½ cups chopped walnuts |
| 1 cup mayonnaise | 1 tsp. salt |
| 1 cup diced celery | ⅓ cup grated Parmesan cheese |
| 1 Tb. grated onion | 1 cup buttered crumbs |
| 2 Tbs. strained fresh lemon juice | Minced parsley |

In a mixing bowl combine chicken, mayonnaise, celery, onion, lemon juice, walnuts and salt. Blend. Turn into a buttered shallow Pyrex baking dish from which it may be served. Combine cheese, crumbs and parsley. Sprinkle this mixture evenly over the "salad." Bake at 400° F. for 20 minutes. Serve hot. Serves 6. This makes a wonderful supper with hot biscuits, cold country-cured ham and pickled peaches.

Real Chicken Salad—cold and with lettuce—seems to present some sort of challenge to Texas housewives, for all of them seem to feel compelled to embellish it with nuts, olives, pickles, even caviar. And often the embellishments are added in combination.

## ★ Chicken Salad

A 5-lb. hen, cooked, skinned, boned and diced
2 cups diced celery
1 tsp. salt, or to taste
1 cup diced sweet gherkins
8 hard-boiled eggs, chopped
¼ tsp. pepper
½ tsp. celery seed
1 small bottle pitted green olives, drained and chopped
1½ cups mayonnaise, or as needed

Combine all ingredients and let stand 2 hours in refrigerator, covered, before serving. If too dry, add more mayonnaise or a little heavy cream. Serve with leaf lettuce. Serves 8 to 12.

As Chicken Salads go in Texas, this is a rather simple one. The addition of the chicken broth adds to its chickeny flavor.

---

### ★ East Texas Chicken Salad

| | |
|---|---|
| 2½ cups cooked chicken, diced | 2 Tbs. minced fresh parsley |
| 2 cups diced celery | 2 tsps. fresh lemon juice |
| ½ cup sliced stuffed olives | Freshly ground black pepper to taste |
| ¼ cup strong chicken broth | Lettuce |
| 1 cup mayonnaise | Hard-cooked eggs for garnish |
| 1 tsp. salt | |

Combine all ingredients except lettuce and eggs in a mixing bowl; blend. Cover and refrigerate at least 1 hour before serving. At mealtime, arrange on a cold platter with crisp lettuce leaves and quartered hard-cooked eggs. Serves 8 to 10.

The avocado, once halved and with seed removed, simply asks to be filled with something. You find it often in Texas with crab meat or a shrimp filling at luncheon. Here it is filled with a chicken mixture, then broiled. Delectable.

### ★ Chicken in Avocados

| | |
|---|---|
| 2 Tbs. butter | ½ tsp. Worcestershire sauce |
| 2 Tbs. flour | Pinch cayenne |
| ½ cup milk | ¼ cup finely chopped canned green |
| 1 cup cream | chilis |
| 2 cups evenly diced cooked chicken | 3 avocados |
| 1 tsp. salt | Paprika |

In a double boiler melt butter over hot water; add flour and blend. Pour in milk and cream and cook, stirring constantly, until smooth and thickened. Add chicken, salt, Worcestershire sauce, cayenne and green chilis. Blend. Do not cook further. Cut avocados in half and discard seeds. Fill with chicken mixture, spreading it over the cut surface of the avocado meat. Arrange in shallow baking dish and brown under broiler 3 to 4 inches from flame. Sprinkle with paprika before serving. Serves 6.

Smothered Chicken, though made today in Texas with birds of 4 pounds or less, was originally another dish that called for older, plumper hens, the steam in the covered baking dish bringing them to tenderness as the liquid reduced to a rich sauce.

## ★  *Smothered Chicken*

A 4-lb. chicken, cut into serving
   portions
½ cup flour
2 tsps. salt
¼ tsp. pepper
Bacon drippings

1 medium onion, sliced
1½ cups milk
½ bay leaf, powdered
Browned flour, if needed (see
   below)

Dredge chicken in flour seasoned with salt and pepper. Brown quickly on both sides in bacon drippings in a heavy skillet. Lay sliced onion in a baking dish just large enough to hold the chicken. Add chicken. Pour on milk. Sprinkle with bay leaf. Cover and bake at 350° F. for 1 hour and 15 minutes. If desired add ½ cup heavy cream 20 minutes before chicken is done. If you want a thicker gravy, thicken pan juices with browned flour rubbed with an equal amount of butter. Use 1 tablespoon flour to each ¾ cup liquid. Serve from baking dish or platter. Serves 3 or 4.

While chicken, because of its convenient size, is among the most popular foods in Texas for out-of-doors charcoal grilling (and so is often called Barbecued Chicken—whether with or without a special sauce), it is also frequently "barbecued" in the kitchen range, either in the oven or under the broiler or in a skillet over the flame. Each cook has his or her own special method for adding crispness and/or flavor. Here are two recipes, both Barbecued Chicken, that give very different results. Serve with Baked Beans or Ranch Beans and a big Potato Salad, Cole Slaw, sliced ripe tomatoes and, of course, additional barbecue sauce of some kind and a bowl of relish or pickles.

★  *Barbecued Chicken*

1 cup catsup
1/3 cup strained fresh lemon juice
1 Tbs. grated or scraped onion
1/3 cup melted butter
1/2 cup Worcestershire sauce

1/2 tsp. black pepper
2 frying chickens, 3½ lbs. each, cut up, or the equivalent weight in chicken parts—breasts, legs and thighs

Combine the first six ingredients and blend. Brush on chicken and let stand 20 minutes. Arrange chicken on foil-lined broiler pan. Broil at moderate heat 6 inches from the flame. Turn several times and baste frequently with the remaining sauce. Allow about 35 minutes cooking time. Serves 6.
NOTE: This chicken, after standing 20 minutes with the sauce, may be placed in a shallow baking pan and baked 45 minutes at 350° F.

★  *Special Barbecued Chicken*

Marinate split broilers or frying chickens in equal parts distilled malt vinegar and salad oil for 4 hours. While still wet with the marinade, place chickens on grill (they may also be broiled) and cook until done, basting frequently with the marinade and turning them several times. About 5 minutes before the chickens are done, sprinkle with salt and freshly ground black pepper. Add a pinch of cayenne just before serving.

I have been told that a typical Texas farm dinner is Fried Chicken, Turnip Greens, Fresh Black-eyed Peas and "churn" milk (buttermilk). This, however, is a dinner you might find anywhere in Texas and in any kind of household.

★  *Fried Chicken*

Frying chicken                    Fine dry breadcrumbs
Buttermilk                        Lard for frying
Salt and pepper

Cut chicken into serving portions; cover with buttermilk and leave 10–15 minutes. Drain. Sprinkle with salt and pepper and dredge in fine crumbs, patting the crumbs on with your fingers so they adhere. Chill on a platter 10 to 15 minutes so the coating has a chance to set. Heat ¼ inch lard in a heavy skillet just large enough to hold the chicken comfortably. When very hot but not smoking, add chicken. Brown quickly on both sides over high heat. Do not burn. Reduce heat to low. Cover and cook very slowly for 20 minutes more, turning the chicken once. Drain on paper before serving.

NOTE: In Texas you will often find evaporated milk used instead of buttermilk for such dishes as this.

Oven-fried Chicken is a comparative newcomer to the Texas cuisine. Here it is made with lemon juice. A very good dish, indeed.

## ★ *Oven-fried Lemon Chicken*

A 3-lb. frying chicken cut into serving portions
½ tsp. salt
1 tsp. grated onion
½ tsp. thyme

½ tsp. marjoram
2 tsps. grated lemon peel
⅓ cup lemon juice
½ cup water
Minced fresh parsley

Sprinkle chicken with salt and let stand 5 minutes. Place chicken in greased baking pan skin-side down. Combine onion, seasonings, lemon peel, juice and water. Pour over chicken. Bake uncovered at 400° F. for about 40 minutes. Turn chicken, baste and continue baking about 30 minutes longer, basting at least once with the pan juices. Remove chicken to heated platter. Moisten each piece with a little of the essence remaining in the pan. Sprinkle with parsley and serve. Serves 2 to 4.

Black Chicken is chicken cooked with molasses. It is a perfect dish for chicken parts and though breasts are used in Texas, I have found it just as good with legs and thighs.

## ★ Black Chicken

4 chicken breasts, halved
Salt and pepper
2 Tbs. butter
1 clove garlic, halved
1 medium-size onion, chopped

½ cup water
2 tsps. bead molasses
1 tsp. Worcestershire sauce
1 tsp. flour

Sprinkle chicken breasts with salt and pepper; brown them in butter with the garlic over moderate heat in a heavy skillet. Remove chicken. Brown onion in remaining butter. Add water, molasses and Worcestershire sauce. Blend. Cook 1 minute. Return chicken to pan; cover tightly; reduce heat to low and simmer 1 hour, basting frequently. About 10 minutes before chicken is done, sprinkle with flour, baste, re-cover and let thicken slowly. Correct seasoning with salt and pepper if necessary. Serve chicken with rice, the remaining pan juices spooned over both. Serves 4 to 8.

These delectable chicken legs are eaten out of hand and are marvelous for an outdoor party. Have an extra supply of napkins on hand.

## ★ Chicken Leg Dip

Judge the number of chicken legs you will need for each person. This means just the leg—*not* leg and thigh. Then for 2 lbs. of legs allow:

1 egg yolk
½ cup sweet milk
1 cup fine dry breadcrumbs
½ cup flour

2 tsps. salt
½ tsp. cayenne
1 tsp. paprika
Deep fat for frying

Arrange chicken legs in a baking dish and bake, covered, 20 minutes at 375° F. Uncover. Remove legs to a rack and cool. Beat egg with milk. Combine crumbs, flour, salt, cayenne and paprika. Dip cooled legs in egg mixture, then dredge with the seasoned crumbs. Coat them evenly all over. Return them to rack so the coating will set. In a deep pot heat 2 inches lard or tasteless vegetable oil to 360° F. Fry legs a few at a time until tender and very crisp. Lift out carefully and drain on paper. Arrange on baking sheet and keep warm—uncovered—until needed. The oven with the heat barely on will do very well.

*For the Sauce:*

Combine ½ cup chili sauce with ½ cup heavy cream. Beat with a rotary beater until thick. Beat in 1 heaping tablespoon Dijon mustard, 1 teaspoon drained prepared horseradish and 1 tablespoon Worcestershire sauce. Add a pinch of cayenne if desired.

Serve the chicken legs hot and the sauce ice-cold. Let your guests eat and dunk as they please.

"Deviled" dishes in Texas almost invariably include chili powder among the required spices, thus making them especially Texan.

## ★ *Deviled Chicken*

| | |
|---|---|
| ½ cup butter (¼ lb.) | 1 tsp. salt |
| Chicken parts for 4 diners—halved breasts, thighs, drumsticks | ½ tsp. dry mustard |
| | 1 tsp. chili powder, or to taste |
| 2 tsps. paprika | ¼ tsp. Tabasco |

Melt butter in a saucepan. Dip chicken parts to coat them all over. Arrange in single layer in baking pan without crowding. Bake at 350° F. for 30 minutes. To the remaining butter add paprika, salt, dry mustard, chili powder and Tabasco. Blend. Dribble this evenly over chicken. Add a little water to the pan (do *not* pour it over the chicken) and bake 30 minutes longer. When done, remove chicken to platter. Swish out pan with additional water and reduce to essence over high heat, scraping up any browned bits and pieces. Spoon over chicken and serve. Serves 4.

Perhaps because of the Texas taste for small game birds, squab recipes turn up more frequently in Texas than elsewhere. Or it well may be that the Texas pocket can better afford them. The dipping in melted butter is a typical Texas touch.

★   *Broiled Squabs*

Have your butcher split squabs down the back and remove breast bones. Flatten. Dip in melted butter to coat the birds evenly all over. Broil 3 inches below flame until done, turning once and basting several times with remaining butter; about 10 minutes on each side.

While the birds are cooking, prepare a whole slice of toast for each bird. Have ready for spreading some peanut butter thinned with Worcestershire sauce. Also have a slice of sautéed lean ham ready to cover each slice of toast.

When birds are done, quickly spread toast with peanut butter mixture. Cover with ham. Lay bird on top. Dribble any remaining pan juices and/or butter over squabs. Serve immediately!

In Texas as elsewhere in the United States, Roast Turkey is a holiday dish. In Texas, however, the bird is often cooked without a stuffing. A *dressing*—which almost always includes cornbread crumbs—is baked instead in a separate pan. Or, this may be baked in the turkey's roasting pan after the bird has been removed to a platter—in which case the dressing absorbs whatever is left in the pan of the turkey juices and drippings. Gravy, at such times, made with a stock from the giblets, will be made in another pan.

When a turkey is cooked *with* a stuffing in Texas, 1 cup of the mixture is allowed for each pound of bird, dressed weight. Both breast and body cavities should be filled, of course, but the stuffing should never be packed too tightly to allow the heat to penetrate and cook it through. When a bird is cooked *without* a stuffing, a quartered onion and several sprigs of celery leaves are usually put into the body cavity to add flavor. Following you will find several typical Texas *dressings* which, made in lesser quantity, serve for chickens as well as the larger birds. These are used also in "made" dishes that require dressing and cooked chicken.

## ★ A Celery-Cornbread Stuffing

4 cups crumbled cornbread
4 cups crumbled baking-powder biscuits
3 eggs, beaten lightly
2 cups finely chopped celery
1 cup finely chopped onion
1 apple, peeled, cored and chopped
½ cup melted butter
Salt and pepper to taste
Turkey or chicken stock to moisten

In a large mixing bowl, combine cornbread, biscuit crumbs, eggs, celery, onion and apple. Toss to mix throughly. Dribble the butter over all and toss again. Season to taste with salt and pepper. Moisten with stock as needed. Do *not* make the dressing soggy. Use to stuff a 10-pound turkey.

## ★ Cornbread-Biscuit Dressing for a 12-Pound Bird

| | |
|---|---|
| 6 cups crumbled cornbread | ⅓ cup drippings |
| 4 cups crumbled baking-powder biscuits | 4 eggs, beaten |
| 4 cups giblet stock | 2 tsps. salt |
| 1½ cups chopped onion | 1 tsp. pepper |
| ¾ cup chopped celery | 1 tsp. rubbed sage |
| ½ cup chopped celery leaves | 2 Tbs. minced fresh parsley |
| | 4 cups (or less) additional stock |

Combine crumbs in large bowl and moisten with giblet stock. (If the giblets themselves are not to be used in gravy, add them, cooked and chopped, to the crumb mixture.) Sauté onions, celery and celery leaves in the drippings until the onions are golden. Add to the crumb mixture with any drippings in the pan. Add the eggs and seasonings. Blend. Add as much of the additional stock as needed to moisten thoroughly. The dressing should *not* be wet, however. Let stand at least 1 hour before stuffing bird. If the stuffing is to be baked separately, place in shallow, buttered baking dish and bake uncovered at 325° F. for 1 hour or until top is crisp and brown. For a richer dressing, dot with extra butter before baking.

Rice dressings are frequently served with turkeys. Here is one of them. It is virtually the same kind of dish as the Baked Rice on page 260.

---

## ★  Rice Dressing

| | |
|---|---|
| 2 cups rice | 1 cup finely chopped celery |
| ⅓ cup melted butter and olive oil, half and half | 2 Tbs. minced celery leaves |
| 1 cup finely chopped onion | 2 cans chicken consommé |
| | 1 can mushroom soup |

In a heavy skillet sauté rice in butter-oil mixture until golden; stir frequently. Add onion and celery and cook 3 to 4 minutes longer. Stir in celery leaves; set aside. Combine consommé with mushroom soup and add enough water to make 4 cups liquid. Heat just to the boiling point. Turn rice mixture and all remaining butter and oil into a greased 2-quart casserole or baking dish. Pour on the hot soup mixture and blend. Cover tightly and bake at 375° F. for 1 hour. Serve from the baking dish. (Additional salt and pepper should not be needed, for the soups have seasonings of their own. Suit yourself, however.) Serves 8 to 10.

## ★  To Prepare a Turkey for Roasting

If bird is to be cooked with the dressing in it, fill both breast and body cavities lightly but fully. If to be cooked without stuffing, simply put 1 quartered onion and a few celery leaves in the body cavity after sprinkling with salt and pepper.

Tuck wing tips down under the bird to fasten them securely. Tie the legs together so the whole bird is firm. Brush all over with melted butter or drippings and sprinkle lightly with seasonings.

★   *To Roast a Turkey*

Place bird breast-side up on a rack in a shallow roasting pan. Add a skimming of water to the pan to prevent charring of the initial drippings. Roast uncovered at 325° F., basting from time to time with the pan juices as they accumulate. If the breast browns too quickly, cover it with several thicknesses of aluminum foil or with a clean dish towel saturated with drippings. Do not wrap the foil tightly around the bird, however, as this will cause it to steam. The doneness of the bird may be judged by whether or not the leg moves easily in its socket and whether the thigh meat is tender to the touch. As for the required time, the chart below gives an approximation only. Small turkeys take a disproportionately long time to cook, while large ones take a disproportionately short time. I have seen charts that estimate 7 hours cooking time for a 20-pound bird but, in actuality, a bird this size will probably be done in a little over 5 hours. A meat thermometer, if stuck into the meatiest portion of the thigh with the tip well away from bone, will give the precise time your bird is done, of course; it will register 180° F. But if you have no thermometer, use the finger test and check any large bird after 3½ hours. Unstuffed birds, for obvious reasons, cook more quickly than stuffed ones. And all birds will be the better for a 20-minute resting period after coming from the oven and before going to the table.

★   *Roasting Time for Turkey at 325° F.*

| | |
|---|---|
| 8-pound bird . . . . . . . . . . | 3½ hours (approx.) |
| 12- to 16-pound bird . . . . . | 4½ to 5½ hours (approx.) |
| 20-pound bird . . . . . . . . . . | 5½ to 6 hours (approx.) |

As I have mentioned before, Texas diners often seem to take meat just for the sake of the gravy. And this is even more noticeable with chicken and turkey. Giblet Gravy is made in prodigious quantities in every household and is consumed in like amounts not only on the chicken or turkey but with rice, potatoes, biscuits —whatever of the sort is handy.

★ *Giblet Gravy*

Turkey giblets
  4 cups water
  2 celery leaves
1¼-inch slice onion

Salt and pepper to taste
¼ cup butter
¼ cup flour
  2 hard-cooked eggs, chopped

Cook the turkey giblets in water with celery leaves, onion and salt and pepper to taste until the gizzard is tender. Drain, reserving stock. Chop giblets and set aside. In a saucepan melt the butter and add flour. Blend and let brown over gentle heat. Stir in 2 cups of the reserved stock, strained. (If there is not enough stock to make 2 cups, add water as needed.) Cook, stirring constantly, until smooth and thickened. Correct seasoning if necessary with additional salt and pepper. Add chopped giblets and heat thoroughly. Stir in eggs a few minutes before serving. Makes about 2½ cups gravy.

Turkey leftovers are frequently used in Texas for precisely the same kind of dishes that require specially cooked chicken. Here are a couple of them:

## ★ Turkey Spoon Bread

½ cup cornmeal
1 Tb. tapioca
2½ cups well-seasoned turkey stock

4 Tbs. butter
3 eggs, separated
2 cups chopped, cooked turkey

Combine meal, tapioca, and stock in the top of a double boiler (if the stock is not well seasoned, add salt to taste). Cook over hot water, stirring frequently, until thick and the meal is cooked. Add butter and blend. Beat in the egg yolks one by one. Add turkey and blend. Beat the egg whites until stiff and fold into the mixture. Turn into a buttered 2-quart baking (or soufflé) dish. Bake at 350° F. about 35 minutes, or until puffed and brown. Serve immediately. Serves 4 to 6.

## ★ Turkey-Hominy Casserole

1 can condensed cream of
  mushroom soup
½ cup sour cream
2 Tbs. diced pimiento
1 tsp. Worcestershire sauce
Salt and cayenne to taste

2½ cups hominy, canned
2½ cups diced, cooked turkey
1 cup toasted fresh breadcrumbs
3 Tbs. melted butter
¼ cup chopped pecans

In a saucepan combine soup, sour cream, pimientos, Worcestershire and salt and cayenne. Heat thoroughly over a low flame, stirring constantly. Remove from heat. Spread hominy in an even layer in a buttered 2-quart casserole. Add the turkey. Pour the hot mixture evenly over all. Make a top crust of the toasted crumbs. Sprinkle with butter and the pecans. Bake at 350° F. for 30 minutes. Serve from the casserole. Serves 4 to 6.

Barbecued Turkey is possibly even better than Barbecued Chicken. For this you can use turkey parts, if you like, instead of the 8-pound bird.

★  *Barbecued Turkey*

¼ cup vinegar
¼ cup peanut oil
 1 Tb. strained fresh lemon juice
½ cup finely chopped onion
½ cup finely chopped, seeded green
    pepper
 1 tsp. celery salt
¼ tsp. oregano

½ tsp. basil
½ tsp. white pepper
¼ tsp. ground cinnamon
¼ tsp. ground cumin
 1 clove garlic, crushed
Tabasco to taste
An 8-lb. turkey

In a stainless steel saucepan combine all the ingredients except Tabasco and turkey. Cook gently until onion is translucent. Remove from heat to cool. Add Tabasco to taste. Quarter the turkey; remove wings and drumsticks. Place parts in large bowl or a larger flat Pyrex baking dish. Pour on the sauce. Cover and let stand 6 hours or overnight, turning the turkey parts frequently. Before cooking, remove turkey and drain. Reserve the marinade. Cook bird on grill or under broiler 4 inches below flame. If a gas broiler is used, have heat at moderate. Cook turkey 20 to 25 minutes on each side. Baste several times with the marinade. Brush with marinade again when done. Serves about 8, with Corn Pudding on the side or Big Hominy.

Meaty turkey breasts are delicious when fried; the thickness of the breast preserves their moisture while the crusty outside comes to a wonderful golden brown.

## ★  Fried Turkey Breasts

Many markets sell turkey parts as well as chicken parts. For this fine dish buy small turkey breasts, minus the wings. Bone them. Dip in batter, then crumbs as in the Fried Chicken recipe (page 164). Fry in lard, like chicken, and when done to a crisp and golden brown, serve with a Cream Gravy (page 232), fresh hot biscuits, a quantity of butter and honey.

Smoked Turkey is very popular in Texas and, provided you have means of smoking it, rather easy to make.

## ★  Smoked Turkey

A turkey for smoking must be first soaked in a "pickle," allowing 30 hours for each pound of bird, dressed weight, and turning the birds in the "pickle" once every 5 days, side to side and end to end.

*For the Pickle You Will Need:*

| | |
|---|---|
| 3 gal. water | 2 Tbs. whole allspice berries |
| 3 lbs. salt | 2 Tbs. whole cloves |
| 2 lbs. brown sugar | 1 blade mace |
| 10 bay leaves | 8 cloves of garlic, halved |

Combine all ingredients and stir until both sugar and salt are completely dissolved. Completely immerse birds and keep them immersed during the entire soaking. Before smoking, drain and dry.

*To Smoke:*

Use any good hard wood or fruit wood. Do not use any wood with resin. Smoke in smokehouse (or equivalent) at 140° F. allowing 16 hours for a 14-pound bird; 20 to 24 hours for a larger one. For birds of 24 pounds or so increase the heat to 160° F. for several hours just before bird is done. Shrinkage will be about 8 percent.

# FIFTEEN

## GAME AND GAME BIRDS

# BECAUSE of the vast open spaces

that the state still boasts, game is more plentiful in Texas than most other parts of this country and, consequently, appears more often at Texas tables. The central flyway of the Mississippi Valley brings clouds of wild duck to coastal waters annually. And across the farmlands and plains, other game birds are available in season in such quantity that recipes for them call not for merely one or two birds as elsewhere but for six, eight or a dozen, as in Chilipitin Doves (page 182). Wild turkeys, though virtually extinct in most of the United States, are still to be found in Texas. And venison, available year round thanks to freezers, is so common that Venison Sausage and Venison Chili are both household standbys. Other wild animals and even reptiles indigenous to the state—the armadillo, for example, and rattlesnake—are also often eaten, though certainly not by all Texans. And squirrels and rabbits, of course, abound.

## ★ *Chilipitin Doves*

| | |
|---|---|
| 6 doves | 6 slices bacon |
| Salt and pepper | ½ cup hot water |
| 12 chilipitins (very small, very hot chili peppers that grow wild in South Texas) | |

Sprinkle doves inside and out with salt and pepper. Place 2 chilis in the body cavity of each. Wrap each bird in a strip of bacon, taking care to have it cover the breast. Arrange birds in a baking dish side by side. Add water. Cover and bake at 350° F. for 1½ hours. Uncover and cook until birds are browned (about 20 minutes longer). Remove to a heated platter. Garnish with watercress if available. Serve with Hominy (page 262) or Spoon Bread (page 261). Serves 3 to 6.

## ★ *Twice-cooked Quail*

| | |
|---|---|
| 12 to 14 quail, dressed | 12 to 14 bacon slices |
| 1 large onion, chopped | 1 cup dry white wine |
| 2 tart apples, cored and chopped (do not peel) | 1½-inch thick slice onion |
| Salt and pepper | 1 small bay leaf |

Stuff birds loosely with a mixture of chopped onion and apple, lightly salted. Fasten body cavities by thread or toothpick. Sprinkle with salt and pepper. Wrap each bird in slice of bacon. Place birds on a hinged grill and cook over charcoal 30 minutes, turning frequently. Remove birds to a baking pan or casserole. Add wine, onion slice and bay leaf. Cover. Bake at 300° F. for 45 minutes to 1 hour. Baste frequently with the pan juices. Serve with Mexican Rice (page 259) or Wild Rice or Spoon Bread (page 261). Serves 4 to 6.

## ★ Wild Duck

Clean, rinse under cold water and dry inside and out. Sprinkle body cavity and skin with salt. Stuff with quartered cored apples and quartered onion. Place in open roasting pan breast-side up; cover breast with strips of bacon and roast at 500° F. for 30 minutes. Reduce heat to 350° F. and cook 30 minutes longer. Discard apple and onion. Remove birds to heated platter. Moisten with pan juices. In a sauce bowl serve the remaining pan juices seasoned to taste with salt and pepper.

## ★ Baked Wild Ducks

| | |
|---|---|
| 3 ducks | ½ tsp. ground cinnamon |
| 1 can tomatoes, #2 size | 1 tsp. salt |
| 2 large onions, chopped | ½ tsp. pepper |
| ½ tsp. ground cloves | |

Place ducks breast-side up in a heavy pot. Pour tomatoes over them; add remaining ingredients; cover and simmer very gently 1½ hours, basting frequently. Remove ducks to an open roasting pan, arranging them breast-up, side by side. Strain the pan juices over them, pressing the tomatoes and onions through a sieve and blending the purée with the liquid. Baste ducks well with the sauce. Correct seasoning as necessary with salt and pepper. Bake at 350° F. for 1½ hours, uncovered, basting frequently. Add a little water or stock to the sauce if it cooks away too quickly. Carve ducks when done and place the portions on a heated platter. Spoon the sauce over all. Serves 6.

★ *Fried Squirrel or Rabbit*

Skin tender young animals, discard entrails, rinse under cold water and pat dry with paper towels. Cut into convenient serving portions. Dredge in flour seasoned with salt and pepper. Fry in about ⅛ inch lard over moderate heat until brown on both sides. Add medium cream to a depth of ¼ inch. Cover pan tightly and cook over lowest heat until tender, turning once and basting several times. About 20 minutes of "steaming" should be sufficient. Serve with remaining pan juices poured over as sauce. Good with Fried Mush (page 53).

Of all the many kinds of game in Texas, venison played the most important role for the early settlers. From the Indians' way of sun-drying long strips of lean venison, the settlers learned to make their jerky—not only of venison but later also of beef. This dried meat was a mainstay of the cowboys on the open range where they would stay for as long as forty or fifty days at a time. And though chuckwagons and camp cooks always accompanied the great cattle drives north from Texas along the Chisholm Trail to Abilene, Kansas, jerky was then, too, always among the stores. It was the early West's chief emergency ration.

Nowadays venison has more sophisticated uses, of course. It is one of the few meats in Texas that is often cooked with wine. Boned venison roasts often have elaborate stuffings. But as with

184

everything else at the Texas table, whether sophisticated or not, it often appears in the company of such Texas specialties as Pickled Peaches, Fried Peaches, Cole Slaw, Sauerkraut Salad, Black-eyed Peas—and often has a chili pepper or two added to give it a Texas flavor.

★ *Roast Venison*

| | |
|---|---|
| A 6- to 8-lb. leg of venison | 1 bay leaf |
| 1 thin slice salt pork | 1 cup water |
| 2 cloves garlic, halved | 1 cup red wine |
| 3 Tbs. lard | Flour and butter in equal parts as |
| Salt and pepper | needed for thickening |
| 4 slices bacon | |

With a small sharp knife, pierce deep holes in meaty parts of venison. Cut salt pork into slivers and press one of these into each of the holes. Rub leg all over with cut cloves of garlic. Then rub with lard and a sprinkling of salt and freshly ground pepper. Lay venison in roasting pan. Cover with bacon slices. Cook at 425° F. uncovered for 45 minutes.

Reduce oven heat to 325° F. Add bay leaf, water and wine to pan. Cover. Roast venison 1½ hours longer (or until tender) basting frequently. If desired, turn meat once during cooking time. Uncover for last 10 minutes of cooking. Skim excess fat from pan juice before making gravy. Thicken the remaining essence as desired with flour and butter rubbed together. Serves 8 to 10.

The caraway seeds in this delicious Venison Pot Roast show German or Bohemian influence. Caraway is also often used with pork and sometimes in meat loaves.

## ★ *Venison Pot Roast*

| | |
|---|---|
| 1 slice venison from haunch, 2½ inches thick | ½ cup chopped onion |
| ¼ cup flour | 1 Tb. minced celery leaves |
| 1 tsp. salt | 1 can tomato sauce, 8-oz. size |
| ½ tsp. pepper | 1 cup water |
| 2 Tbs. lard | 2 tsps. caraway seeds |
| | 2 bay leaves |

Wipe venison with a damp cloth. Rub thoroughly all over with a mixture of the flour, salt and pepper. Heat lard in a heavy iron skillet or Dutch oven. Brown the venison on both sides over moderate heat. Add onion and celery leaves. Cook until onion is golden. Add remaining ingredients. Blend. Cover tightly. Reduce heat to lowest. Simmer 2½ hours or until meat is tender. This, of course, will depend on the age of the venison. Baste frequently. If the sauce cooks away too quickly, add a *little* more hot water. There should be just enough sauce, when the meat is done, to moisten the slices. Serves 6. This is delicious with *Frijoles Refritos* (page 252).

One might suppose that the seasonings of a good chili would completely hide the presence of venison, but such is not the case. In fact the meat you use in any chili makes a great difference to its finished taste. Combinations of meats do likewise.

## ★ Venison Chili

3 lbs. ground venison  
2 lbs. ground beef  
3 Tbs. lard  
2 cloves garlic, minced  
3 large onions, chopped  
1 qt. water  
2 cans tomatoes, #2 size  

1 Tb. salt  
1½ tsp. black pepper  
6 Tbs. chili powder  
1½ tsps oregano  
1½ tsps. *comino*  
3 Tbs. paprika  

Brown venison and beef together in lard in large heavy pot over moderate heat. Add garlic and onions and cook until golden, stirring frequently. Add water and tomatoes and blend. Reduce heat to low. Cover loosely and simmer 3 hours. Add seasonings and cook 1 hour longer. Serve as is or let stand, covered, until needed or refrigerate over night. Reheat gently before serving. Serves 8 to 12.

## ★ Venison Sausage

Venison Sausage is generally made "to taste," so specific directions for it are hard to come by. You need 3 parts venison to 1 part lean pork and 1 part fat pork. Grind these together, using a medium grinder blade, then mix in your seasonings by hand—red pepper, garlic, salt and freshly ground black pepper. Fry bits of the sausage at intervals to ascertain its taste; it should not be a definitely *hot* sausage, but it should have a noticeable pepper bite to it. Pack it in gut casings and tie off in lengths as desired, leaving some room for expansion. Hang to smoke for several days over a cool fire (not more than 140° F.) of oak and mesquite wood or hickory or fruit wood. Fry or grill as needed. Serve with Soft-fried Potatoes, Fried Eggs and Cornbread or Popovers.

Snake meat—if you can bring yourself to try it—has a very good flavor, indeed. Canned rattlesnake meat, in fact, is widely sold in both Florida and Texas and is served frequently as an appetizer.

★ *Vibora de Cascabel (Rattlesnake)*

A snake of 3 to 4 feet has the best quality meat. To prepare: Cut off the snake's head and let the body drain. Skin as though removing a glove. Slit snake up middle. Discard entrails. Rinse under cold water and pat dry. Cut body crosswise in 1- to 2-inch lengths. Dredge in lightly salted cornmeal. Let stand a few minutes for the coating to set. Fry in hot lard, ⅓ inch deep, until brown on both sides. When crisp, drain on paper. Serve as soon as possible or reheat in a hot oven. If any fried food must wait, do *not* cover it. This will make the crust soggy for the meat tends to steam. And when reheating, arrange meat on a baking sheet or in shallow pan in a single layer.

# SIXTEEN

## *MEATS*

# MEAT

MEAT in Texas today is virtually synonymous with beef. This is natural enough considering the number of acres devoted to raising beef cattle and the quantities of beef consumed annually by Texans. In the early days, however, pork was far more common among the Anglo-Texans than beef and as popular among them as *cabrito,* young goat (kid), is today among the Texas Mexicans. Pork is still popular, of course—especially pork chops, spareribs and fresh sausage; and ham and bacon and salt pork are more or less taken for granted as household necessities.

But beef is *the* meat—rare, medium or well done. I mention the last specifically for there is more well-done meat served in Texas by preference than in any other part of the country, so far as I know. And much of this is cooked in ways that have been handed down for generations, often ways that have passed out of general use elsewhere. Pot roasts, for instance, are especially popular, as also are fried steaks and braised shortribs. A host of dishes were developed from the barbecue, and another host evolved from the Mexican dishes which developed, in turn, from ones popular with the indigenous Indians and the Aztecs.

In the old days, before refrigeration was general, all the beef was fresh-killed so long cooking was in order for the less tender cuts, many of which are today tenderized by cold-storage hanging. In the old days, too, all of everything was used, so many of the parts and oddments of beef now seldom purchased found their ways into the soup or stew pot. In clinging to these old-fashioned dishes, Texans have been winners in many gastronomic respects. All of these dishes are home-made and to have them at all (and most Texans have them frequently) means that housewives cook. And living as they do among other housewives who also cook, they share an interest in food which has brought them a repertoire of dishes that stand in this country in relation to sophisticated urban dishes in much the same way many provincial dishes of France relate to the best cuisine of Paris or Lyon or Dijon.

Texas, as I have said, has basically a meat-and-potatoes cuisine. It's food is rib-sticking, man's food. And beef is the focal point of the vast majority of meals. I have treated the marvelous steaks and roasts only briefly for, on the whole, they are cooked in much the same way as elsewhere. There is a difference, however: one cook in giving advice on party fare suggested that the best way to assure a sufficiency of beef cooked to different degrees of doneness for a large gathering was to cook three large roasts at the same time but for different lengths of time. This, of course, is Texan to the core. And she meant what she said seriously enough. In Texas, people do cook three roasts at once. Here, however, you will find simpler fare—but no less delicious!

★ *Rib Roast of Beef*

Rib Roast in Texas is cooked in much the same way as elsewhere in this country, but as you might suppose, the roasts all tend to be on the large size (which is all to the good, of course), a 3-rib roast being thought of as the passable minimum.

*To Cook:*

Rub the surface of the meat lightly with flour. Place it rib-side down in a roasting pan; add a skimming of water to prevent the pan's charring and roast at 325° F.—18 minutes per pound for rare, 22 minutes per pound for medium, and 26 minutes per pound for well done. Sprinkle with pepper and salt about 20 minutes before the meat is to come from the oven. Baste at intervals with the pan drippings for best results. If desired, place 1 quartered onion and 1 bay leaf in the pan at the start of cooking. Baste the pan juices over the onion when you baste the meat.

Remove roast to a heated platter when done and let stand at room temperature at least 20 minutes before serving. Make a pan gravy with a part of the drippings, adding an equal quantity of browned flour and water or stock as desired. Serve the gravy in a sauceboat. Serve the roast with hot rolls, Hominy in Cream, Cole Slaw, Baked Fresh Corn, sliced ripe tomatoes, Creamed Spinach and either a Peach Pie or Peach Cobbler. Horseradish Sauce is also frequently served with Roast Beef either along with or instead of pan gravy. This, of course, is both the German and Central European way which, in Texas, has been extended to all tables.

Leftovers seem not to pose the problem in Texas that they do elsewhere. This may stem from a natural inbred rural thrift that Texans show at their tables (even though the tables may be in palaces), or it may stem from the fact that they simply like well-done meat and hence find no fault with it when it's twice cooked. Roast Beef Hash, for instance, is thought of as a breakfast delicacy in Texas. And it is.

## ★ Roast Beef Hash

For every 2 cups of chopped (not ground) leftover lean beef, allow 1 large boiled potato, diced, 1 small onion, chopped very fine, and ¼ cup leftover roast beef gravy. Allow also 1 teaspoon salt, ¼ teaspoon pepper (rounded), and ½ teaspoon very finely minced, seeded, *jalapeño* pepper.

Combine all these ingredients and blend. Heat a skimming of bacon drippings in an iron skillet. Add the hash mixture. Spread it out evenly with a spatula and press it down gently. Cook, covered, over moderate heat 20 minutes. Turn with a spatula. Press down again. Cook until the hash is browned on the bottom and crusted. Add 2 to 3 tablespoons heavy cream, dribbling it over the hash evenly, and cook 10 minutes longer. Turn out on a heated platter and serve with fried eggs. The hash made with 2 cups of beef will serve 2 modestly.

Pot Roasts of many kinds and tastes are popular everywhere in Texas; some show the influence of different ethnic groups, some (like the one below) the imaginative flair of housewives, while others with their Texan seasonings are simply Texan to the core.

## ★ Black Pot Roast

4 lbs. boneless rump pot roast in a
    solid chunk
3 to 4 cloves garlic cut in slivers
Salt and pepper
1 cup cider vinegar

2 Tbs. lard or drippings
2 cups strong black coffee
2 cups hot water
Butter and flour for thickening

194

Pierce deep gashes in meat on all sides and insert slivers of garlic. Rub meat thoroughly with salt and pepper. Tie if necessary in a firm round shape. Place in deep bowl just large enough to hold it. Pour on vinegar. Cover and let stand 24 hours. Turn meat several times. Before cooking, remove meat from bowl and pat dry with paper towels. Heat drippings or lard in an iron pot. Brown meat on all sides over high heat—really brown it. Add coffee and hot water. Cover pot and just barely simmer 4 to 6 hours, or until very tender; or, roast, covered, 4 hours at 275° F. The slower the oven and the longer the cooking, the better the meat. When done remove to a heated platter. Skim off all grease from remaining pan juices. Thicken with 1 tablespoon flour rubbed with 1 tablespoon butter for each cup of liquid. Cook, stirring constantly, until smooth and of desired consistency. Serves 6 to 8.

★   *Barbecue Pot Roast*

| | |
|---|---|
| 3 lbs. boneless rump pot roast in solid chunk | 1 can tomato sauce, 8-oz. size |
| 2 tsps. salt | 2 Tbs. brown sugar |
| ½ tsp. pepper | 1 tsp. paprika |
| 3 Tbs. bacon drippings or rendered salt pork | ½ tsp. dry mustard |
| | ¼ cup lemon juice |
| 3 medium onions, chopped | ¼ cup cider vinegar |
| 2 cloves garlic, minced | 1 Tb. Worcestershire sauce |
| ½ cup water | Butter and flour as needed for thickening |

Rub beef with salt and pepper. Heat drippings in a heavy pot just large enough to hold meat without crowding. Brown meat on all sides. Remove from pot, add onions and garlic. Cook over moderate heat until golden. Return meat to pot. Add water and tomato sauce. Blend. Cover tightly; reduce heat to low and simmer 1 hour and 30 minutes. Turn meat. Combine all remaining ingredients and pour over meat. Cover and cook 1 hour longer or until tender. Baste several times. When meat is done, remove to a heated platter. Skim grease from remaining pan juices. The remaining sauce should be quite thick, but if you want it thicker, add 1 tablespoon flour moistened with 2 tablespoons water *or* rubbed with 1 tablespoon butter. Cook, stirring constantly, until of desired consistency. Spoon a bit of the sauce over the meat and serve the rest in a sauceboat. Serves 6.

Beefsteak, as you'd expect, is one of the most popular meats in Texas for outdoor cooking—either the true barbecue (the steak for this being cut extra thick) or the casual backyard cookout. The difference between these methods of cooking, bear in mind, is chiefly a matter of the fire itself, a barbecue fire being primarily for long, slow cooking of large cuts of meat (or meats that take to slow cooking) and the backyard grill fire being primarily for smaller cuts that cook more quickly. Here, however, I am dealing only with kitchen-cooked beefsteak.

## ★ To Broil a Beefsteak

Allow ½ pound of meat for each diner. Have your butcher cut your steak at least 2 inches thick, preferably from the sirloin. A thin steak, you will find—if you have not found out already—simply cannot be properly broiled. By the time the outside is browned and crisp, the inside will have become gray, tasteless and dry. And though most Texans like their beef thoroughly cooked through, as I have said, they want it merely well done, not overdone. Those exceptional Texans who profess to a liking for "rare" beef think of rare as pink, not red. Beef with a raw look to it is considered downright uneatable. "I seen steers hurt worse than that that got well," said one Texan when served a blood-red steak.

Slash edges of steak to prevent curling and place on a greased rack in broiler pan. Broil 3 inches from flame in broiler preheated to about 350° F. Adjust broiler flame (if gas) to a little more than medium and for a *rare steak* cook 6 minutes on each side, turning once; for a *medium steak,* 10 minutes on each side, turning once; and for *well-done steak,* 15 minutes on each side, turning once. Sprinkle with salt and pepper (freshly ground) about 5 minutes before steak is taken from the broiler. Remove to a heated platter immediately when done and dot with a generous quantity of butter. If you like garlic with your steak, rub the platter with a cut clove of garlic and dot this with butter just before taking your steak from the broiler. Then turn the steak once or twice as this butter melts. Sprinkle again with salt and pepper and serve as soon as possible.

In Texas, many steaks are marinated before broiling and some of these are delectable, indeed. But let me say that if a steak is really of top quality, it needs no embellishments or special treatment to give it savor. Lesser steaks, however, are another matter. And a marvelous marinade to help these along can be easily made as follows:

★ *Whiskey Marinade for Beefsteak*

Combine 1 part bourbon whiskey with 2 parts strained, fresh orange juice and 2 halved cloves garlic. Pour over steak and let stand 2 hours before broiling, turning once or twice in the process. Drain steak and pat dry before cooking. Baste with remaining marinade several times. Or, if you like, try this:

197

## ★  *A Butter-marinated Steak*

Have your butcher cut boneless sirloin, 1 inch thick, into serving portions. Marinate the steak for 1 hour in a mixture of:

| | |
|---|---|
| ¼ lb. butter, melted | 2 crushed cloves garlic |
| 5 Tbs. Worcestershire sauce | Salt and pepper |

Do not dry meat before broiling. Lay on grid (or broiler rack) and cook until done, turning the meat once, and basting 2 or 3 times with remaining marinade. Sprinkle with salt and pepper just before serving. If any of the buttery marinade is left over, dribble a little over each portion.

Though Texas is a world in itself, it is also a Southern world, and many of its favorite dishes are wholly Southern. Fried Steak, for instance, of which there are many varieties.

## ★  *Fried Round Steak*

Have the butcher cut a slice of round steak about ¾ inch thick, its weight depending on the number of diners. With a rolling pin or bottle, pound the steak to ½-inch thickness. Cut it into convenient serving portions. Dip in buttermilk, then dredge in flour that has been seasoned with salt and pepper. Heat lard or drippings in a large iron skillet. When almost at the smoking point, add the steak and sear very quickly on both sides. Reduce heat and fry until brown on one side, turn and brown the other. Drain quickly on paper. Serve with a White Gravy.

Onion Steak is another Texas specialty and though always the same in one sense, it is always different in another—as the following recipes will show you.

### ★ *Onion Steak #1*

| | |
|---|---|
| 1½ lbs. lean round steak, ¾ inch thick | 1 cup flour |
| 1 tsp. salt | 3 Tbs. drippings |
| ¼ tsp. pepper | 3 medium-large onions, sliced |
| ¼ tsp. MSG | ½ cup hot water |
| | 3 Tbs. minced fresh parsley |

Cut steaks into serving portions. Sprinkle evenly with salt, pepper and MSG. Dredge with flour. Pound pieces to even ½-inch thickness, using a wooden mallet or a bottle. Heat drippings in heavy iron skillet large enough to hold meat easily in one layer. Brown meat on both sides over high heat. Remove pan from fire. Spread onions over meat. Sprinkle with a little additional salt. Add hot water. Cover tightly and bake at 300° F. for half an hour. Remove steak and onions to heated platter. Correct seasoning of remaining pan juices with salt and pepper and spoon over all. Sprinkle with parsley and serve immediately, with plenty of creamy mashed potatoes. Serves 6.

### ★ *Onion Steak #2*

| | |
|---|---|
| 2 lbs. round steak in 1½-inch-thick slice | Lard |
| Salt and pepper | 2 cups sliced onions |
| Flour | 3 Tbs. flour |
| | 2 cups milk |

Cut steak into serving portions. Pound to an even thickness of about ¼ inch. Sprinkle with salt and pepper. Dredge in flour. Shake off excess. Heat ½ inch lard in a large iron skillet. When hot, fry the steaks quickly, turning them to brown both sides. When brown and tender, remove to platter and keep warm. Drain off most of the lard. Fry onions over moderate heat until golden. Sprinkle with flour (about 3 tablespoons) and blend. Add milk. Blend. Cook over low heat, stirring constantly, until thickened. Reduce to lowest possible and cook 5 minutes. Season with salt and pepper to taste. Pour over steak and serve. Serves 4 to 6.

Barbecued steaks—of which there are many in Texas—are merely miniature editions of Barbecued Pot Roast. Here is a typical recipe:

## ★  *Barbecue Steak*

| | |
|---|---|
| 1½ lbs. round steak cut into 4 serving portions | ¾ cup chili sauce (bottled) |
| ¾ cup flour | 2 Tbs. vinegar |
| 1 tsp. salt | 2 Tbs. brown sugar |
| ½ tsp. pepper | 2 Tbs. Worcestershire sauce |
| 3 Tbs. lard | 1 dash Tabasco |
| 2 tsps. chili powder | ¼ cup water |

Trim any outer gristle or tough membranes from steak. Combine flour, salt and pepper. Pound the mixture into the steak on both sides, using a wooden mallet, rolling pin or bottle. Heat lard in a 10-inch iron skillet. Brown the steak quickly and thoroughly on both sides over moderately high heat. Remove to shallow baking dish large enough for the steak to lie in a single layer.

Combine the remaining ingredients and pour over meat. Cover and bake at 325° F. for 1 hour. Baste several times. Uncover and bake 15 minutes longer. Serves 4.

Among the best beef cuts for oven barbecue are short ribs. They are vastly popular in Texas.

★ *Barbecued Beef Ribs (Short Ribs)*

4 lbs. beef ribs
2 medium onions, finely chopped
1 cup catsup
2 cups water
½ cup cider vinegar
1 Tb. Worcestershire sauce
1 rounded Tb. chili powder

1 crushed clove garlic
1 tsp. salt
1 tsp. freshly ground black pepper
2 Tbs. brown sugar
½ tsp. cayenne or a generous dash or two of hot pepper sauce

Place ribs in a heavy pot with about ½ inch water; cover and steam over moderate heat until almost tender (about 1 hour). Turn the ribs several times. Drain, reserving the pan juices. Separate the ribs into serving portions as desired. Skim most of fat from broth.

While the ribs are steaming, combine all the remaining ingredients in a heavy saucepan and bring to a boil. Cook uncovered about 25 minutes, stirring frequently. Correct seasoning as desired.

When ribs are done, place them in a roasting pan. Pour on the sauce, cover and bake at 325° F. for 30 minutes. Uncover, reduce heat to 275° F. and bake 30 minutes longer, basting frequently and adding the reserved broth if more liquid is needed. If the ribs are not *very* tender by this time, cook 10 to 15 minutes longer. The whole process may be done ahead of time, for the ribs are even better when reheated. Serves 4 to 6.

★ *Laredo Short Ribs*

2 lbs. beef short ribs cut in serving portions
½ cup catsup
½ cup good red wine
½ cup chopped onion
1 minced clove garlic
1 tsp. salt
½ tsp. pepper
1 rounded tsp. oregano

Fold a double thickness of aluminum foil large enough to wrap around all the ribs. Press the center of this down into a shallow baking dish. Arrange the ribs in this well. Combine all the remaining ingredients and pour over the ribs. Bring up the sides of the foil to meet over the ribs and fold carefully to seal. Bake at 350° F. for 1 hour. Open the foil so the ribs are exposed; baste and bake, uncovered, about 40 minutes longer or until the ribs are brown. Most of the liquid will have cooked away. Serves about 4.

Whether or not this hash was ever actually made by a camp cook, I do not know. But if it was, there were at least some cowboys with reason to be envied.

★ *Chuck-wagon Hash*

2 lbs. Irish potatoes, peeled and diced
2 lbs. lean beef cut in ¾-inch cubes
2 Tbs. drippings
1 lb. onions, coarsely chopped
2 cups water
Salt and pepper
Hot pepper sauce to taste

Boil potatoes until about halfway tender; drain and set aside. Brown the beef in the drippings over high heat. It should be really brown on all sides. Add onions and let them color slightly. Reduce heat to medium. Add water and let reduce by half, stirring meat from time to time. Add potatoes. Blend. Cover and cook over low heat until meat is tender. The potatoes by this time should be somewhat mushy. Season with salt, pepper and hot pepper sauce to taste. There should be very little remaining liquid. Serves 6.

Cider has never been much used in American cookery. In Texas, however, you find quite a few recipes such as this:

## ★ *Cider Stew*

| | |
|---|---|
| 3 large onions, chopped | ½ tsp. pepper |
| 3 Tbs. bacon drippings | ½ tsp. thyme |
| 3 lbs. lean beef cut in 2-inch chunks | 1½ cups cider |
| 3 Tbs. flour | 1 Tb. tomato catsup |
| 1 Tb. salt | |

In a large iron skillet, brown onions in bacon drippings over moderate heat. When done, push them to one side, add beef and brown that also. Combine flour, salt, pepper and thyme. Sprinkle evenly over meat. Toss. Add cider and catsup. Blend. Cover tightly. Cook over low heat until beef is tender, stirring from time to time and adding more cider if necessary. There should not be too much sauce when the beef is done. Takes about 2½ hours all told. Serves 6 to 8. Serve with noodles or rice.

*Tamale* pies always include corn in some form, but they do not always contain *tamales* as you might suppose. More often than not the name stems from the fact that the dish is baked in a shell of cornmeal either cooked or blended to mush consistency. And the filling, if not an outright *chili,* is at least reminiscent of one and has *chilis* in it. As a rule, cheese is also an ingredient. In most households, though *tamale* pies may be party dishes (and good ones, too), they are family affairs in which leftover meats can fill the requirements quite as easily as fresh ones.

## ★ *Tamale Pastel*

*For the Mush:*

| | |
|---|---|
| 2 cups water-ground cornmeal | 5 cups boiling water |
| 2 tsps. salt | 1 rounded Tb. lard |

Combine ingredients in top of double boiler and cook 15 minutes over boiling water, stirring frequently. Make sure there are no lumps. If the mush seems very dry, add a bit more boiling water. (If too dry, the finished dish will be brick hard.) Line bottom and sides of a well-buttered baking dish with a ½-inch layer of the mush. The extra mush will be spread over the top.

*For the Filling:*

| | |
|---|---|
| ¼ cup chopped onion | ½ cup beef or chicken stock |
| 2 cloves garlic, minced | 1 tsp. salt |
| 2 Tbs. bacon drippings | 1 tsp. sesame seeds |
| 2 cups chopped lean cooked beef | ¼ tsp. *comino* |
| ½ cup chopped pitted ripe olives | 1 generous pinch coriander, if |
| 1 rounded Tb. chili powder | available |
| 1 cup canned tomatoes with most of the juice drained off | 2 Tbs. butter |

204

Brown onions and garlic in drippings. Add all remaining ingredients except butter and cook over moderate heat 20 minutes, stirring from time to time. Fill center of baking dish. Spread top of meat mixture with remaining mush. Bake at 325° F. for 1 hour. After 30 minutes dot top with butter. Serve from the baking dish. Serves 4 to 6.

Many dishes somewhat similar to *Tamale* pies have the cornmeal mush in alternate layers with the filling.

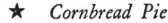 ★ *Cornbread Pie*

| | |
|---|---|
| 1 cup yellow cornmeal | 1 lb. ground lean beef |
| 2 eggs | 1 large onion, chopped fine |
| 1 cup sweet milk | 2 Tbs. additional drippings |
| ½ tsp. soda | 4 hot *jalapeño* peppers, chopped |
| ¾ tsp. salt | Salt |
| 1 can cream-style corn, #2 size | ½ lb. grated sharp Cheddar cheese |
| ½ cup bacon drippings | |

In a mixing bowl combine the first 7 ingredients. Blend thoroughly. In a skillet, brown the beef and onion in the additional drippings. Crumble the meat with a fork as it cooks. Stir in the hot pepper. Drain off any excess fat. Add salt to taste. In a greased rectangular Pyrex baking dish (or any rather shallow casserole) spread half the cornbread mixture. Cover this with all of the meat mixture. Sprinkle meat with the cheese. Top with remaining cornbread mixture. Bake at 450° F. for 45 minutes or until done. Cut into squares to serve directly from the baking dish. Serves 4 or 6. While it is not required, I find this at its best if the top of the bread is spread lavishly with butter the minute it is taken from the oven.

Hominy appears most often in Texas as an accompaniment to meat in a separate dish, taking the place of rice or potatoes or such. Here it is combined with chili in a delectable casserole.

## ★ Chili and Hominy

¼ cup chopped onion
1 clove garlic, minced
3 Tbs. butter
4 lbs. ground lean beef
2 Tbs. chili powder

2 cups beef bouillon
Salt to taste
2 to 3 cups canned hominy
2 cups grated Cheddar cheese

Sauté the onion and garlic in butter until onion is transparent. Add beef and chili powder; cook 4 to 5 minutes, separating the meat with a fork. Add bouillon and blend. Simmer 5 minutes. Add salt if needed. In a casserole arrange layers of the meat mixture, hominy and cheese, ending with the cheese on top. Bake at 350° F. for 45 minutes. Serves 8 to 10.

Ground beef is used in a host of Texas dishes, which all bear a resemblance or at least a relation to chili. Here are three of them:

## ★ Amarillo Ground-beef Delight

1 lb. ground lean beef
1 medium onion, chopped
3 Tbs. butter
1 small green pepper, seeded and chopped

¼ cup chopped green chili peppers (canned)
1 can cream of mushroom soup
½ soup can water
1 pkg. cream cheese, 3-oz. size
Salt to taste

206

Sauté beef and onion in butter in a heavy skillet over moderate heat until onion is golden. Break up and separate the meat with a fork as it cooks. Add chopped green pepper and cook 3 to 4 minutes. Add green chilis, mushroom soup and water. Blend. Simmer 20 minutes, stirring frequently. Add the cream cheese, broken into bits, and stir gently until melted. Serve with rice or wild rice or toast spread with chili butter. Serves 6.

NOTE: To make Chili Butter, simply work butter and chili powder together with a fork in a mixing bowl until thoroughly blended. One tablespoon chili powder to ¼ pound butter should be your point of departure.

 ## Ranch Stew

| | |
|---|---|
| 6 slices bacon, diced | 2 cans tomatoes, 1 lb. each |
| 1 cup chopped onion | 2 tsps. salt |
| 1 clove garlic, minced | ½ tsp. pepper |
| ½ cup chopped, seeded green | 1 heaping Tb. chili powder |
| pepper | 1½ cups whole kernel corn |
| 1½ lbs. ground lean beef | 2 cups diced potatoes |

In a large heavy pot sauté bacon until almost crisp. Add onion, garlic and pepper. Cook until onion begins to brown. Add beef and brown on all sides. Add tomatoes, salt, pepper and chili powder. Cover and simmer 1 hour. Uncover and add corn and potatoes. Simmer until potatoes are tender (about 15 minutes). Serves 6 to 8.

★ *Washday Dinner*

1 lb. ground chuck
1 tsp. salt
¼ tsp. pepper
1 medium onion chopped
2 cups cooked red beans, drained
1 cup tomato sauce

¼ tsp. oregano
½ tsp. ground cumin
12 small potato balls cut out with a
    ball cutter, cooked and drained
Minced parsley

In a heavy skillet brown the beef over low heat, crumbling it as it cooks. Season with salt and pepper. Add onion and blend. Cook 5 minutes. Add beans and tomato sauce. Blend and cook 10 minutes. Add oregano, cumin, and potatoes and cook until potatoes are heated through. Serve in bowls with a generous sprinkling of minced parsley. Serves 4 to 6.

Recipes for *Picadillo* appear throughout all of Spanish America and though usually made with diced or cubed beef instead of ground, they have much the same taste as this recipe from Texas.

★ *Picadillo*

2 Tbs. butter or drippings
1 lb. ground lean beef
1 medium onion, chopped
1 small green pepper, seeded and
    chopped
1 clove garlic, mashed
½ cup tomato paste
1 small bay leaf
½ tsp. cumin, ground

1 Tb. cider vinegar
½ cup beef or chicken stock
    (bouillon)
¼ cup seedless raisins
¼ cup sliced stuffed green olives
1 tsp. sugar
1 tsp. salt
Pepper to taste
1 dash hot pepper sauce

Heat fat in a heavy skillet, add beef, onion, green pepper and garlic; cook over moderate heat until the onion is golden. Add all the remaining ingredients, blend and simmer 20 minutes, stirring frequently. If more liquid is needed, add a small amount of stock. The dish when done should not be too moist. Serve with rice. Serves 4 to 6.

Sloppy Joes in Texas are all more or less visually alike—living up to their name—but their seasonings vary greatly, some being rather plain and predominantly beefy while others may be more like (if not identical to) chili. Here is a middle-ground recipe.

## ★ *Sloppy Joes*

| | |
|---|---|
| 1 lb. ground chuck | 1 tsp. liquid barbecue smoke |
| 1 lb. onions, chopped | Salt and pepper to taste |
| ⅔ cup catsup | 6 or 8 hamburger buns |
| ½ cup chopped, seeded green pepper | |

In an iron skillet brown the ground beef and chopped onions. Do *not* add any fat. The fat in the meat should be sufficient. If it sticks to the skillet at first, scrape it up with a spatula. When meat is brown, add catsup, green pepper and liquid smoke. Blend. Reduce heat to low. Simmer 1 hour, stirring frequently. As fat renders from the meat, skim it off. Add salt and pepper to taste. Serve either in or on split buns. Messy but nice! Serves 6 or 8.

Meat loaf has a peculiar position in American cuisine, for while most people feel compelled to avow dislike or contempt for the dish, you will find that secretly they are very fond of it indeed. And why not? It can be and often is delicious. Texas is the only place I know of, however, where an admiration for meat loaf is voiced publicly. Here is the basic meat loaf that you'll come across all through the state.

★ *Family Meat Loaf*

1½ lbs. ground beef
¾ cup freshly crumbled cracker
  crumbs
2 eggs, beaten
¼ cup chopped onion
2 tsps. salt

½ tsp. mixed herbs (marjoram and
  thyme)
¼ tsp. freshly ground black pepper
½ cup tomato juice
1 can tomato sauce, 8-oz. size

Combine all ingredients except the tomato sauce in a mixing bowl and blend thoroughly. Pack firmly into a well-greased small loaf tin. Smooth top with a knife or spatula. Pour on the tomato sauce. Bake at 350° F. for 1 hour. Serve hot or cold as desired. Serves 4 to 6.

Many meat loaves are given the Texas taste with chili powder; sometimes with a considerable amount of it. Some have hot chili peppers in addition.

★   *Chili Meat Loaf*

3 lbs. ground chuck                    1 Tb. salt
3 large onions, ground                 ½ tsp. coarsely ground black pepper
1 cup fine cracker crumbs              2 cups canned tomatoes
1 large egg                            Minced fresh parsley
1 Tb. (rounded) chili powder, or to
    taste

Combine beef, onions, crumbs, egg and seasonings in a mixing bowl. Blend thoroughly. Work the mixture with your hands. Form into a roll. Place in a greased baking pan. Cover with the canned tomatoes. Bake at 350° F. for 1¼ hours. Baste several times with the pan juices. Sprinkle with parsley before serving. For sauce, serve a tomato sauce or *Salsa Verde* (pages 78–79). This is as good cold as hot. Excellent cold with Potato Salad.

The so-called *variety meats*—innards—have always been used extensively in Texas. This is true also of any community that lives close to the soil. Though today they appear in the growing cities less frequently than a generation or two ago, they still turn up more often than elsewhere and usually with a typically Texan show of pride. Many of the dishes made from them are wholly Texan, which no doubt accounts for the feelings they engender; they are tangible evidence, you might say, of Texas history and legend—the Son-of-a-Gun Stew, for example. Many others are dishes that spring from a particular ethnic background.

If one wonders why in the early days in Texas, when there were an estimated six hundred head of cattle for every human, the settlers bothered with innards at all (what with the mountains of beef they had available), I can only say that rural thrift the world over demands that all of everything of an edible sort be used in the best way possible. And having used all of everything— which here means absolutely all—and found all good, the Texans simply kept on using all as the Texas way.

Today in Texas one finds many variety meats unheard of elsewhere in the country—narrow gut, for instance, diaphragm, mountain oysters (the latter found not infrequently as calf fries in Texas markets packaged and frozen).

The following is a Texas-German way with liver:

## ★ *Fried Calves' Liver*

Dip thin slices of liver in cornmeal seasoned with salt. After dredging slices, pat the meal on to hold it firm. Brown lightly and quickly on both sides in bacon drippings. Do not overcook. Drain slices on paper. Keep hot until all are done. Serve with a White Gravy (page 231) or Coffee Gravy made by adding ¾ cup strong black coffee to the skillet after all the liver has been fried. Blend with drippings. Cook over moderate heat several minutes. Serve in a bowl or sauceboat on the side.

In the old days in Texas when a steer was slaughtered on the range to furnish meat for the cowboys, every scrap of the carcass was used. And the innards all went into a stew that is still made in Texas today, although its name has been polished for book purposes into Son-of-a-Gun Stew. (As long as I'm being euphemistic, let me say that the camp cooks in the old days also made a bread called Son-of-a-Gun-in-a-Sack. This was an ingenious bread to say the least. Flour was precious when the cowboys were on the trail for forty or fifty days at a time, so to conserve it, the cook slit the flour sack and put directly into it whatever shortening, seasoning, liquid and leavening agent was needed for the loaves or loaf. Working quickly with his hands buried in the flour, he molded the wet central mass with just the right amount of surrounding flour getting the proper feel of the dough with his hands. Then he would draw the dough out of the sack, leaving the remaining flour completely dry. He would mold his loaves as desired, then bake them in a preheated Dutch oven. But back to our stew.)

Son-of-a-Gun Stew appears today at all kinds of Texas tables and with all kinds of variations, most of the latter depending on either changed proportions or the inclusion of rather special bits of innards such as the diaphragm, the narrow gut (a glandular tissue), and tripe (the stomach lining). Even the different ethnic groups of Texas have taken to Son-of-a-Gun Stew and in the West, predominantly Bohemian, one housewife has her own version which she has given a Bohemian name, *matchka,* meaning a kind of gravy. She has in fact joined the Texas love of its native stew and the Texas love of gravy, for her *Matchka* is thought of in her household really not as stew at all but as a rich, flavorful moistener to be served with rice or something similar. Her touch of caraway seed is, of course, wholly Bohemian.

## ★ *Matchka*

| | |
|---|---|
| 2 Tbs. oil or lard | ¼ tsp. caraway seeds |
| Heart, liver, tongue, kidneys of calf or hog, cleaned and cut into small pieces | 3 whole allspice |
| | 1 bay leaf, crumbled |
| ½ cup chopped onion | ¼ cup flour, or as needed |
| | Salt and pepper to taste |

In a heavy pot heat oil or lard and brown the meat over moderate heat. Add onion and cook until golden. Add caraway seeds, allspice and bay leaf. Cover with water. Cover pot and cook over low heat until the meat is tender (1½ to 2 hours; without the heart, the meat cooks more quickly). Add flour that has been mixed to a paste with a little cold water. Cook, stirring constantly, until thickened. Add salt and pepper to taste and serve with rice, grits, Spoon Bread, or hominy. The number of servings depends on the quantity of meat.

★ *Calf Fries*

| | |
|---|---|
| **Calf fries** | **White water-ground cornmeal** |
| **Salt and pepper** | **Lard for frying** |

Dip frozen calf fries in hot, not boiling, water, and leave 3 to 4 minutes; drain. Peel off outer membrane. Cut into equal-size, bite-size chunks. Pat dry if necessary. Sprinkle with salt and pepper. Dredge in cornmeal, pressing the meal on with your finger tips so that it adheres. Shake off any excess. Let stand 10 to 15 minutes so the coating will have a chance to set. Heat about ¼ inch lard in a large heavy skillet. Fry the calf fries a few at a time until crisp and brown on all sides. Skim out and drain on paper. Keep hot until all are cooked. Serve with scrambled eggs or (though this is not Texan—I take full responsibility) *Chili con Queso*. Delicious.

Texas cooks love to fry things in batter or crumb or cornmeal coatings and anything of a convenient size to coat is sooner or later fried. But this does not mean that of necessity it is greasy.

★ *Batter-fried Wieners*

| | |
|---|---|
| 1 cup sifted flour | 1 egg |
| 1½ tsps. baking powder | ¾ cup milk |
| ½ tsp. salt | 2 Tbs. melted lard |
| ¾ cup cornmeal | 16 hot dogs |
| 2 Tbs. sugar | |

In a mixing bowl combine all ingredients except the hot dogs and blend thoroughly. Dip hot dogs in batter to coat them all over. Have deep fat ready at 375° F. Carefully lower coated hot dogs into the fat, cooking only a few at a time, and fry until golden brown on all sides. Serve with a barbecue sauce.

Like Sloppy Joes (page 209), S.O.B.'s are inclined to be messy—but good.

★ *S.O.B.'s*

| | |
|---|---|
| 12 finger rolls | 4 Tbs. Worcestershire sauce |
| ¼ cup melted butter | ½ lb. sharp Cheddar cheese, coarsely |
| 1 can tomatoes, #2 size | grated |
| 3-oz. jar chipped beef | 6 eggs, beaten |
| 2 Tbs. Tabasco | |

Cut top off finger rolls and scoop out soft crumbs. Brush center with melted butter. In saucepan, cook tomatoes with chipped beef until most of liquid has cooked away. Stir in Tabasco and Worcestershire. Add cheese and melt over low heat. Fold in eggs and cook 2 minutes. Set aside.

Now on a baking sheet heat the rolls at 325° F. When hot, fill with some of the cheese mixture. Return to oven. As the mixture in the rolls cooks down, add more from the pot, but do not let it run over. Cook until the filling is very thick. Serve rolls on individual plates (2 to each diner) or platter on a bed of shredded lettuce. Serves 6.

Veal seems to appear rather infrequently in Texas. There are the usual veal roasts, of course, and stews (often seasoned with chili powder or chili pepper); cutlets (which become Chicken-fried Steaks when cooked like the steaks on page 198) and chops, but they are not regarded as being in any sense *special*. As a matter of fact, more is made over such dishes as the following Veal Loaf than the choice and invariably expensive cuts. I can only assume that this is further evidence of Texas independence.

★   *Old-fashioned Veal Loaf*

3½ lbs. boneless shoulder of veal, mostly lean, chopped fine. Do *not* grind.
⅛ lb. salt pork, diced very fine
¼ cup chopped celery
2 Tbs. minced fresh celery leaves
½ cup fine cracker crumbs
⅓ cup melted butter
2 eggs, beaten lightly
2 tsps. salt
1 tsp. pepper
1 tsp. rubbed sage
Additional fine crumbs for topping

Combine all ingredients in a mixing bowl. Blend by hand. Pack into a large, greased, loaf pan. Sprinkle top with additional fine crumbs. Cover pan with double thickness of aluminum foil. Press down edges over pan to seal. Bake at 325° F. for 2 hours.

Uncover. Cook 15 to 20 minutes longer. Let stand in pan at room temperature 20 minutes before turning out. Serve hot or cold, but preferably the latter. Serves 6 to 10.

Lamb is considerably less popular than beef in Texas and this well may stem from the way sheep were regarded by the old-time cattlemen. The open range in Texas in the early days was all for cattle, longhorn steers for the most part. When sheep were brought in, it was soon discovered that they cropped the grass so close that none was left for cattle feed and even if there had been any left, the cattle would not have touched it because of the odor left by sheep wherever they grazed. That the conflicting interests of cattlemen and sheepmen could have led to war may seem hard for non-Texans to believe—but it is true. And though today hundreds of thousands of head of both sheep and cattle are raised in Texas, there is still remembrance of the bygone strife. And in this remembrance, sheep (which are lamb and mutton) come out a very poor second to cattle (which is beef). But Texas tables do have lamb dishes anyway and good ones, too. Here is one of them:

★   *Barbecued Lamb Shanks*

For 6 shanks use the same ingredients as for the Barbecued Beef Ribs (page 201), using 2 teaspoons dry mustard instead of the chili powder and increasing the sugar to 4 tablespoons instead of 2. Make the sauce as directed, but do *not* steam the shanks. Place shanks in roasting pan, pour on the sauce, cover and bake 2 hours at 325° F. Baste several times and turn the shanks at least once. Uncover and remove to a heated serving platter 15 minutes before serving. These may be cooked ahead of time and reheated. Serves 6.

Pork, in the early days of Texas settlement, was more widely used and more popular than beef. Today it is still widely used and vastly enjoyed, but Texas, regardless of its annual pork consumption in pounds per capita, is not thought of as a pork state. Texas means beef. Here, however, are some pork favorites:

## ★ Sue's Barbecued Spareribs

| | |
|---|---|
| 2 sides of trimmed spareribs | 1 tsp. celery seed |
| 1 tsp. salt | ¼ cup brown sugar |
| ¼ tsp. pepper | ¼ cup cider vinegar |
| 1 lemon sliced very thin and seeded | ¼ cup Worcestershire sauce |
| 1 large onion, chopped | 1 cup tomato catsup |
| 1 tsp. chili powder | 2 cups water |

Cut ribs into serving portions. Lay in shallow roasting pan meaty side up. Sprinkle with salt and pepper. Put a lemon slice on each piece of ribs, or two if the portions are cut large. Scatter chopped onion over all. Bake 45 minutes at 450° F. While ribs are cooking, combine all other ingredients in saucepan and simmer 20 minutes. Remove ribs from oven when done and drain off all drippings. When ribs are drained, pour sauce over all. Return to oven and bake 1¼ hours longer at 350° F. Baste every 15 or 20 minutes. Serve with Cole Slaw and Fried New Potatoes. Serves 4 to 6, depending on appetites.

# ★ Pork Chop and Corn Casserole

6 shoulder pork chops cut 1 inch thick
1 can whole-kernel corn, drained, (12-oz. size)
1 Tb. minced fresh parsley
¼ tsp. oregano

1 cup fine soft white breadcrumbs
1 tsp. salt
¼ tsp. pepper
1 dash hot pepper sauce
¾ cup rich milk or half-and-half

In a heavy skillet, brown pork chops on both sides over high heat. Reduce heat to medium and cook chops 5 minutes on each side. Remove chops to a baking dish large enough to hold them in a single layer. Combine corn, parsley, oregano, crumbs, salt, pepper and hot pepper sauce. Toss. Sprinkle over chops evenly. Pour in milk. Bake at 350° F. for about 50 minutes. Serve from baking dish. Serves 6.

# ★ Baked Pork Chops

6 pork chops
Salt and pepper
2 apples, peeled, cored and sliced
2 Tbs. sugar

2 Tbs. cornstarch
½ cup cold water
2 cups cider
½ cup white raisins

Cut most of the fat from chops. Brown them on both sides in a heavy skillet over high heat. The fat remaining on the chops should give grease enough for the pan. When chops are brown, remove them to a casserole. Sprinkle with salt and pepper. Cover with apple slices. Combine sugar, cornstarch and cold water; blend. Add cider and raisins. Pour over chops. Bake, covered at 350° F. for 45 minutes; uncover and bake 15 minutes longer. Serves 3 to 6.

*Tomatillos* are tomatoes of sorts but have a special flavor. They are available, canned, at all stores that deal in Spanish-American foods and in many chain stores located where there is a Spanish-American population. This casserole may be made with regular tomatoes, of course, but I like the *tomatillo* taste; I suggest you try it.

★ *Green Chili and Pork Casserole*

| | |
|---|---|
| 10 *tortillas* | 2 cups sour cream |
| Oil for frying | 1 can chopped green chilis |
| 1 medium-size onion, chopped | 1 cup chopped, cooked lean pork |
| 2 cloves garlic, crushed | 1 cup sliced, drained, parboiled |
| 1 Tb. olive oil | zucchini |
| 2 cans *tomatillos* (10 ozs. each) | ½ cup sliced, pimiento-stuffed |
| pressed through a sieve | green olives |
| Salt to taste | |

Cut *tortillas* into quarters and fry lightly in oil. Drain on paper. Set aside. In a saucepan, sauté onion and garlic in olive oil until golden. Do not brown. Add *tomatillos* and blend. Simmer over low heat 15 minutes. Add salt to taste. Set aside. Combine sour cream and green chilis, drained. Butter an 8-cup (2-quart) casserole and in it arrange alternate layers of the fried *tortillas,* *tomatillos* mixture, pork, zucchini, sour-cream mixture and sliced olives. Repeat until all have been used, but end with sour cream on top. Bake at 325° F. for 30 to 40 minutes. Serve from the casserole, cuting the contents as though a cake. Refried beans (which sound better as *frijoles refritos*) make a fine accompaniment. Serves 4 to 6.

★  *Pork Tamale Loaf*

| | |
|---|---|
| 3 slices bacon, finely diced | 3 eggs, beaten |
| 1½ lbs. ground lean pork | 1 Tb. salt |
| ½ cup chopped onion | ¾ tsp. coarsely ground pepper |
| 1 can tomatoes, #2 size | 1 tsp. ground *comino* |
| 1 cup chicken broth | 1 tsp. paprika |
| 1½ cups cornmeal | 4 tsps. chili powder |
| 1½ cups whole-kernel corn | |

In a heavy pot or skillet sauté bacon until almost crisp. Add pork and onion. Cook, stirring frequently, until pork is well browned. Add tomatoes and broth. Bring to a boil. Gradually sprinkle in the cornmeal. When blended, remove from heat and stir in all the remaining ingredients. Pack evenly into a large greased loaf pan. Bake at 325° F. for 1½ hours. Let stand in pan at least 15 minutes before turning out. Serve hot with a tomato sauce or *Guacamole*. Excellent with salad. Serves 6 to 8.

Sausages of all kinds and dishes made with sausages or sausage meat are popular everywhere in Texas. Of the sausages themselves, the kinds are legion, for not only do you find those which are typically American and similar to sausages found elsewhere throughout the country, but also those typical of each ethnic group long settled in the state—German, Spanish, Mexican, Bohemian, Polish. And then there are sausages that seem to reflect intermarriages—German with Mexican, American with Polish, ad infinitum. One of the most popular sausages of East Texas is known as East Texas Hot Guts. Here it is:

## ★ East Texas Hot Guts

4 lbs. predominantly lean beef
1 lb. predominantly lean pork
1 lb. fat pork
3 Tbs. salt

2 tsps. freshly ground black pepper
½ tsp. red pepper
1 Tb. rubbed sage
½ tsp. ground saltpeter

Cut up the meats and fat and put them through a medium grinder blade together. Combine seasonings. Blend the seasonings into the ground meat by hand and, if desired, add more to taste. To get the right taste, fry small cakes of the sausage from time to time as you work on it. When properly seasoned, this may be used either as bulk sausage meat and so fried in cakes, or it may be stuffed into a gut casing and tied off in links.

Mexican sausages are frequently very hot and highly seasoned with cumin, oregano, and garlic. Those similar to the Spanish *chorizos* are sold everywhere throughout the state and are widely used by all Texans. Here is a relatively mild Mexican Sausage.

## ★ Mexican Sausage

3 lbs. lean pork
1 lb. fat pork
4 large cloves garlic
3 tsps. crushed *comino* seeds

1 tsp. coarsely ground black pepper
1 Tb. salt
¼ tsp. cayenne
2 tsps. rubbed sage

Cut up lean and fat pork and put them through a meat grinder together with the garlic. Combine all seasonings. Mix sausage meat with seasonings by hand. Form into small (but relatively thick) patties. Grill or fry over moderate heat. Baste during cooking with *Salsa de Chile* (page 60) as desired. This gives extra fire to the finished sausage.

Sausage meat is often combined with beef in Texas meat loaves, but here it is used only with crumbs, tomatoes, mashed potatoes, egg and seasonings. An excellent dish.

★ *Sausage Loaf*

| | |
|---|---|
| 2 cups well-seasoned country sausage | 2 cups soft breadcrumbs |
| 1 cup canned tomatoes | 1 tsp. salt |
| 2 cups mashed potatoes | ¼ tsp. pepper |
| | 1 egg, beaten |

Fry sausage, crumbling it as it cooks, for 10 minutes over low heat. Drain. Combine sausage with all the remaining ingredients. Mix thoroughly, working it with your hands. Press into lightly greased 5 x 8-inch loaf pan. Bake at 400° F. for 1 hour. Drain off excess fat once or twice during cooking. Turn out on platter if to be served hot. Cool in the loaf pan if to be cold. Delicious either way. Makes wonderful sandwiches. Serves 6 as main meat dish.

Hams, both fresh and cured, are served on festive occasions everywhere in Texas. The fresh ones are often boned and stuffed to make for marvelous eating or, as in the following recipe, they may be oven-barbecued—or anyway so called in Texas.

★ *Oven-barbecued Fresh Ham*

| | |
|---|---|
| 1 fresh ham, 12-lb. | 1 bay leaf |
| 2 cups brown sugar | 1 tsp. mustard seed |
| 2 cups wine vinegar | 6 whole allspice |
| 2 cups water | ½ tsp. celery seed |
| 2 cups condensed consommé | 1 tsp. coarsely ground black pepper |

Score the fat surface of the fresh ham in a criss-cross pattern with the cuts running down slightly into the flesh. Place it in a large enamel pot or preserving kettle. Combine all the remaining ingredients in a saucepan and bring to a boil; simmer 5 minutes. Pour over the ham while still hot; cover and let stand in a cold place overnight, turning the ham several times to marinate it evenly.

Place ham in an open roasting pan fat-side up. Roast at 350° F. for 5 hours, basting with the marinade at 20-minute intervals and draining excess fat from the roasting pan as it accumulates. When ham is done, serve with Candied Sweet Potatoes, Fresh Black-eyed Peas, a "Grand" Salad (page 291), pickles and Cherry or Peach Cobbler.

Cured hams, which nowadays even in Texas are more often of the commercially processed sort than country cured, may be either oven-baked to finish with a sugar glaze or barbecued (grilled over charcoal). As all processed hams are at least partially cooked, the grilling is primarily for giving the wanted charcoal-grilled flavor. But it should be born in mind that all of these hams (including the so-called *ready-to-eat* ones) are improved by cooking in the oven, uncovered, at 300° F. for from 2 to 4 hours, depending on their kind and whether or not they will subsequently be grilled. This cooking not only improves their texture but their flavor, too. And while they are cooking, they may be basted with any of a variety of liquids, the most popular in Texas being some fruit juice or the ubiquitous Dr. Pepper—which latter makes for a delicious ham indeed.

Ham leftovers pose no problem in Texas. Fried ham being *the* favorite Texas breakfast meat, the term leftovers really doesn't apply where ham is concerned. Country-cured ham, because of its somewhat dry, waxlike texture, provides the best ham for frying by far, but a good-quality, commercially processed ham will result in *good* fried ham if the slices are patted dry with paper towels before frying. They should be cooked in a pre-heated, heavy, ungreased iron skillet for best effect. The crisp browned bits of the ham that adhere to the skillet are the makings of your gravy (see page 231).

Then, too, hams in Texas are used to provide such excellent dishes as this Ham Loaf with Pineapple.

Pineapple, you will find, is used extensively at Texas tables, not only in desserts and fruit salads but in main meat dishes, as meat accompaniment, too, and even for pickles.

## ★ *Ham Loaf with Pineapple*

1½ cups drained crushed pineapple
1 lb. lean well-flavored ham, ground (preferably country-cured)
1 lb. lean fresh pork, ground
1½ cups crushed corn flakes

1 cup milk
3 eggs, beaten
Salt to taste (this depends on the ham you use)
1 tsp. coarsely ground black pepper
1 tsp. cornstarch

In a large mixing bowl, combine 1 cup of the pineapple with all the other ingredients except the cornstarch. Blend thoroughly, working the mixture to a smooth paste. Pack firmly in a greased 5

225

x 8-inch loaf pan. Smooth the top with a spatula. Bake at 350° F. for 30 minutes; reduce heat to 275° F. and bake 1½ hours longer. Baste every 20 minutes with a little of the Basting Sauce given below. Turn loaf out into a baking pan. Mix remaining pineapple with cornstarch. Spread mixture evenly over loaf. Return to oven and bake 30 minutes longer. Remove loaf carefully to a heated platter. Serve hot or cold. Serves 6 to 8.

Special basting sauces are widely used in Texas to give meats a sweet-sour taste. Here is one of them:

## ★ Basting Sauce for Meat Loaf, Ham, Pork

½ cup brown sugar  
½ cup water  
1 tsp. dry mustard

1 Tb. Worcestershire sauce  
Vinegar to taste

Combine all ingredients in small saucepan and boil until sugar has melted. Keep warm until needed. Store leftover sauce, covered, in refrigerator. Makes 1¼ cups.

*Cabrito* (goat) is a popular dish among all the Mexicans of Texas, especially along the border. And when it is cooked with *Sangre Fritada* (literally fried blood), it is thought particularly delectable. And it is delectable—as anyone can easily discover with the following, which takes its name from its sauce:

---

## ★   *Cabrito Sangre Fritada*

### For the Stew:

½ cup lard
3 lbs. *cabrito* (goat), cubed
1 goat's heart, cleaned and sliced
1 goat's liver, sliced
2 Tbs. lard, additional
2 cloves garlic, minced
3 shallots (or 6 scallions), chopped

1 Tb. *pasta de chili*
2 Tbs. minced fresh parsley
½ tsp. minced mint leaves
½ tsp. marjoram
1 pinch rue (if available)
2 tsps. salt

Melt the ½ cup lard in a heavy iron pot; add cubed meat, heart and liver. Stir to brown evenly over moderate heat. Reduce heat to low. Cover. Cook 1 hour. Add more lard if needed. Meanwhile, heat the 2 tablespoons lard in a small skillet and sauté the garlic and shallots (or scallions) until golden. Add them to the meat with all the seasonings. Blend. Cook over lowest possible heat while preparing the sauce.

### For the Blood Sauce:

1½ cups fresh goat's blood
1 Tb. minced fresh parsley

1 generous pinch salt

Combine blood and salt in a saucepan. Bring just to boil. Reduce heat immediately to low. Simmer until all redness has gone from the blood. Break up the blood as it coagulates. When brown, add to the meat. Blend. Cook 4 to 5 minutes. If dish is too dry, add a few tablespoonfuls of boiling water. Cook over lowest possible heat 10 minutes, stirring frequently. Sprinkle with minced fresh parsley before serving. Serves 4 to 6.

# SEVENTEEN

## SAUCES AND GRAVIES

# THOUGH Texans on the whole are

dedicated gravy eaters, they tend to be disinterested in those more-or-less-standard French sauces that have elsewhere become integral parts of the American cuisine. Texans do have their own sauces, of course, and those of Mexican origin. And they use some of the sauces that were first brought into the state by German settlers of the mid-nineteenth century. But most of the Texas dishes that require something in the way of sauce when they appear at table have this made as a part of the dish. Then, too, many Texas dishes are themselves of a somewhat saucelike consistency. So the lack, if it can be called such, is really not noticeable to the casual observer.

The more sophisticated urban tables in Texas, of course, tend increasingly to seem like sophisticated tables anywhere, presenting the whole gamut of French sauces. But these tables, though *of* Texas are really not Texas tables at all; they are international. Even so—and with or without sauces—they tend to be more regional here than elsewhere. And sooner or later White Gravy will turn up at all of them.

★ *White Gravy*

In a small iron skillet blend 6 tablespoons flour with 6 tablespoons sausage drippings. Place skillet over medium heat and brown the mixture very lightly. Stir in ½ teaspoon salt and ¼ teaspoon white pepper. Add 1½ cups rich milk. Cook over low heat, stirring constantly until gravy is smooth and thickened. Add extra milk and blend if gravy is thicker than you like. Cook gravy gently 4 minutes before serving. Serves 4. In Texas this gravy is served with eggs, biscuits, breaded veal cutlets, pork chops, mashed potatoes and sausage. It is especially good with fried ham.

White Gravy, obviously, is not the same thing at all as White (or Cream) Sauce, which is one of the standard sauces (or perhaps I should say *ingredients*) of every Texas household. Just to refresh your memory, here is the way to make it:

## ★ *White (Cream) Sauce*

| | |
|---|---|
| 2 Tbs. butter | 1 cup milk |
| 2 Tbs. flour | Salt and pepper (or cayenne) to taste |

Melt the butter in the top of a double boiler over hot water. Stir in flour and let the mixture cook for a few minutes. Do not let it color. Add the milk and cook, stirring constantly, until the sauce is smooth and thickened. Add salt and pepper to taste and remove from heat. If the sauce is to be left standing some time before using, float 1 tablespoon melted butter over the top to prevent a skin from forming. Stir this into the sauce before you use it. Makes about 1¼ cups.

Another "gravy" that turns up at virtually all Texas tables to be used as "gravy" or "sauce"—depending on the point of view—is Raised Gravy, the Red Gravy of the Deep South.

232

★ *Raised Gravy*

Raised Gravy is made in a skillet immediately after frying ham. While the pan is still hot (but with the drippings drained off), pour in 1 to 1½ cups of strong, hot, black coffee. With a spatula, scrape up all the browned ham bits left clinging to the skillet and simmer 4 to 5 minutes. Season to taste with black pepper. Salt, as a rule, is not needed. Serve with ham and eggs and hot biscuits and grits or Fried Mush. Serves 4.

The following so-called Spanish Sauce (or a facsimile thereof) is used with many dishes in Texas. Whether it is indeed Spanish or even Mexican is a moot point, for a similar sauce was used in the nineteenth century virtually everywhere in the United States. In Texas, however, it seems to have a more truly Spanish taste.

★ *Spanish Sauce*

| | |
|---|---|
| ½ cup chopped onion | 2 tsps. salt, or to taste |
| 1 clove garlic, minced | 1 tsp. sugar |
| ¼ cup chopped celery | 1 Tb. minced fresh parsley |
| ½ cup diced, seeded green pepper | 1 tsp. minced celery leaves |
| 2 Tbs. olive oil | ¼ tsp. ground cloves |
| 2½ cups canned tomatoes | 1 tsp. flour |
| 1 bay leaf | |

In a heavy saucepan sauté onion, garlic, celery and green pepper in olive oil over moderate heat until the onion is golden. Add tomatoes and all the remaining ingredients. Blend. Simmer over low heat 1 hour, or until very thick. Makes about 3 cups sauce.

Many of the "made" sauces of the Texas cuisine are spicy ones such as this:

## ★ Steak Sauce

3 Tbs. butter
1 Tb. scraped onion
1 Tb. walnut catsup
1 Tb. chili sauce
1 Tb. Worcestershire sauce

1 Tb. paprika
1 tsp. prepared mustard
½ tsp. pepper
1 tsp. salt

Melt butter in small saucepan. Add the remaining ingredients. Blend. Cook about 2 minutes. Keep hot until needed. Spoon over a *very* rare steak just before serving.

Horseradish Sauce, a German import, is served usually with either roast or boiled beef. It is also delectable with roast pork.

## ★ Horseradish Sauce

½ cup heavy cream
1 Tb. vinegar

4 Tbs. ground horseradish*
Salt to taste

Whip cream until stiff then whip in vinegar. Add ground horseradish to taste. Blend. Add salt as needed. Chill thoroughly before serving. Do not make too long in advance of using. Makes about 1 cup.

* If prepared horseradish is used, drain it thoroughly before blending it with the cream.

234

This Garlic Sauce is often served with beef and very often with *cabrito*.

★ *Garlic Sauce*

| | |
|---|---|
| 2 cups beef broth | 2 cloves garlic, minced very fine |
| 2 cups dry white wine | 1 tsp. fresh lemon juice |
| Salt | 1 Tb. olive oil |
| 2 Tbs. minced fresh parsley | |

Combine broth and wine in a saucepan and cook until reduced by half. Add salt to taste, parsley and garlic. Cook over low heat 30 minutes. Add lemon juice and oil and more salt if needed. Makes about 1½ cups sauce.

Sweet-sour sauces are other German additions to the Texas cuisine. This one is usually served with tongue or ham.

★ *Sweet-Sour Currant Sauce*

| | |
|---|---|
| 1 Tb. cornstarch | ¾ cup water |
| ¼ tsp. dry mustard | ½ cup red-currant jelly |
| ¼ cup brown sugar | ½ cup raisins |
| 2 Tbs. vinegar | 2 Tbs. slivered zest* of orange |

In a small saucepan, combine cornstarch, mustard and sugar. Stir in vinegar and water. Add currant jelly. Blend. Add raisins

* Zest: the outer orange part of the orange rind with none of the bitter under white part.

and zest. Cook over low heat, stirring constantly, until thick and clear. Keep warm until needed. Makes 1½ cups sauce.

This Parsley Sauce (or one similar to it) is often served with fish and sometimes with bland meat.

★ *Parsley Sauce*

2 Tbs. butter
2 Tbs. flour
1 cup milk
½ tsp. salt

2 Tbs. scraped onion pulp
¼ cup very finely minced fresh parsley
1 hard-cooked egg, chopped

Melt butter in top of double boiler over hot water; add flour and blend. Stir in milk and continue stirring until sauce is smooth and thickened. Add salt, onion pulp, parsley and chopped egg. Blend. Cook 3 to 4 minutes over moderate heat and serve from a sauceboat.

# EIGHTEEN
## *ACCOMPANI-*
### *MENTS*

SIDE dishes and accompaniments are essential to all Texas meals. And while the latter most frequently are preserves of various kinds and pickles and relishes (a great many of which are home-made), they may also be a specially prepared fresh or canned fruit. And sometimes they are fresh, raw vegetables.

The raw vegetable accompaniments to meats are often similar to salads. They are not thought of as such, however. Their form and use probably stems from those Mexican *salsas* such as *Guacamole* (page 102) and *Salsa de Aguacate* (page 76). Texas Caviar (Pickled Black-eyed Peas) and Pickled Okra are both served with meats in precisely the same way as these Mexican sauces. So also are such simple creations as Salted Cucumbers and Onions.

★ *Texas Caviar*

2 cans black-eyed peas, 1 lb. each, drained
½ cup olive oil
¼ cup wine vinegar
2 cloves garlic, mashed
1 medium onion, sliced paper-thin

1 tsp. salt, or none
Freshly ground black pepper to taste
1 small bay leaf
¼ cup minced fresh parsley
2 hard-cooked eggs, chopped
Watercress

239

In a glass jar or bowl, combine all ingredients except the parsley, chopped egg, and watercress. Cover and refrigerate 3 days, turning the jar upside down several times each day. To serve, drain off some of the oil and vinegar. Pour black-eyed peas into a glass serving dish. Top with parsley and chopped egg. Garnish with watercress. Serve with cold meats or hamburgers. Serves 6 to 8.

★ *Pickled Okra*

| | |
|---|---|
| 2 pkgs. frozen okra, 10-ozs. each | ¼ cup water |
| 2 hot-red-pepper pods | 3 Tbs. salt |
| 2 cloves garlic, halved | 1½ tsps. celery seed, bruised |
| 2 cups white vinegar | ½ tsp. mustard seed, bruised |

Thaw okra. Pack carefully into 2 hot, sterilized 1-pint jars. Put a pepper pod in each. Add also a halved clove garlic. In a small saucepan, bring vinegar and water to a boil. Add salt, celery seed and mustard seed. Pour over okra. Seal. Let stand 4 weeks before using. If whole pepper pods are not available, add ¼ tsp. crushed, dried, hot red pepper to each jar. Excellent with cold roast beef or cold roast pork.

★ *Salted Cucumbers and Onions*

| | |
|---|---|
| 1 large cucumber | 1½ cups cold water |
| 1 medium-size onion | ½ cup cider vinegar |
| 2 Tbs. salt | Minced fresh parsley |

240

Pare cucumber; slice paper-thin into bowl. Cut onion into similar slices. Combine with cucumber. Add salt and cold water. Cover and chill 4 or more hours. Before serving, drain off all the water, reserving ¼ cup. To the reserved liquid add cider vinegar. Pour over cucumbers and onions, cover and keep chilled until needed. Sprinkle liberally with minced fresh parsley before taking to the table. Serves 4 to 6. Very good with pork or any barbecue or with chili dishes.

Bowls of relish appear on Texas tables as a matter of course—and sometimes several at once.

## ★ *Green Tomato Relish*

| | |
|---|---|
| 6 qts. small green tomatoes, quartered | 1 large sweet red pepper, seeded and chopped |
| 3 qts. medium onions, quartered | 10 tsps. salt |
| 1 qt. medium-size hot green chili peppers, chopped (use canned if you like) | 8 cups sugar |
| | 4 cups cider vinegar |
| | 4 cups water |

Combine all the ingredients in a large enamel or agateware kettle, bring to a boil and then simmer until the onions are clear (about 20-25 minutes). Ladle into sterilized pint jars and seal. Yield about 1 dozen pints. Serve with ham, pork, chicken or any white-meat fish.

★  *Cranberry Relish*

| | |
|---|---|
| 4 cups fresh cranberries (1 lb.) | ¼ tsp. cinnamon |
| 2 oranges, quartered, seeded but *not* peeled | ¼ tsp. allspice |
| | 1 cup chopped pecans |
| 2 cups sugar | |

Put cranberries and oranges through the medium blade of food grinder together. Add remaining ingredients and blend. Cover and chill several hours before using. In tightly covered container this will keep in refrigerator for several weeks. Makes 2 pints.

★  *Pepper-Onion Relish*

| | |
|---|---|
| 1 doz. sweet red peppers | 2 cups sugar |
| 1 doz. sweet green peppers | 2 cups cider vinegar |
| 1 doz. medium-size white onions | 1 Tb. salt |
| Boiling water | |

Remove stems and seeds from peppers. Peel and quarter onions. Put peppers and onions together through medium blade of food grinder. Place in heavy pot; cover with boiling water and let stand 5 minutes. Drain. Add sugar, vinegar and salt. Bring to boil over high heat. Cook 5 minutes, stirring frequently. Pour into hot sterilized jars and seal. Makes approximately 8 pints.

Many of the pickles popular today in Texas are ones that were first made in the English colonies of the Atlantic seaboard. Bread-and-Butter Pickles, for instance.

242

---

## ★  *Uncooked Bread-and-Butter Pickles*

1 gal. unpeeled cucumbers, sliced crosswise thinly
2 sweet green peppers, seeded and slivered
8 small onions, about 1 inch diameter, thinly sliced
½ cup salt

5 cups cider vinegar
4 cups sugar
2 Tbs. white mustard seed
½ tsp. ground cloves
1½ tsp. turmeric
1 tsp. (rounded) celery seed

Combine sliced vegetables in large bowl. Toss to blend. Sprinkle with ½ cup salt. Pack bowl in ice if possible. Cover and let stand 4 hours. Drain.

While the vegetables are standing, make a syrup of the remaining ingredients in a large saucepan. Cook until thick, stirring frequently with a wooden spoon. When the vegetables have been drained, pack them in hot, sterilized pint jars. Pour the hot syrup over them to cover completely. Seal and let stand 2 weeks at least before using. Makes about 12 pints.

## ★  *Sour Pickles*

15 medium-size cucumbers
1 qt. cider vinegar
1 cup water

¼ cup salt
¼ cup sugar
¼ cup white mustard seed

Select cucumbers of equal size, of a good green color and free of blemishes. Wash and dry them well. Combine all other ingredients in a deep kettle and bring to a full rolling boil. Pack cucumbers in hot sterilized jars. (They *must* be hot to prevent cracking). Pour hot pickle solution over them to cover completely. Seal. This amount of pickle should do for about 4 quarts.

Preserves of one kind or another are standard fixtures of the Texas breakfast table. But they appear at other meals almost as often and, in a German way, side by side with pickles and relishes.

## ★ *Green Tomato Marmalade*

| | |
|---|---|
| 4 lbs. green tomatoes | 2 lbs. sugar |
| 5 lemons | ½ tsp. salt |

Wash tomatoes and drain. Cut away the stem end. Cut tomatoes into chunks. Peel lemons and cut the peel in thin slivers. Boil cut peel 5 minutes in 1 cup water. Drain. Repeat and drain again. Cut up the lemon pulp, discarding all seeds. Combine tomatoes, lemon peel, pulp, sugar and salt in a preserving kettle. Heat slowly. Stir until the sugar is dissolved. Bring to a boil and cook 1 hour, stirring frequently. When done, the marmalade should be very thick and the fruit transparent. Pour into hot, sterilized ½-pint jars to ¼ inch from the top if paraffin is to be used. If not, fill to the top. Seal and store. Makes 8½ pints.

## ★ *Pear Honey*

| | |
|---|---|
| 8 parts ground fresh pears | 1 part canned grated pineapple, |
| 6 parts granulated sugar | drained |
| | Pecans (optional) |

In a heavy pot or saucepan cook the ground pears and sugar together over moderate heat until *very* thick, stirring frequently. Add pineapple. Cook 4 minutes. Pack into sterilized jars and seal.

If pecans are added (as they may be), use 2 parts chopped pecans in proportion to pears, sugar and pineapple.

## ★ *Apple Butter*

Select sound, tart apples. Wash, peel and slice them. Combine in large, heavy pot with an equal measure (by volume) of sweet cider. Cook, stirring frequently, until apples are very soft. Purée through a colander with holes small enough to hold back the apple seeds. Season to taste with ground allspice, cinnamon and sugar as desired. Reduce if necessary over moderate heat. Anyway bring almost to the boil, pour into hot, sterilized ½-pint jars and seal. Six pounds of apples will make 12 ½-pint jars.

Though one thinks of Texas as being Southern to the core, it exhibits a marked New England influence as well. At table, this shows up in such things as the Cranberry Sauce that is a *must* with turkey. Being from Texas, however, this sauce (like the one below) is often spicy.

## ★ *Whole Cranberry Sauce*

2 cups sugar
2 cups water
4 cups fresh cranberries (1 lb.)

1 cup finely chopped candied orange peel
¼ tsp. cinnamon
¼ tsp. allspice

Combine sugar and water in saucepan and bring to a boil. Add cranberries and orange peel. Cook, without stirring, 6 to 8 minutes or until berries pop open. Remove from heat. Stir in spices. Cool, then chill or store in covered jars. Makes about 2½ pints.

Preserves, jams and jellies in Texas are often given a touch of hot chili. The effect is altogether delectable. This jelly is wonderful with cold meats.

## ★ *Hot Pepper Jelly*

¾ cup chopped, seeded bell peppers    1½ cups cider vinegar
   (almost 2 large peppers)        6 cups sugar
¼ cup chopped hot green peppers    1 small bottle Certo (pectin)

Combine the peppers in a blender with ½ cup of the vinegar. Blend at high speed. Turn into enamel or stainless steel saucepan. Rinse blender with remaining vinegar and add to peppers. Add sugar. Bring to rolling boil and cook 3 minutes. Stir constantly. Remove from heat. Skim. Stir in Certo and skim again. Pour into 5 sterilized ½ pint jars and seal.

Specially prepared fruits and fruit dishes are often served with birds and meats. The following one is delicious with pork, ham or turkey.

## ★ Prune Aspic

2 Tbs. unflavored gelatin
½ cup cold water
3½ cups canned prune juice, heated
4 cups stewed prunes, pitted and chopped

2 Tbs. lemon juice
2 cream cheeses, 3-oz. size
Sweet or sour cream as needed

Soften gelatin in cold water. Add the hot prune juice and stir until gelatin is completely dissolved. Let cool. When thick but not set, stir in prunes and lemon juice. Pour into a ring mold that has been rinsed in cold water and chilled. Put the mold in the refrigerator until the mixture is set. Turn out on a cold serving plate. Fill center with cream cheese that has been whipped to creamy consistency with a little cream or sour cream. Serves 10 to 12.

## ★ Fried Peaches

3 barely ripe freestone peaches
6 tsps. brown sugar

2 Tbs. butter

Peel peaches; cut in half and discard stones. Put 1 teaspoon brown sugar in each half. Melt butter in skillet. Add peaches, cut side up. Fry over low heat until tender. Baste with the butter from the pan. Serve hot with Roast Pork. Serves 3 to 6.

# NINETEEN

## *FRIJOLES AND OTHER LEGUMES*

# BEANS

are as characteristic of Texan cuisine as chili peppers, and *beans* in this connection means *dried beans*—usually pinto beans (*garbanzos*). One way or another, beans may appear at any kind of Texas meal, although they are a *must* only with barbecue and certain Texas-Mexican combinations. They may be merely boiled to tenderness (with seasonings, of course) or they may be mashed or baked or fried. They may be served as appetizer, vegetable, side dish, sauce of some kind or salad. Sometimes they even appear pickled. And though, as I say, pinto beans are the ones most commonly used and are THE *frijoles* of the Mexicans, black beans and red beans and cranberry beans and white Navy beans also put in appearances. And dried limas, too.

Although beans elsewhere in the United States will be served in lieu of other starchy vegetables, they are served in Texas (as though no one had ever heard of calories) side by side with potatoes or rice (or both) or hominy or even pasta (done in some English way). Here are a few of the many hundreds of Texas bean recipes:

★ *Frijoles*

2 cups (1 lb.) dried pinto beans
1 large onion, chopped
2 cloves garlic, minced
1 tsp. ground *comino*

1 *chili ancho* (canned) mashed to a paste (or more if desired)
3 Tbs. bacon drippings
Salt and pepper to taste

Pick over beans carefully; cover with cold water and let stand overnight. Before cooking, add more water, covering beans again. Combine in heavy pot with onion, garlic, *comino,* chili and drippings. Simmer until tender, adding a little more water when needed. When the beans are done, however, virtually all the liquid should have cooked away. If some of the beans are mashed during cooking, so much the better. Add salt and pepper to taste when done. The longer the cooking, the better your beans so cook over the slowest fire possible. Serves 4 to 8 depending on the portion size.

*Frijoles Refritos* (fried, cooked pinto beans) are probably the most popular and generally useful beans in Texas. So good are they and so fond of them do non-Texans become during even a short stay in Texas that one wonders why they are not served elsewhere. They are marvelous with any chili or barbecue, and with ham or pork of any kind, superb.

★   *Frijoles Refritos*

Cook pinto beans as described in the previous recipe or use leftover or canned ones. For 2 cups of cooked beans, heat 6 tablespoons lard or bacon drippings in a heavy iron skillet over moderate heat. Add the beans. As they fry, mash them with the back of a wooden spoon. Continue to fry and mash them until they are dry enough to shake loose from the bottom of the pan in a mass. The inner portion of this mass will (or should) be moist. The bottom surface will be slightly crusty. The consistency is not necessarily smooth like a purée, though it may be. Serves 4.

The various ethnic groups in Texas have all contrived dishes of their own from pinto beans. Here is one from a Swedish family.

## ★ Swedish Brown Beans

| | |
|---|---|
| 2 cups pinto beans | 1 tsp. cinnamon |
| 1 tsp. salt | 2 Tbs. molasses |
| 1 Tb. vinegar | 3 Tbs. butter |
| 1 Tb. sugar | |

Place beans in heavy pot. Cover with cold water. Add all remaining ingredients except butter. Cover. Cook over low heat until beans are tender, adding a little *hot* water if necessary. When beans are done, correct seasoning with more salt and pepper, if desired, and stir in butter. Serve with pork, ham or barbecue. Serves 6.

Barbecued Beans are very similar to the so-called Ranch Beans in Texas and, as you'd expect, they have the characteristic *barbecue* taste.

## ★ Barbecued Baked Beans

| | |
|---|---|
| 2 cups dried Navy or pinto beans | 1 small hot red chili pepper |
| 8 slices bacon, diced | ¾ cup tomato catsup |
| ½ cup chopped onion | 2 Tbs. prepared mustard |
| 2 Tbs. corn syrup | 1 tsp. salt |
| 2 Tbs. chili powder | 1 generous dash hot pepper sauce |

Soak beans overnight in cold water to cover. Fry bacon until crisp. Drain drippings from bacon into baking dish or small bean pot. Add all remaining ingredients to fat and blend. Drain beans and add to mixture. Blend. Crumble the crisp bacon over top. Add water just to cover beans. Cover dish or bean pot and bake at 325° F. for 2 hours. Add more *hot* water if needed. Uncover beans during last 20 to 30 minutes. Serve from baking dish. Serves 6 to 8.

A slice of smoky bacon rind used instead of the sliced bacon will give a more decidedly country flavor. Brown sugar to taste may replace the corn syrup. And canned tomatoes may take the place of the catsup—but if so, correct the seasoning as necessary with a little sugar, salt, cayenne and a pinch of ground allspice.

In many Texas bean dishes you will find a considerable quantity of cheese and a dominant seasoning of either chili powder or chopped chilis.

## ★ Red Fire

4 cups red kidney beans
½ lb. butter
½ lb. grated mild Cheddar cheese
4 *jalapeño* peppers, chopped very fine (available canned, be sure of the name; these are *hot*)

1 tsp. juice from peppers
¼ cup scraped or grated onion
1 large clove garlic put through a garlic press
Salt to taste
Paprika optional

Cover beans with cold water, bring to a boil, reduce heat and simmer until tender. Drain and purée through sieve or food mill. Place in large double boiler or saucepan over hot water, add remaining ingredients and cook until cheese is melted. Paprika may be added if desired for a redder red. When serving, keep hot over candle warmer or in chafing dish with *tostados* or fried *tortillas;* or serve on small individual plates over *fritos;* or as a filling for split broiled hot dogs. This is also delectable over very rare hamburgers.

Chili Beans may also be a very simple dish such as this. They are especially good with pork and with barbecue.

★ *Chili Beans*

| | |
|---|---|
| 1 lb. pinto beans | 3 Tbs. chili powder |
| ¼ lb. salt pork | Salt to taste |
| 1 medium onion, chopped | |

Pick over beans carefully, then put them to soak overnight in a heavy pot with 1 quart water. Next day add water as needed to make up the original amount. Cut rind from pork; cut the remaining meat in 3 equal pieces and add to beans. Cook over low heat until beans are almost tender. (If water cooks away too fast, add a little more, but whatever liquid remains when the beans are done should be very thick.) Add onion and chili powder. Cook until onion is limp. Add salt to taste and serve or reheat gently later. The beans are actually the better for standing and reheating. Serves 6 to 8.

★ *Barbecued Lima Beans*

| | |
|---|---|
| 2 cans lima beans, 1 lb. 13 oz. each | ¼ cup dark brown sugar |
| ⅔ cup evaporated milk | 1 Tb. Worcestershire sauce |
| 5 slices bacon, diced | 1 tsp. chili powder |
| 1 cup chopped, seeded, sweet green pepper | 1 Tb. cornstarch |
| | 1 Tb. prepared mustard |
| 1 clove garlic, minced | 2 cans tomato sauce, 8 ozs. each |
| ¼ cup vinegar | |

Drain limas and put them in a mixing bowl. Add milk and set aside. In a skillet sauté bacon until cooked but *not* crisp. Add green pepper and garlic. Cook 10 minutes over moderate heat. Add vinegar, sugar, Worcestershire sauce, chili powder, cornstarch (moistened with a little cold water), mustard and tomato sauce. Blend. Cook until thickened, stirring constantly. Add salt if needed. Combine sauce with beans and milk. Turn into a 9½ x 13½-inch baking dish or casserole. Bake at 350° F. for 50 minutes. Serve with beef, ham, chicken, pork or hot dogs. Serves 6.

# TWENTY

## *RICE, PASTA AND SUCH*

AS I mentioned in connection with beans, Texas meals are not limited to one main meat accompaniment. Nor is there any limit to the number of starchy dishes that may appear together. And although the cuisine is figuratively a *meat-and-potatoes* affair, potatoes actually appear rather less frequently than you'd expect, their place being taken by rice or hominy or pasta (done in some non-Italian manner)—with a Spoon Bread in addition. And often you will find one or another of these served with potatoes—sweet or white.

Rice is the favored vehicle for gravy in Texas. In certain parts of East Texas it is said that regardless of whatever else may appear at table, the rice and gravy make or break the meal. And in most cases, the rice referred to is plain boiled rice, white and fluffy, with each grain standing separate and apart. Here, however, I will give you Mexican Rice, a dish that is made in countless variations in as many Texas households.

## ★ *Arroz Mejicano (Mexican Rice)*

2½ cups chicken stock
 1 medium onion, chopped fine
 1 clove garlic, crushed
 ¼ tsp. oregano
 2 medium-size ripe tomatoes, peeled, seeded and chopped
 1 small sweet green pepper, seeded and chopped

¼ tsp. dried hot chili pepper
Salt and pepper to taste
1½ cups rice
 1 rounded Tb. lard
 ¼ tsp. saffron
 2 Tbs. warm water

Heat stock in a saucepan; add onion, garlic, oregano, tomatoes, sweet pepper, hot chili pepper and salt and pepper to taste. Simmer 30 minutes. Meanwhile sauté rice in lard in a heavy 10-inch skillet, stirring frequently, until browned. Moisten saffron with warm water and set aside. When rice has browned evenly, pour on the stock and vegetables. Blend. Cover tightly. Cook over lowest heat until all the liquid has been absorbed. If rice is not tender, add a bit more chicken stock. Cover and continue to cook until additional stock is absorbed.

When rice is done, stir in saffron, using a fork. Cover again and let rice steam for 5 minutes. Serves 6 to 8.

There are many versions of Baked Rice in Texas and, on page 171, you will find a Rice Dressing that is very similar.

★ *Baked Rice*

| | |
|---|---|
| 2 cups long grain rice | 2 cans consommé |
| ½ cup finely chopped onion | Pepper |
| ¾ cup butter | Salt, if needed |

Brown rice and onion in butter over moderate heat in a heavy 10-inch skillet; really brown it, but do not burn it. It should be a deep, rich color. Turn rice, onion and remaining melted butter into a casserole from which rice may be served. Combine consommé with enough hot water to make 4 cups all told. Add to rice. Add pepper to taste. Since the consommé is salted, additional salt will probably not be necessary. Stir rice once with a fork. Cover tightly. Bake at 350° F. until all the liquid has been absorbed (about 30 minutes). Stir again lightly with a fork. Cover again and return to oven for 5 minutes more. Serves 6 to 8.

Spoon Bread (which is really not a bread at all but rather a kind of pudding) is Southern in origin and, along with Fried Chicken, one of the chief Southern touches added to the basic Texas table. It may be made in either of two ways, depending on whether whole eggs are beaten into the batter or eggs first separated, the stiffly beaten whites making of the *bread* a kind of soufflé. The latter, though a dressier dish, is no better than the former. My personal preference, in fact, is for the plainer of the two and I like it made with lard, not butter. Here is an excellent Spoon Bread.

## ★ Spoon Bread

| | |
|---|---|
| 1 cup (scant) water-ground cornmeal | 1 tsp. salt |
| 3 cups sweet milk | 1 Tb. baking powder |
| 3 eggs | 1 rounded Tb. lard, melted |

Combine cornmeal with 2 cups of the milk in the top of a double boiler; cook, stirring frequently, until of a thick, mushlike consistency. Beat eggs and then beat with remaining cup of milk. Stir into the cornmeal mixture. Remove from heat. Stir in salt, baking powder and lard. Pour into a well-greased 2-quart baking dish and bake at 350° F. for 30 minutes. Serve from the baking dish with any poultry, pork or ham. Serves 6 to 8.

Hominy is a great favorite in Texas as, indeed, it should be everywhere. It is available canned and virtually ready to eat in stores the country over. And it's delicious with ham, pork, chicken, barbecue and, in fact, almost any meat. Fried Hominy, in Texas, is usually served at breakfast.

## ★ Fried Hominy

| | |
|---|---|
| 3 Tbs. bacon drippings | Salt and pepper to taste |
| 2 cups hominy (canned) | |

Heat drippings in a heavy skillet. Add hominy. Cook over low heat, stirring gently but frequently, until a golden brown. Add salt and pepper to taste. Excellent with ham or sausages. Serves 3 or 4 . . . modestly.

Hominy in Cream is especially good with chicken and ham. No dish could possibly be simpler.

## ★ Hominy in Cream

Separate the contents of 2 cans of hominy and, if necessary, rinse in a sieve under cold water. Drain. Arrange the drained hominy in a wide, rather shallow, well-buttered baking dish. Sprinkle with pepper and salt. Pour on heavy cream to come just barely level with the top of the hominy (it will not require very much). Sprinkle the top with fine buttered crumbs (bread or cracker). Bake at 325° F. until the cream is very thick and the crumb topping is browned and crisp. Serve from the baking dish. Serves 6 to 8.

Condensed cream of mushroom soup is a favorite cooking ingredient of Texas housewives and it is often used in such casseroles as this:

## ★ Hominy Casserole

2 cans hominy
1 can condensed cream of
 mushroom soup
1 cup grated sharp Cheddar cheese
 (or as needed)

Salt and pepper to taste
Cayenne if desired

In a shallow, greased casserole place a layer of half the hominy. Spread with half the soup and half the cheese. Sprinkle with salt and pepper. Add a touch of cayenne if you like the bite. Repeat layers ending with cheese and seasonings on top. Bake at 350° F. for 20 minutes or until browned and bubbly. Serves 6.

Although noodles appear in or with many dishes made in Texas by housewives of Central European background, pasta—generally speaking—is of minor culinary importance in the state. And when it is cooked, it is served as often as not in such an Anglo-Saxon dish as the following:

## ★ Baked Macaroni

8 ozs. macaroni
Salt
2 Tbs. butter
1 egg
1 tsp. salt (additional)

1 Tb. prepared mustard
2 to 3 cups grated sharp Cheddar
 cheese (as desired)
1 cup light cream

Cook the macaroni in water with salt according to package directions until tender; drain. Immediately stir in the butter.

263

While the macaroni is cooking, beat egg with salt, mustard and cream. Set aside. Toss buttered macaroni with all but ⅓ cup of the grated cheese. Arrange it in a buttered baking dish. Pour on the cream mixture. Top with remaining cheese. Bake at 350° F. for about 40 minutes. Serve as soon as possible when done. Excellent with beef, turkey, chicken, pork. Serves 6 to 8.

Noodles are often used in such typically Texas dishes as this:

 ## *Sour Cream Noodle Bake*

| | |
|---|---|
| 1 lb. ground lean beef | 1 cup sour cream |
| 1 clove garlic, minced | 1 cup slivered scallions with part |
| 1 Tb. butter | of their green tops |
| 1 tsp. salt | ¼ cup minced fresh parsley |
| ¼ tsp. pepper | 1 pkg. noodles, 8-ozs., cooked and |
| 1 cup tomato sauce | drained |
| 1 cup creamed cottage cheese | 1 cup grated mild Cheddar cheese |

Brown meat with garlic in butter. Add salt, pepper and tomato sauce. Blend and simmer 5 minutes. Combine the cottage cheese with sour cream, scallions and parsley. Add noodles. In a buttered baking dish alternate layers of the noodle mixture and the meat mixture. Begin and end with the noodles. Sprinkle top with grated Cheddar. Bake at 350° F. for 25 minutes. Serve from the baking dish. Serves 6 to 8.

# TWENTY-ONE

## *VEGETABLES*

# FRESH

FRESH vegetables are immensely important in the Texas cuisine and while they certainly appear twice a day, they may appear three times. You not only find frozen vegetables at all tables, but canned ones, too. In fact, you find more canned vegetables (which I rarely like) at more *good* tables in Texas than anywhere else I know of. Canned cream-style corn is a kitchen staple; so also are English peas, as they are called— mature green peas differentiated as *English* from tiny peas (called *petit pois*), black-eyed peas and dried yellow ones.

Many fresh vegetables are simply cooked in Texas as elsewhere to be served, equally simply, with salt, pepper and butter. But many are made into rather complex, often pudding-like dishes in combination with other vegetables, crumbs, cheese, cream or sour cream and seasonings. Many—especially tomatoes, onions, corn and sweet peppers—are also often made into hearty dishes in combination with poultry or meat. Many Texas vegetable dishes would elsewhere be considered main dishes. At the other extreme you find perfectly plain sliced raw vegetables—onions, tomatoes, cucumbers, radishes—at all tables, too, as vegetables, not salads. And both these and the big dishes are in the company of starch dishes; quite an array. Here is a sampling of them:

Aside from the salad vegetables and greens that appear daily at Texas tables, and those vegetables such as spring onions which are standard seasonings, corn is probably the Texas favorite. It appears with equal ease at breakfast, lunch and dinner, and Texas housewives have a hundred ways to cook it. Here is an old-fashioned way that is still one of the best:

★ *Fried Corn*

4 cups scraped corn (see below)          Half-and-half (about 1 cup)
4 slices bacon, diced                    2 Tbs. butter
Salt and pepper to taste

For this dish you should use either green field corn (the best choice) or very mature fresh golden bantam. If the former, open the husk of the corn and cut into a kernel to ascertain whether or not it is milky. It should be. (Sweet corn—golden bantam, etc.—is always green when sold, hence always milky.) Remove husks from about 1 dozen ears. Strip off the silk. With a sharp knife, slice the kernels into a bowl. With the dull side of the knife blade, scrape down the cob to get all remaining milk and pulp. Do *not* scrape off the clinging tough husks if you can avoid it. Measure out 4 cups milk, pulp and kernels. Set aside.

In a heavy 10-inch iron skillet fry the bacon over moderate heat until crisp. Skim out bacon and reserve. Add the 4 cups measured corn to the drippings in the skillet. Sprinkle with salt and pepper. Fry over low heat, stirring frequently, for 4 minutes. Add the half-and-half; press the corn down gently to level it with a spatula. Dot with butter. Cover and cook over lowest heat until corn is tender and the liquid has cooked away. Taste for seasoning. Turn out on a heated platter. Sprinkle with reserved bacon and serve immediately. Serves 4 to 6.

This Baked Corn is a Texas specialty—and a good one, too.

## ★ Baked Fresh Corn

| | |
|---|---|
| 6 ears fresh corn | 1 tsp. sugar |
| 4 slices bacon, diced | ¼ cup water |
| Salt to taste | 6 Tbs. butter |

Holding corn upright and using a sharp knife, cut kernels from ears, then scrape the ears, getting what remains of each grain. Fry bacon in an 8-inch iron skillet. When crisp, skim out and drain on paper. Add corn to the bacon drippings. Add salt to taste, sugar and water; blend. Place skillet in oven at 350° F. Bake 30 to 40 minutes, stirring occasionally, adding butter bit by bit and more water—but only a little—when needed. The corn, when done, should be very thick and creamy. Stir in bacon just before serving. Serves 4 to 6.

This Chili Corn is delicious with any barbecue or grilled meat.

## ★ Chili Corn

| | |
|---|---|
| 6 ears of fresh corn | 1 tsp. paprika |
| ¼ cup butter, melted | Salt and pepper |
| 1 Tb. (rounded) chili powder | |

Remove husks and silk from cobs. Combine butter with chili powder, paprika and salt and pepper to taste. Brush mixture over entire surface of corn. Wrap each ear in aluminum foil. Fold foil to seal. Place wrapped ears on cookie sheet. Bake at 350° F. for 1 hour. Serve either in the foil or unwrapped. If the latter, dribble any butter mixture from the wrappers over the corn before serving. Messy but delectable.

Corn puddings and casseroles, sometimes plain, sometimes fancy, are popular everywhere in Texas.

★ *Sour Cream Corn*

1 medium-size onion, chopped
1 small green pepper, seeded and
 chopped
2 Tbs. butter
1 can cream-style corn, 1-lb. size
1 can white whole-kernel corn,
 12-oz. size

1 can pimientos, drained and
 chopped, 4-oz. size
1 cup sour cream
1 tsp. cornstarch, rounded
1 tsp. salt
¼ tsp. pepper

Sauté the onion and green pepper in butter over moderate heat until the onion is golden. Do *not* brown it. Add creamed corn, white corn kernels, and chopped pimientos. Blend. Combine sour cream with cornstarch, salt and pepper. Stir into corn mixture. Pour all into a shallow, buttered Pyrex baking dish. Bake at 350° F. until lightly browned (about 20 minutes). Serve from the baking dish. Serves 6 to 8.

Soda crackers are widely used in Texas for their special kind of crumbs. There is something very pleasantly old-fashioned and homey about what they do to a dish. Here they are used with eggplant.

270

## ★ Scalloped Eggplant

| | |
|---|---|
| 1 large eggplant | ½ cup chopped onion |
| 8 soda crackers (Uneeda or such) | 1 Tb. each, butter and olive oil |
| 3 Tbs. heavy cream | 1 egg, beaten |
| Salt to taste | ⅓ cup fine cracker crumbs |
| Generous sprinkling of black pepper | ¼ cup grated Parmesan cheese |
| ¼ cup butter | |

Peel and dice eggplant; cook in water to cover until just tender. Drain off virtually all the water (but do not let the eggplant drain dry). Add crumbled crackers and cream to eggplant. Stir to blend thoroughly. Add salt, pepper and butter. Blend. Fry chopped onion in butter and oil until golden. Add to eggplant mixture. Add beaten egg and blend. Turn into a greased casserole or Pyrex baking dish. Top with fine crumbs (you may not need all of them) and cheese. Bake at 400° F. for 30 minutes. Serves 4.

At the more sophisticated, urban tables of Texas you find a preference for tender young green beans, Frenched and just barely cooked to tenderness. But all Texans have a hankering just the same for the more mature beans cooked in the old-fashioned Southern way with salt pork or fat back. Such beans may well be lacking in vitamins when done, but they certainly are delicious.

## ★ Green Beans

Snap and string 2 pounds mature (but not old and leathery) green beans. Place in ¼-pound piece of salt pork in a heavy saucepan; add the beans; add about 1 inch of water and sprinkle the beans with ¼ tsp. salt. Cover, bring to a boil, reduce heat to medium-low and cook until the beans are tender, turning them gently with a fork every once in a while. Cooking time will be about 2½ hours. Drain the beans before serving, but reserve the "pot likker." Slice the salt pork and use it to garnish the beans. Moisten all with 2 to 3 tablespoons of the "pot likker." Use the remaining "pot likker" for soup. Serves 6.

Okra is another favorite Texas vegetable. A popular breakfast of the old days consisted of ham, black-eyed peas, fresh hot corn-bread with a quantity of butter and okra, fried as in the fol-lowing:

## ★  Texas Fried Okra

Wash okra, cut off stems and cut diagonally into ¼-inch slices. Sprinkle with salt and pepper, then dredge in cornmeal, tossing and turning the okra in the meal until thoroughly coated. Heat ¼ inch lard in a heavy skillet, the size depending on the quantity of okra. Add okra and fry over moderate heat. When the pieces on the bottom are brown, turn with a spatula so the rest can brown evenly. When done, skim out with perforated spatula. Drain on paper before serving. One pound of okra serves 4.

Whole Fried Okra is also a delicious dish. The bit of vinegar added to the cooking water in the initial step keeps the okra from excessive "stringing."

# ★ *Whole Fried Okra*

| | |
|---|---|
| 1 lb. whole fresh okra pods, not too large | 1 Tb. cider vinegar |
| 1 tsp. salt | Cornmeal |
| | Lard |

Place okra in a saucepan with water just to cover, salt and vinegar. Boil until barely tender. Do *not* overcook. Drain. While okra is still moist, roll in cornmeal. Be sure the pods are coated thoroughly and evenly all over. Heat ¼ inch melted lard in a heavy skillet. When *very* hot (but not smoking) add the okra carefully. Take care that the cornmeal coating remains intact. Fry over moderately high heat until crisp and golden brown on all sides. Drain on paper. Serve immediately. Serves 4.

# ★ *Onions*

Onions, though the major crop of thirty Texas counties, are not as much used for special onion dishes as one might expect. Creamed onions appear frequently, of course, and fried onions are virtually a staple of diet. But other "made" onion dishes are rare. Texans like their onions raw. Chopped or sliced raw onions are served constantly. And they love spring or green onions (scallions) as a seasoning with anything.

Black-eyed peas—fresh, canned or dried—are served everywhere in Texas. And they appear at family and company meals alike. They *are* Texas and Texans love them. Here is an old-time recipe that is still in use today.

273

## ★ Fresh Black-eyed Peas

Select mature pods with peas all of a size. Shell. Place peas in saucepan with water to cover by half an inch. Add 1¼-inch slice salt pork, diced. (Do not add extra salt until peas are almost done, then add to taste.) Cover pot and cook gently until peas are tender (about 2 hours). Drain off most of liquid and reserve for soup or stock.

Serve peas in individual deep dishes with some of their cooking liquor and topped with a slice of the pork. Pass hot, buttered cornbread and chopped raw onion on the side. To eat: break the cornbread into the dish with peas and spoon the peas and their "likker" over it.

## ★ Black-eyed Peas with Honey

1 medium onion, chopped
6 slices bacon, diced
2 cans (#303) black-eyed peas
  (about 4 cups)
1 tsp. salt

½ tsp. pepper
1 tsp. dry mustard
2 Tbs. finely chopped preserved
  ginger
¾ cup strained honey

In a heavy skillet, sauté the onion and bacon together over moderate heat for 5 minutes. Drain off all but 2 tablespoons drippings. Add peas, salt, pepper, mustard and ginger. Blend. Turn into a deep casserole (with lid) or bean pot. Pour the honey evenly over all. Cover. Bake at 325° F. for 1½ hours. Serve from the baking dish with pork of any kind or ham or any barbecued meat. Serves 4 to 6.

274

Fried Potatoes are not only popular as a breakfast dish in Texas but with barbecue, grilled meats and pork chops any time. Here is a Fried Potato recipe from Burleson:

## ★ *So-good Soft-fried Potatoes*

Peel as many white potatoes as you will need and cut as for French fries, making the pieces a little thicker. Or if you like, cut the potatoes in even ½-inch dice. Sprinkle with salt. Put enough lard in a heavy skillet to just cover the bottom with a film when melted. When fat is *very* hot, add the potatoes. Cover skillet. Reduce heat to medium. Turn potatoes with a spatula every 5 minutes to brown evenly. When all are tender, drain. Sprinkle with more salt, if needed, and pepper. Serve immediately. The total cooking time will be 20 to 30 minutes.

These wonderful potatoes take a bit of time and watching, but they're well worth the trouble.

## ★ *Fried New Potatoes*

Scrub small new potatoes of even size, but do not peel them. Dry thoroughly. Heat a generous skimming of butter and peanut oil (half and half) or butter and lard in an iron skillet. Add potatoes. Cook over moderate heat, shaking the pan frequently, until potatoes are tender and crisp on all sices. When done, drain on paper. Sprinkle with salt and minced fresh parsley. Serve immediately with any beef or roast or barbecue.

Here is another wonderful potato recipe, this one of German extraction.

## ★ *Fredericksburg Potatoes*

Wash, pare and slice potatoes lengthwise into eighths. Soak in cold water 1 hour. Drain and pat dry. Allowing 1 teaspoon melted butter or bacon drippings for each potato, dribble the fat over slices, turning them so they are evenly coated. Use more fat if needed. Arrange in a single layer on baking sheet. Bake at 400° F. until brown. Turn occasionally. When done, sprinkle with salt, pepper and a few caraway seeds.

Many Texas recipes make you wonder whether calories have ever been heard of in the state. Here is one of them—but how good it is!

## ★ *Party Potatoes*

| | |
|---|---|
| 10 medium-size old potatoes | Salt and white pepper to taste |
| 8-ozs. cream cheese | Melted butter |
| ¼ cup sour cream | Paprika |

Boil potatoes in their jackets until tender; drain, peel and mash them. Soften cream cheese at room temperature. Cream it with the sour cream. Gradually beat the cheese mixture into the potatoes. Salt and pepper to taste. Pile in shallow baking dish. Brush surface of potatoes with melted butter. Sprinkle with paprika. Bake 20 to 25 minutes at 325° F. Serve from the baking dish. Serves 8.

276

Sauerkraut in Texas is not only widely used as a vegetable but as salad, too—or anyway, cold accompaniment to meat—as is the way in Germany and Central Europe. Though much of this today is either canned or commercially processed, much is also still home-made, also in the way of Germany and Central Europe. Shredded cabbage and salt are packed layer on layer in large crocks or barrels (the latter of special cypress wood), then stomped down by barefoot boys; more cabbage and salt are then added, then stomped again and so on until the crocks or barrels can hold no more. The cabbage cores, called nubbins, are laid on top; the kraut is covered with a heavily weighted lid and left to ferment. Such home-made sauerkraut has an incomparably better flavor than any commercial variety. Here is a recipe of Bohemian origin for a special kraut to serve with pork:

★ *Bohemian Kraut*

1 qt. sauerkraut  
1 tsp. caraway seeds  
1 tsp. sugar  
2 Tbs. bacon drippings  
2 slices bacon, diced very fine  

1 medium-size onion, chopped  
1 medium-small potato, peeled and grated  
Salt and pepper

Rinse sauerkraut under cold running water and place in heavy saucepan while still dripping. Add caraway seeds, sugar and drippings; blend. Cook over moderate heat until bubbling. Add diced bacon and cook 15 minutes, stirring from time to time. Add onion and cook 10 minutes. Stir in grated potato and cook until sauerkraut has thickened, stirring frequently. Season with salt and pepper as necessary just before serving. Serves 6.

Spinach in most sections of the United States appears most frequently simply as spinach—*en branche,* chopped or puréed. In Texas, on the other hand, it is often cooked in some special way. Creamed spinach is popular; so is spinach soufflé. You find many spinach casseroles made sometimes with eggs, sometimes with garlic and cheese. And then there are many Spinach Loaves. Here is one of them:

★   *Spinach Loaf*

2 cups chopped, well washed,
   drained spinach
1 cup toasted soft breadcrumbs
1 medium onion, grated
1 clove garlic, crushed
1 medium green pepper, seeded
   and chopped

3 eggs, beaten
¼ cup butter, melted
Salt and pepper to taste
Hard-cooked egg yolk, sieved

In a mixing bowl combine all the ingredients except hard-cooked egg yolk and blend them thoroughly with a wooden spoon. Turn into a buttered 5 x 8-inch loaf pan. Set in a larger pan with 1 inch warm water and bake at 325° F. for about 1 hour. When done, let cool for a few minutes in pan, then turn out on a heated platter. Sprinkle with hard-cooked egg yolk. Serve with chicken, turkey, ham or lamb. Serves 6 to 8.

Squash was an important Indian food when the first white settlers arrived in Texas, and it is still a Texas favorite, particularly the yellow squash. Often Texas housewives combine it with other vegetables and sometimes they combine it with another variety of squash and cheese, as in this recipe.

---

## ★ *Squash and Cheese Casserole with Chilis*

| | |
|---|---|
| 4 lbs. yellow squash | 1 cup grated Cheddar cheese |
| 2 lbs. zucchini | (sharp) |
| 1 large onion, chopped | 1 cup shredded Velveeta cheese |
| 2 Tbs. sugar | 4 Tbs. canned chopped green chilis |
| 1 tsp. salt | 1 cup light cream |
| 2 cups water | Butter |

Slice yellow squash and zucchini and combine with onion in saucepan; add sugar, salt and water. Cover and cook over moderate heat until tender, 15 to 20 minutes; drain. Mash but do not purée. Combine the two cheeses. Arrange alternate layers of squash and cheese in greased casserole. Sprinkle layers as you go with green chilis. Pour cream over all. Dot with butter and bake at 325° F. until bubbly. Serve from casserole. Serves 8 to 12.

Virtually all of the Indian tribes of this continent had a dish similar to succotash when the white man first arrived. The one in use by the Texas Indians was made of meat, hominy, peppers and beans. Here is one made in Texas today.

## ★ *Mexican Succotash*

| | |
|---|---|
| 1 lb. medium to small zucchini | 1 medium onion, chopped |
| 4 ears corn | 4 Tbs. butter |
| 1 lb. tomatoes (about 3 of them) | Salt and pepper to taste |

Dice the zucchini without peeling. Cut the kernels from the ears of corn with a sharp knife and then, using the dull side of the

279

knife blade, scrape off any remaining pulp and the milk. Peel and dice the tomatoes. Sauté the onion in butter until just barely golden. Add the other ingredients. Blend. Cover tightly and cook over low heat 30 minutes, stirring from time to time. Uncover and let any accumulated liquid cook away. Season to taste with salt and pepper. Serves 4 to 6.

Sweet potatoes are cooked and served in Texas in hundreds of ways. And as in the South, it is the habit of Texas cooks to make them sweeter than they are by nature with sugar, syrup or molasses—and richer with pecans and marshmallows—and spicier with cinnamon, cloves, allspice and/or nutmeg. Here is a relatively simple sweet-potato recipe:

## ★  Sue's Candied Sweets

| | |
|---|---|
| 6 medium-size sweet potatoes | 3 Tbs. water |
| 1½ cups brown sugar, firmly packed | ½ tsp. cinnamon |
| | 3 Tbs. butter |

Boil potatoes until just barely tender; drain, cool and peel. Halve and arrange in shallow Pyrex baking dish. Combine sugar, water and cinnamon in small saucepan. Bring to a boil. Cook until sugar is dissolved. Add butter. Blend. Pour over potatoes. Bake at 350° F. for 15 minutes. Baste several times. Serve from baking dish. Serves 6.

Though seen less often than pan-fried sweet potatoes, these are certainly no less delicious.

## ★ *Deep-fried Sweets*

Allow 1 medium-size sweet potato for each person. Peel and cut in thin, even, crosswise slices. Soak 3 hours in *ice water*. Drain and dry thoroughly. Fry in deep fat at 375° F. Sprinkle with sugar and salt while still hot just before serving. Wonderful!

The Christmas turkey in Texas is invariably accompanied by such a sweet-potato dish as this:

## ★ *Sweet Potatoes with Marshmallows and Pecans*

| | |
|---|---|
| 3 cups mashed cooked sweet potatoes | ¾ tsp. salt |
| 3 Tbs. honey | 3 Tbs. butter |
| 1 tsp. ground cinnamon | 1 package marshmallows |
| | ½ cup chopped pecans |

Beat potatoes until light, then beat in honey, cinnamon, salt and butter. Spread half of the potatoes in a buttered baking dish. Over these arrange a layer of marshmallows, touching or not as you wish. Spread chopped pecans over marshmallows. Cover with remaining potatoes. Top with second layer of marshmallows and bake, covered, at 375° F. for 10 minutes. Uncover and let marshmallows brown. Serve immediately with ham, turkey or chicken. Serves 6 to 8.

These Stuffed Sweet Potatoes are excellent with ham, pork, chicken, turkey, venison, duck and goose—which is equivalent to saying, good with anything.

★ *Stuffed Sweet Potatoes*

| | |
|---|---|
| 4 large sweet potatoes | ¼ cup chopped pecans |
| 1 can crushed pineapple, drained, | Salt and pepper |
| 8½-oz. size | Nutmeg to taste |
| ½ cup brown sugar | Additional butter |
| 3 Tbs. butter | |

Boil sweet potatoes in their jackets until just tender. Peel and cut in half lengthwise. With a teaspoon scoop out a pocket from the cut side of each potato half. Place the scooped-out meat in a mixing bowl. Add pineapple, sugar, butter, pecans and blend thoroughly. Add salt, pepper and nutmeg to taste. Mound this mixture in the scooped-out potatoes. Dot with extra butter. Keep hot or warm until just before serving. Slip under the broiler to brown. Serves 8.

Though yams are somewhat richer than sweet potatoes and of a deeper orange color, they may be used in any sweet-potato recipe.

★ *Yam Cakes*

| | |
|---|---|
| 2 cups flour | ½ cup corn oil |
| 2½ tsps. baking powder | ½ cup milk |
| 1½ Tbs. sugar | 1 cup mashed cooked yams |
| 1 tsp. salt | |

Sift flour, baking powder, sugar and salt together into a mixing bowl. Pour oil and milk into the same measuring cup; do *not* mix any more than you have to. Add liquid to mashed yams. Blend.

Add this to flour mixture. Stir lightly with a fork until the dough just holds together. Turn onto a lightly floured board. Knead gently. Roll out to ¼-inch thickness. Cut out with a cookie cutter. Arrange on a lightly greased baking sheet. Bake at 425° F. for 12 minutes. Serve with pork chops, roast pork or ham. Serves 6 to 8. Tomatoes, like onions, are served everywhere in Texas, and virtually every day, but there are relatively few dishes specifically made of them. Stewed tomatoes, of course, appear at every table, as do scalloped or baked tomatoes. And sometimes you will find stuffed ones. But usually they are served sliced and raw, either as a simple side dish (sometimes with sliced raw onions) or in a salad. And chopped, peeled raw tomatoes appear in many of the Texas-Mexican sauces. Fried Green Tomatoes are a special favorite.

★  *Fried Green Tomatoes*

Allow 2 firm well-shaped green tomatoes for each serving. Cut off stem end and a thin slice at blossom end as well; discard. Slice tomatoes in ⅓- to ½-inch-thick slices. Sprinkle slices on both sides with salt and pepper. Dredge in cornmeal to coat evenly. Press on with finger tips. Shake off excess. Heat ¼ inch fat or oil in a large heavy skillet. Fry slices over moderate heat until both sides are evenly browned. Turn carefully so the crust remains unbroken. Drain on paper towels and serve with ham, pork, or chicken.

## ★ Turnip Greens

Choose tender young turnip greens and remove all the coarse stems. Wash leaves in 4 changes of cold water. Drain. Place in large pot with 1 quart of water and cook, stirring occasionally, until water is dark green. Drain off water. Add fresh water, 1 teaspoon salt and 3 tablespoons bacon drippings. Cover and simmer very gently 1½ to 2 hours or until greens are tender. Drain and chop if desired or serve as is. Many use the "pot likker" as a broth. Two pounds of greens will serve 3 people. If desired, turnip and mustard greens may be used half and half. Either way, greens are always served with a hot pepper sauce on the side.

## ★ Vegetable Gumbo

3 slices bacon, diced
1 large onion, chopped
3 cloves garlic, minced
4 large tomatoes, peeled and
  quartered

3 stalks celery with leaves, stalks
  sliced, leaves chopped
1 green pepper, seeded and sliced
Salt and pepper to taste
2½ cups whole, medium-size okra
  pods (or more if desired)

In a heavy pot or skillet fry bacon until almost half cooked; add onion and garlic. Cook over low heat until golden. Add tomatoes, celery and celery leaves, and green pepper. Cook 5 minutes. Add water to barely cover; salt and pepper to taste. Cover pan and cook gently until celery is tender. Add okra. Cover pan tightly and cook until okra is just tender. Do *not* overcook. By the time the okra is done, most of the liquid will have cooked away. Serves 4 to 6. Excellent with beef, pork or barbecue.

# TWENTY-TWO

## *SALADS*

# SALADS in Texas may appear at any

time during a meal, but they are seldom served as a separate course following meat, as is the way elsewhere. And salads may be composed of virtually any fruit and leaf vegetable in combination, or a leaf vegetable in combination with other vegetable, or of vegetables with meats or poultry, and served as main dish, side dish, hors d'oeuvre, vegetable or dessert. Their number is indeed legion if all of these creations are, indeed, salads. It is *as* salads that Texans think of them, however, and so they are treated here.

The most common Texas salads are of lettuce and sliced ripe tomatoes (with or without sliced raw onions). The next most common salads are of fruit and/or avocado and some green. The former are served with any and every kind of meal, including both barbecue and Texas-Mexican. The latter appear most frequently with birds of all kinds and game.

The dressings for both kinds of salads tend to be rather more complicated than elsewhere and to be more highly and sometimes very highly seasoned. In fruit salad dressings, the influence of Miss Helen Corbitt has been felt all over the state; housewives everywhere try to duplicate the exotic tastes she has made so vastly popular. Mayonnaise for all kinds of dressings is used more frequently as an ingredient among several than as a dressing by itself. Old-fashioned "cooked" salad dressing is as widely used today as a hundred years ago for cabbage salads and Cole Slaw. Here, to begin the dressing roster, is a typical Texas French Dressing—really not French at all, but delectable.

## ★ *Red French Dressing (#1)*

| | |
|---|---|
| 2 tsps. salt | 2 Tbs. tomato catsup |
| 1 tsp. paprika | ¼ cup cider vinegar |
| ½ tsp. dry mustard | 1 cup olive oil |
| 1 dash Worcestershire sauce | 1 clove garlic, split |
| 1 generous dash hot pepper sauce | |

Combine all ingredients in jar and shake well. Let stand 2 hours before using. Discard the garlic. Makes about 1½ cups.

## ★ *Red French Dressing (#2)*

| | |
|---|---|
| 1 pimiento (canned) | 1½ Tbs. best paprika (fresh and |
| ¼ cup tomato sauce, canned | Hungarian if possible) |
| | ¾ cup mayonnaise |

Mash the pimiento to a paste and combine with tomato sauce and paprika. Beat bit by bit into the mayonnaise. Chill. Serve on lettuce or any cooked-green-vegetable salad or any bean salad. Makes 1 cup plus.

Miss Helen Corbitt's Poppy Seed Dressing is perhaps her most famous single culinary creation. It has been copied not only in Texas but virtually everywhere in America. It is unbeatable for fruit salads.

---

## ★ *Helen Corbitt's Poppy Seed Dressing*

1½ cups sugar
  2 tsps. dry mustard
  2 tsps. salt
 ⅔ cup cider vinegar

3 Tbs. onion juice*
2 cups salad oil (*not* olive oil)
3 Tbs. poppy seeds

Mix sugar, mustard, salt and vinegar. Add onion juice. Blend. Bit by bit add the oil, beating vigorously and constantly. Continue beating until thick. Add poppy seeds and beat a minute or two longer. Store covered in a cool place until needed. Do *not* let it get too cold. Use on fruit salads. It is especially good with grapefruit. Makes 3½ cups.

This dressing also calls for poppy seeds, but it obviously is not a copy of Miss Corbitt's. It is also excellent on fruit salads.

## ★ *Poppy Seed Dressing*

⅓ cup sugar
 1 tsp. flour
 1 egg yolk
½ cup strained fresh orange juice

2 Tbs. lemon juice
2 tsps. poppy seeds
1 cup heavy cream

Combine sugar, flour, egg yolk and orange juice in top of double boiler. Stir until smooth. Cook over hot water, stirring constantly, until thickened. Add lemon juice and poppy seeds. Pour into bowl and chill. Just before serving, whip cream until stiff. Fold into poppy seed mixture. Serve with fresh fruit salad. Makes 2 cups.

* To get onion juice, grate a large white onion or purée it in a blender. Turn into fine sieve and drain off juice.

Currant jelly is used in Texas in many sauces and occasionally you will find it added to stews, pot roasts and "made" dishes. Here it is used in a delicious salad dressing.

## ★ *Sour Currant Dressing for a Fruit Salad*

¼ cup currant jelly          2 Tbs. peanut oil
2 Tbs. vinegar               1 tsp. scraped onion pulp
1 pinch salt

Beat jelly with a fork until smooth. Then add remaining ingredients and beat again. Serve over grapefruit or orange or a combination of the two with watercress.

This is a typical "plain" salad in Texas.

## ★ *Lettuce and Tomato Salad*

½ head lettuce, medium-size          3 Tbs. olive oil
2 ripe tomatoes, medium-size         1 tsp. salt
¼ cup sliced radishes                Vinegar to taste
¼ cup slivered scallions with part
   of their green tops

Tear lettuce into bits and place in salad bowl. Peel tomatoes and cut into bite-size chunks. Combine tomatoes, radishes and scallions with lettuce. Toss. Dribble olive oil over all and toss again. Let stand in cool place until needed. Just before serving sprinkle with salt and just enough vinegar to give a tart taste. Toss again and serve. Serves 4 to 6.

Many cabbage salads in Texas are made with fruits, a Central European touch. This is a typical one.

## ★ A "Grand" Salad

½ cup grated (not shredded) cabbage
½ cup chopped, peeled, cored apples
1 can crushed pineapple, 8½-oz. size

¼ cup raisins
¼ cup chopped pecans
1 Tb. (rounded) mayonnaise
1 Tb. vinegar (optional)
Salt

Combine cabbage, fruits and nuts. Toss to blend. Add mayonnaise and toss again. A tablespoon of vinegar may be added if desired and a pinch of salt adds to the flavor. Serves 4.

The chopped vegetables in this Mexican Salad are reminiscent of many of the Texas-Mexican sauces and accompaniments.

## ★ Mexican Salad with Chili Dressing

3 green peppers, seeded
4 medium tomatoes, peeled
1 medium onion
4 slices bacon, diced

⅓ cup cider vinegar
1 rounded tsp. chili powder
Salt to taste
Lettuce

Chop the peppers, tomatoes and onion separately. Then combine and chop them together. Fry bacon until crisp. Add vinegar, chili powder and salt to taste. Bring just to boil. Remove from heat. Tear as much lettuce as you want into small bits. Toss with the chopped vegetables. Pour on bacon-chili dressing and toss again. Serve immediately for 4.

Texas has a special Potato Salad recipe for every individual taste in the state. One or another appears at every barbecue.

★    *Potato-Parsley Salad*

2½ cups cubed hot boiled potatoes    Salt to taste
½ cup finely chopped onion          Vinegar
⅓ cup minced fresh parsley          Olive oil

In a bowl combine potatoes, onion, parsley and salt to taste. Toss to blend. Do *not* mash the potatoes in tossing. Dribble with vinegar to moisten—just moisten. Toss again. Let stand 30 minutes. Then dribble with olive oil. Let stand in refrigerator until cold. Dribble once more with olive oil. The potatoes should be shiny with the oil. Serve just colder than room temperature with watercress or young lettuce and mayonnaise on the side. Wonderful with any rare beef or barbecue. Serves 4.

★    *Country Potato Salad*

5 lbs. old potatoes, preferably of some waxy variety
1 cup mayonnaise
½ cup chopped seeded green pepper
½ cup chopped green onions
⅓ cup chopped pimientos (canned, drained)
⅓ cup sour-pickle relish
⅓ cup prepared mustard (French's or Gulden's as desired; they will give quite different salads)
Sugar to taste, if desired (and sugar is desired in Texas)

292

Boil potatoes in their jackets until just tender. Peel and cut as desired. Combine with all other ingredients. Cover and refrigerate 2 hours before serving. Serve with or without lettuce. Good with cold meats, barbecue, hamburgers. Serves 8 to 10.

## ★  Perfect Potato Salad

2½ cups sliced, cooked potatoes
 1 tsp. sugar
 1 tsp. vinegar
 ½ cup chopped sweet onion
1½ tsps. salt

1½ tsps. celery seed
 ¾ cup mayonnaise
 2 hard-cooked eggs, sliced
Cherry tomatoes
Extra mayonnaise

Sprinkle potatoes with sugar and vinegar. Toss to blend. Let stand a few minutes. Add onion, salt, celery seed and mayonnaise. Blend gently. Fold in the sliced eggs. Chill at least 1 hour. Serve on crisp lettuce leaves with a sprinkling of minced fresh parsley. Garnish the salad with cherry tomatoes. Pass extra mayonnaise on the side. Serves 4 to 6.

## ★  German Potato Salad

8 medium-size potatoes (*not* Idahos)
3 medium-size white onions, sliced paper-thin
Salt and pepper
Celery salt
8 slices bacon
2 Tbs. sugar

1 cup cider vinegar
1½ cups water
2 rounded Tbs. flour
1 tsp. dry mustard
1 rounded Tb. prepared mustard
½ cup evaporated milk
2 hard-cooked eggs

293

Boil potatoes in their jackets until just tender. Do not overcook. They should be firm and waxy. When done, peel and slice evenly. Arrange potatoes and onions in alternate layers in a bowl while potatoes are still hot. Sprinkle each layer of potatoes with salt, pepper and celery salt.

While potatoes are cooking, prepare the dressing. Dice bacon and fry until crisp in a *saucepan*. Skim out bacon and drain on paper; to the drippings add sugar, cider vinegar and all but ¼ cup of the water; blend. Add the remaining water to flour and stir to paste consistency. Stir in dry mustard and prepared mustard. Add evaporated milk and blend. Stir into vinegar mixture and cook over low heat, stirring constantly, until smooth and thickened. While hot, pour over potatoes as much as you need to moisten them thoroughly. Serve warm or cold sprinkled with chopped hard-cooked egg and the crisp bacon. Serves 6 to 8.


Sauerkraut Salads, as I mentioned in the introduction, have become popular with all the ethnic groups of Texas. Here are two of them:


## ★  *German Sauerkraut Salad*

| | |
|---|---|
| 1 can sauerkraut, #2 size | 1 medium green pepper, seeded and |
| 1 Tbs. mustard seed | slivered |
| 1 Tb. celery seed | 1 cup sugar |
| 1 Tb. *comino* seed | 1 cup white vinegar |

Rinse kraut in collander under cold running water 3 minutes. Drain thoroughly. Squeeze out as much moisture as you can with your hands. Combine with all remaining ingredients. Cover and chill 3 hours. Serves 6. Wonderful with pork or barbecue.

NOTE: Another version of this salad omits the celery seed and adds ½ cup slivered celery and 1 cup slivered scallions.

---

## ★ *Sauerkraut Relish Salad*

| | |
|---|---|
| 1 can sauerkraut, #2 size | 1 cup chili sauce (the commercial |
| 1 small green pepper, seeded and | sort) |
| chopped | ⅓ cup brown sugar |
| 1 small onion, chopped | 1 tsp. paprika |
| 3 small stalks celery, chopped | 3 Tbs. fresh lemon juice |
| 2 Tbs. minced celery leaves | |

Drain sauerkraut, rinse under cold water and drain again. Combine in a bowl with green pepper, onion, celery and celery leaves. Toss to blend. Combine chili sauce with brown sugar, paprika and lemon juice. Pour over sauerkraut. Toss again. Cover and chill several hours before serving. Whatever is left over may be stored in a covered glass jar in the refrigerator and will keep for 1 week. Serves 6 to 8.

Cole Slaw, like shredded lettuce, turns up everywhere in Texas in many different forms. Sometimes—what with assorted ingredients—it is a major-production number; sometimes it verges to sweetness; sometimes it is definitely sweet; sometimes it is sour. Here is a very good, very plain version.

## ★ *Plain Cole Slaw*

| | |
|---|---|
| 2 cups finely shredded cabbage | ⅓ cup olive oil |
| ⅓ cup cider vinegar | ¾ tsp. salt |
| 2 tsps. sugar | ¼ tsp. pepper |

Combine all ingredients in a mixing bowl and toss to blend thoroughly. Refrigerate, covered, for 3 hours. Toss again before serving. Serves 3 or 4.

Cooked Dressing is the general favorite for Cole Slaw.

## ★ *Dressing for Cole Slaw*

| | |
|---|---|
| 2 eggs | ¼ cup cider vinegar |
| 1½ tsps. sugar | ½ cup heavy cream |
| 2 Tbs. melted butter | Salt and pepper to taste |
| 1 tsp. dry mustard | |

In the top of a double boiler, away from all heat, beat eggs with sugar until thick, then beat in butter, mustard and vinegar. Place over hot water and cook, stirring constantly, until very thick. Remove from heat. Strain into small bowl. Stir in cream. Add salt and pepper to taste. Pour over shredded cabbage while still hot, toss, then chill several hours before serving. Makes about 1 cup dressing.

Molded salads are immensely popular in Texas. While some are definitely salads of sorts, others are more jellied meat-accompaniments and still others are very definitely desserts. This one is excellent with ham.

## ★ *Pickle Salad*

| | |
|---|---|
| 1 Tb. gelatin | 2 cups crushed canned pineapple |
| ¼ cup cold water | ½ cup chopped pimientos (canned, |
| 1 cup boiling water | drained) |
| ½ cup sugar | ½ cup chopped gherkins |
| ¼ cup cider vinegar | |

Soften gelatin in cold water. Stir into boiling water and continue stirring until dissolved. Add sugar and vinegar. Stir until sugar is dissolved. Cool until very thick but not quite set. Add remaining ingredients and blend. Turn into a 6-cup mold that has been rinsed in cold water. Chill several hours. Turn out on a cold plate before serving and garnish with leaf lettuce or watercress. Serve with a Boiled Dressing. Serves 6 to 8.

Though Katherine Schwartz of Weslaco, Texas, calls this her "24-Hour Salad," it is really a dessert—and a delectable one, too.

★ *24-Hour Salad*

| | |
|---|---|
| 1 pkg. large marshmallows | ½ cup sugar |
| 1 can crushed pineapple, #2 size | ½ cup heavy cream |
| ½ lb. shelled pecans | Pinch salt |
| 1 lb. green seedless grapes | Strained juice of 1 lemon |
| 4 egg yolks | 1 cup whipping cream |

Cut marshmallows into quarters. Drain pineapple. Chop pecans so that some pieces are large, others fine. If some are almost a powder, so much the better. Combine marshmallows, pineapple, nuts and grapes. Toss to blend. In a double boiler, combine egg yolks, sugar, cream and salt. Cook, stirring constantly, until smooth and very thick. Stir in lemon juice. Cool. When cold, fold in the 1 cup cream, whipped stiff. Blend this mixture with the fruit mixture. Chill 24 hours (covered) in mold or bowl. Turn out on cold dish to serve. Serves 10 to 12.

The following molded "salads" are, of course, desserts—or, if they are not, they should be! They are excellent in hot weather.

## ★  Frosted Fruit Salad

| | |
|---|---|
| 1 envelope plain gelatin | ¾ cup fresh cut-up seeded orange |
| ¼ cup cold water | sections, white membrane and |
| 1 cup strained fresh orange juice | pith removed |
| 1 bottle Dr. Pepper, 6½ ozs. | ½ cup pitted dark cherries, drained |
| ¾ cup canned crushed pineapple, | 3 ozs. cream cheese |
| drained | 3 Tbs. lemon juice |

Soften gelatin in cold water. Heat orange juice, add gelatin and stir until dissolved. Add Dr. Pepper and blend. Cool until very thick. Stir in the fruits. Turn into a mold and chill until set. Turn out on a chilled serving dish and frost with cream cheese softened to spreadable consistency mixed with lemon juice. Serves 6.

## ★  Frozen Fruit Salad

| | |
|---|---|
| 2 pkgs. cream cheese, 3 ozs. each | 2½ cups small marshmallows |
| 1 cup mayonnaise | Few drops red vegetable coloring or |
| 1 cup whipped cream | some maraschino cherry juice to |
| 1 can fruit cocktail, #2½, drained | taste |
| ½ cup maraschino cherries, halved | Watercress |

Cream the cheese with mayonnaise. When smooth, fold in whipped cream. Combine fruit cocktail, cherries and marshmallows. Fold into the cream mixture. Add coloring as desired or the cherry juice. Turn into mold or freezer trays and freeze. Serve garnished with watercress. Serves 10 to 12.

# TWENTY-THREE

## *DESSERTS*

I N the matter of Texas desserts—a term used to include all sweet dishes served at the close of a meal—one is faced by something of a problem when it comes to saying what is and what is not acceptable. In their choice of desserts, you see, Texans are as free-wheeling and independent as they are in their choice of main-course dishes. Some dinners and luncheons come to a close with so simple a sweet as pralines, which came originally from Louisiana and are generally thought of as candies. (They are delectable as the final touch to a buffet, however.) Or you might find the Mexican *Leche Quemada,* a rich creamy candy of milk and sugar, passed with coffee. On the other hand, all kinds of pudding-like dishes are vastly popular, as though no one had ever heard of a calorie. Banana Pudding is a great favorite. And great favorites, too, are such old-fashioned dishes as the Cobbler (cherry or peach), Sweet-Potato Pone (which with less sugar also serves as a vegetable), apple or peach Betty, and Fried Pies of all kinds.

Pies, of course, are served in every Texas household and not only Pecan Pie (every Texas housewife or cook claims the best in the state) but Osgood Pie—similar but with raisins added—and Chess Pie, Black Bottom Pie and Old-timey Vinegar Pie.

Cakes are everywhere in Texas, too, and not just for special occasions. With cakes, as with all else in the Texas cuisine, many of the ones made for party use are daily fare as well. You find a host of old-time Southern cakes in constant use—blackberry jam cake, for instance. And every household has a repertoire of spice cakes—some plain, some fancy, some actually fruit cakes. And then, of course, you have hundreds of nut cakes.

Throughout the dessert recipes you will find again a widespread use of canned milk of one sort or another. Many good desserts are made almost in their entirety of sweetened condensed milk. Some of these are so good in fact that one wonders why they seem to have been limited to Texas usage. The Lemon Pie, for instance. This is a marvel. Eating these rich sweet dishes one becomes conscious of the fact that this country, gastronomically, has really much to offer—despite the dicta of those dedicated to the French cuisine.

I have already mentioned several times the frequent use of certain "salads" as dessert in Texas and I must mention it here again. For the life of me, I cannot see why such a dish as the Frozen Fruit Salad on page 298 must be called *salad* at all; it bears no gustatory relation to salads known as such elsewhere, but it does indeed bear a relation to desserts. It *is* a dessert. And many other Texas "salads" are desserts also. All of these are either molded or frozen; all are sweet and most are made of fruit in some proportion.

The problem lies in deciding where the line must be drawn between the dishes of this sort that *are* desserts and are served as such and those which are *almost* desserts but are actually served as salads, especially at luncheons and buffets. I admit frankly that I have not yet learned where this line appears. Texas cooks and housewives seem to know by second nature, however, for given two recipes that seem virtually identical, they will pick one to serve as salad and the other to serve as dessert. As for the recipes that follow, they are what I think of as dessert and, if wrong, I must take the consequences.

When Ambrosia first appeared on the Colonial scene in Virginia, it was a simple fruit dessert, given a festive appearance with grated coconut. It was served usually on Christmas as an alternative to the heavy plum pudding. In Texas, it is served not only as dessert but also as a main-course accompaniment. As a dessert,

however, it contains more dessert-like ingredients such as marshmallows. And though I am not a marshmallow aficionado, I must
admit that this Ambrosia, thoroughly chilled, is thoroughly good.

## ★ *Ambrosia*

| | |
|---|---|
| 1 cup miniature marshmallows | ½ cup shredded coconut |
| 1 small can crushed pineapple | 3 bananas, sliced |
| 1 can fruit cocktail, drained, 1-lb. size | 1 Tb. lemon juice |
| | 1 pt. heavy cream |
| 1 small can mandarin oranges | ½ cup sugar |
| ½ cup pecans, coarsely chopped | 1 tsp. vanilla |

Combine marshmallows, pineapple, fruit cocktail, mandarin
oranges, pecans and coconut; chill. One hour before serving slice
bananas, brush with lemon juice and blend with other fruit;
return to refrigerator. Whip cream until stiff, then whip in sugar
and vanilla. Chill. Just before serving fold cream into fruit and
pile in a deep round dish. Serves 6 to 8.

A dessert quite similar to this Baked Fruit was known in the old
days in the South as Simple Fruit, but the name was in no sense
derogatory.

## ★ *Baked Fruits*

| | |
|---|---|
| 1 can pears, 1-lb. size | ⅓ cup butter |
| 1 can peach halves, 1-lb. size | 1 cup brown sugar |
| 1 small can pineapple chunks | 2 tsps. curry powder |
| 1 small jar maraschino cherries | |

Drain fruits, reserving syrups for some other use. Arrange fruits in buttered shallow baking dish. Combine butter, sugar and curry powder in saucepan. Cook over low heat until butter melts. Blend. Pour carefully over all the fruit. Bake at 325° F. for 1 hour. Cool, then chill. Serve as is or with whipped cream or simply cold heavy cream. Serves 6 to 8.

Marshmallows are widely used as dessert ingredients in Texas.

## ★ *Marshmallow Delight*

26 marshmallows
1 cup hot milk
1 tsp. vanilla
1 cup heavy cream, whipped

1 cup finely crumbled vanilla wafers
½ cup very finely chopped pecans

In a saucepan over low heat, melt the marshmallows in hot milk. Cool. When cold, stir in vanilla. Fold in whipped cream. Chill until *very* thick. Fold in the crumbled vanilla wafers. Chill 2 hours. Turn out in glass bowl. Sprinkle with pecans. Serves 8.

Banana Pudding seems to have a special place in many Texas hearts. It is easy to make, very good to eat and, unfortunately, fattening.

★ *Banana Pudding*

| | |
|---|---|
| ½ cup sugar | 1 tsp. vanilla |
| ¼ cup flour | 1 banana, mashed |
| 1 generous pinch salt | 18 vanilla wafers |
| 1 cup milk | 1 banana, sliced |
| 2 eggs yolks, beaten | 2 egg whites |
| 1 Tb. butter | ½ cup sugar |

In a saucepan combine sugar, flour, salt and milk. Blend. Cook over low heat, stirring constantly, until smooth and thickened. Add some of this hot mixture to the beaten yolks, then add yolks to the remaining mixture. Return to fire and cook 2 minutes, stirring constantly. Stir in butter, vanilla and mashed banana. Remove from heat. Now fill a 6-cup baking dish with alternate layers of the cooked custard, vanilla wafers and sliced banana, starting and ending with the custard on top. Cool. Top with a meringue made of egg whites and ½ cup sugar. Bake at 325° F. for 20 minutes. Serve hot or cold. Serves 6.

Such old-fashioned puddings as this are relatively common today in Texas.

★ *Molasses Pudding*

| | |
|---|---|
| 1 egg | 1 tsp. warm water |
| 2 Tbs. sugar | ½ cup molasses |
| 2 Tbs. melted butter | 1½ cups sifted flour |
| ½ cup boiling water | 1 generous pinch salt |
| 1 tsp. baking soda | |

Beat egg with sugar until thick. Add butter and boiling water. Blend. Dissolve soda in warm water. Stir into egg mixture. Add molasses. Beat in flour and salt. Grease top of a double boiler. Pour in batter. Cover and cook over *simmering* water 1¼ hours, or until done . . . at which point the pudding will be firm. Turn out into a deep serving dish. Serve hot with rather runny preserved peaches and very heavy ice-cold cream. Serves 6.

Plain puddings of a cakelike consistency also frequently appear in Texas. They are served usually with a Hot Pudding Sauce like this.

## ★ Hot Wine Pudding Sauce

| | |
|---|---|
| ½ cup sugar | 1 cup boiling water |
| 2 Tbs. cornstarch | 2 Tbs. fresh lemon juice |
| 1 pinch salt | 1 small strip bruised lemon peel |
| 1 pinch ground allspice | 2 Tbs. butter |
| 1 pinch ground nutmeg | ¾ cup port |

In a small saucepan combine sugar, cornstarch, salt, allspice and nutmeg. Pour on boiling water. Place over low heat and cook, stirring constantly, until thick and transparent. Add lemon juice, peel, butter and wine. Heat gently. Do *not* boil. Serve hot. Makes 1½ cups sauce.

In Texas fruits find their way into all kinds of desserts that elsewhere would be relatively simple. This Rice Pudding is said to be of Norwegian origin, but what with its pineapple and Bing cherries I make it out to be wholly Texas—and good!

## ★ Rice Pudding

| | |
|---|---|
| 4 cups water | ¾ cup whipping cream |
| ½ tsp. salt | 1 tsp. vanilla |
| ½ cup sugar | 1 cup drained crushed pineapple |
| 2 cups milk | ½ cup drained Bing cherries |
| 1 cup rice | |

In a large heavy saucepan, bring water to a boil; add salt, sugar, milk and rice. Reduce heat to low. Cover tightly. Cook 30 minutes. Stir once or twice with a fork. Turn rice into a glass bowl when done. (Be careful that the bowl doesn't crack; warm it first with warm water and dry!) Cool, then chill. When ice cold, and just before serving, whip cream and then whip in vanilla. Fold in pineapple and cherries. Spread over chilled rice and serve. Serves 8.

This is a rather special Sweet Potato Pone. In the old days it was a stand-by for picnic lunches.

## ★ Old-fashioned Sweet Potato Pone

| | |
|---|---|
| Sweet potatoes (5 or 6) | ¼ tsp. ground nutmeg |
| ½ cup sugar | ¼ tsp. ground cloves |
| ½ cup softened butter | Milk as needed |
| ½ tsp. ground cinnamon | |

Peel and grate enough sweet potatoes to yield 4 cups. Combine grated potatoes with sugar, butter and spices. Blend. Moisten with milk as needed to form a stiff doughlike mixture. Pack into a small greased loaf pan or oblong mold. Bake at 250° F. for 4 hours. Let cool in the pan if to be served cold. Turn out immediately if to be served hot and serve with a quantity of butter and brown sugar. Serves 6.

No collection of Texas recipes is complete without a Cobbler.

★ *Sue's Cherry Cobbler*

*For the Filling:*

| | |
|---|---|
| 2½ cups pitted sour red cherries (canned) | 3 Tbs. cornstarch |
| | ¼ tsp. cinnamon |
| 1 cup sugar | ¼ cup butter |

Drain the cherries, reserving the syrup. Mix sugar, cornstarch and cinnamon. Stir in the reserved syrup. Cook, stirring constantly, until thickened. Add cherries and butter. Stir until butter has melted. Remove from heat.

*For the Pastry:*

| | |
|---|---|
| 2 cups flour | ⅔ cup butter |
| ¼ tsp. salt | 5 Tbs. water |
| 1 tsp. baking powder | |

Combine dry ingredients and sift together into bowl. Cut in the shortening. Add water and blend. Take half of the dough and roll out to ⅛-inch thickness on a lightly floured board. Cut into 2-inch squares.

Pour ⅓ of cherry mixture into a deep Pyrex baking dish. Add a layer of pastry squares. Pour in carefully another ⅓ of the cherry mixture. Add a second layer of pastry squares. Add remaining cherry mixture. Roll out remaining pastry and place over top of baking dish. Seal edge and crimp with fingers. Cut 2 slits in top for the escape of steam. Brush pastry with cream. Sprinkle lightly with sugar. Bake at 325° F. for 30 to 40 minutes. Serve hot from the baking dish. Pass ice-cold cream in a pitcher. Serves 6.

For a Peach Cobbler, use 2½ cups peeled sliced fresh peaches, 1 tsp. lemon juice, 1 cup sugar, 3 Tbs. cornstarch and ¼ tsp. cinnamon. Mix peaches with lemon juice and sugar and let stand half an hour before adding other ingredients and cooking at 325° F. for 30 to 40 minutes. Then proceed as above.

# ★ *Apple Dumplings*

*For the Pastry:*

2 cups flour
1 tsp. salt
2 tsps. baking powder

¾ cup lard
½ cup sweet milk

Combine dry ingredients and sift together into a bowl. Cut in the lard until the mixture is pebbly. Add milk and blend. Roll out on lightly floured board to a rectangle about ¼ inch thick. Cut into strips 3 inches long and 1½ inches wide.

*For the Sauce:*

2 cups sugar
¼ cup flour
¼ tsp. cinnamon
¼ tsp. nutmeg

2 Tbs. strained fresh lemon juice
½ cup water
6 apples, peeled, cored and sliced

In a saucepan combine all the ingredients and boil until thick. One by one slide in the cut pastry strips. When all are in, pour carefully into a baking dish. Bake at 375° F. for 40 minutes. Serve from the baking dish. Pass a pitcher of heavy cream or a bowl of whipped cream. Serves 8.

This is not only a delicious dessert but a beautiful one, to boot.

## ★ *Pecan Meringues for Fresh Berries*

| | |
|---|---|
| 6 egg whites | Ripe berries |
| 6 rounded Tbs. powdered sugar | Sweetened whipped cream |
| 1 cup ground pecans | |

Beat egg whites until stiff; then slowly beat in the sugar. Continue beating until very thick and satiny. Fold in ground pecans. Arrange a sheet of brown paper on a baking sheet. Make 6 nests of the meringue on the paper, dropping the mixture in a pile from a large spoon, then indenting the center with the bowl of the spoon. Place in a cold oven. Turn on heat to 250° F. Cook until thoroughly dry, turning the heat off now and again if the meringues show signs of browning. It will take at least 2 hours. Cool at room temperature if they are completely dry when taken from the oven; if not quite dry or you are in doubt about them, let cool in the oven with the heat off. To serve, place meringues on individual plates. Fill centers with ripe berries (washed and drained), top with sweetened whipped cream. Makes 6 meringues.

# TWENTY-FOUR
## CAKES

❧❧❧

———————————————————————————————

AS I mentioned in the introduction to the preceding chapter, home-made cakes are found everywhere in Texas. In fact, I know of no other part of this country that can boast such a number or so many good ones. Pecans and dates add to the richness of many of them.

★ *Chewy Pecan-Date Cake*

| | |
|---|---|
| 4 eggs | 1 heaping tsp. baking powder |
| 1 cup sugar | ¼ tsp. salt |
| 2 tsps. vanilla | 2 lbs. pitted dates, cut up |
| ½ cup sifted cake flour | 1 lb. chopped pecans |

Beat eggs thoroughly, then beat in sugar and vanilla. Sift flour, baking powder and salt together over dates and pecans in a bowl. Pour egg mixture over the nut mixture and blend with a wooden spoon. Grease a large loaf pan and line it with brown paper. Grease the paper also. Pour in batter. Set pan in *cold* oven. Turn heat to 300° F. Bake 1¾ to 2 hours. Cover cake with paper or foil if the top browns too quickly. Test for doneness after 1¾ hours.* Remember that this cake is meant to be chewy. It is also delicious!

* The best test is the simplest. The cake is done when a straw inserted at the center comes out clean.

## ★ *Marshmallow-Date Fudge Cake*

3 ozs. (squares) unsweetened
    chocolate
½ cup butter
1¼ cups brown sugar, firmly
    packed
2 eggs, beaten
1½ cups flour
1 tsp. soda

½ tsp. salt
½ cup diced marshmallows
1 cup diced, pitted dates
1 tsp. grated orange peel
1 cup chopped pecans
¼ cup additional flour
1 cup milk
1 tsp. vanilla

Melt chocolate over hot, not boiling, water. Set aside. Cream butter and sugar together until light and fluffy. Add beaten eggs and beat together. Combine flour, soda, and salt and sift together into a bowl. Combine diced marshmallows, diced dates, orange peel, chopped pecans and additional flour; toss to blend thoroughly. Add chocolate to egg batter and beat well. Add dry ingredients and milk alternately to chocolate mixture. Stir in nut mixture and vanilla. Turn into 2 greased 5 x 8-inch loaf pans. Bake at 350° F. for about 1¼ hours or until the cakes test done (page 313). Cool 20 minutes in pans when taken from oven, then turn out on rack to cool completely. Do not slice until cold. This is delicious with an orange frosting.

## ★ *Pecan Sponge Cake*

½ lb. shelled pecans*
6 Tbs. flour
1 tsp. cream of tartar

10 eggs, separated
1¼ cups sugar
1 tsp. vanilla extract

Line bottom of a 10-inch tube pan with wax paper. Grease the paper. Grind the nuts in a food grinder, using medium blade. Stir flour and cream of tartar together and mix with the ground nuts. Beat the egg yolks, adding the sugar gradually. This requires about 15 minutes with electric mixer. Add vanilla flavoring. The yolk mixture should be light in color, thick and very smooth. Beat egg whites until they hold a precise peak. Sprinkle flour-nut mixture over beaten egg yolks, pile beaten egg whites over this and gently fold all ingredients together, but only enough to disperse all patches of egg white. Pour batter into pan, leveling the top with a rubber spatula. Bake 50 minutes at 375° F. or until cake tests done (page 313). Invert cake on wire rack. Cool about 1 to 2 hours. Serves 8 to 10.

Cakes with fruit flavorings—but not really *fruit cakes*—are popular everywhere in the state. Here is one made with mashed banana.

## ★  Banana-Nut Loaf Cake

| | |
|---|---|
| 3 cups sifted flour | 6 Tbs. buttermilk |
| ¾ tsp. soda | 1 tsp. vanilla |
| ¾ cup butter | ¼ tsp. allspice |
| 2 cups plus 2 Tbs. sugar | 1 cup mashed bananas |
| 3 eggs | 1 cup finely chopped pecans |

Sift flour and soda together. Cream butter with sugar. Beat eggs one at a time into butter mixture. Starting with the dry ingredients, add them and the buttermilk alternately to the butter mixture. Blend thoroughly. Stir in vanilla and allspice, then the bananas and chopped nuts. Turn into a greased and floured 10-inch tube pan. Bake at 325° F. for 1 hour. Test as described on page 313. Cool 10 minutes in pan when done, then turn out on a

---

* Be sure to measure shelled nuts here by weight and *not* by cup.

cake rack to cool completely. Frost with a lemon or orange frosting or serve simply sprinkled with powdered sugar. You can give this cake a marvelous extra richness if you will dribble over it, while it is still hot, ½ cup of Crème de Banane or, for a different flavor, Curaçao or Grand Marnier.

★ *German Orange Cake*

*For the Cake:*

| | |
|---|---|
| 1 cup butter | 3½ cups sifted flour |
| 2 cups sugar | Pinch of salt |
| ⅓ cup buttermilk | 2 Tbs. grated orange peel |
| 1 tsp. soda | 1 cup cut up, pitted dates |
| 4 eggs, separated | 1 cup chopped pecans |

Cream butter and sugar together until light and fluffy. Beat in buttermilk in which soda has been dissolved. One by one beat in the egg yolks. Add 3¼ cups of the flour and the salt. Blend. Dredge orange peel, dates and pecans with remaining ¼ cup flour and add to the batter. Beat egg whites until stiff but not dry and fold in gently. Pour batter into a greased and floured 10-inch tube pan. Bake at 325° F. for 2 hours. Cover with paper if the top seems to brown too much toward the end of cooking.

*For the Orange Syrup:*

| | |
|---|---|
| 1 cup fresh orange juice | 1 Tb. grated orange peel |
| 1⅓ cups sugar | |

Meanwhile combine the ingredients for the syrup. Stir until sugar is dissolved but do not cook. As soon as the cake is removed from the oven, and while it is still in the pan, pour on ⅓ of the syrup. Let stand until this has been completely absorbed. Turn cake out on a cold plate and pour another ⅓ of the syrup over what is now the top of cake. Let it stand until this has been absorbed. Turn cake over again and pour on remaining ⅓ of syrup. When this has been absorbed and cake is cold, wrap in wax paper. Store in refrigerator 4 days before cutting, making certain that all the while the cake is tightly wrapped. Serves 10 or more.

Old-fashioned Pound Cakes may be too rich for the rest of the country but not so in Texas. There you even find them with the extra richness of coconut and/or pecans.

★ *Coconut Pound Cake*

| | |
|---|---|
| 1 lb. butter | 2 Tbs. fresh orange juice |
| 3 cups sugar | 1 tsp. grated orange peel |
| 9 eggs | 1 can coconut (Angel Flake), 4-oz. |
| 3 cups sifted cake flour | size |

Cream butter and sugar until light and fluffy. One by one, beat in the eggs, beating at least 3 minutes after each addition. Add the sifted flour bit by bit, folding it into the batter as you go. When all is in, add orange juice, grated peel and coconut. Blend. Pour into a greased and floured tube pan—about 3-qt. capacity. Bake 1 hour and 45 minutes at 325° F. Cool 15 minutes in pan when done before turning out on rack to cool completely. Serves 12.

## ★ Pecan Pound Cake

| | |
|---|---|
| 1 lb. sweet butter | ¼ tsp. mace |
| 3 cups sugar | ⅓ cups milk |
| 6 eggs | 1 lb. shelled pecans, chopped |
| 4 cups flour | 2 tsps. vanilla |
| ½ tsp. salt | |

Cream butter and sugar together until very light and fluffy. Beat in the eggs, one at a time, beating well after each addition. Combine flour, salt and mace and sift together. Add flour mixture and milk alternately to egg batter, again beating after each addition. Stir in chopped pecans and vanilla. Pour into an ungreased 10-inch tube pan and bake at 275° F. for 1½ hours. Cool cake in pan 10 minutes before turning out on rack to cool completely. When cold, wrap in wax paper and refrigerate overnight before cutting. Makes 20 slices.

So widely are spices used in Texas cakes that it is sometimes difficult to decide which cakes are *really* Spice Cakes. Here is one of them.

## ★ Coffee Spice Cake

| | |
|---|---|
| ½ cup butter | 1 tsp. ground cinnamon |
| 1 cup sugar | ½ tsp. ground allspice |
| 2 cups flour | 2 eggs, separated |
| 1 Tb. baking powder | ⅔ cup very strong cold black coffee |
| ⅛ tsp. salt | |

Cream butter and sugar together until light and fluffy. Combine dry ingredients and sift together. Beat egg yolks until thick and lemon-colored. Add them to butter mixture and beat in thoroughly. Add coffee and dry mixture alternately to egg batter, beating after each addition. Beat egg whites until stiff but not dry and fold in gently. Pour into greased 9-inch tube pan and bake at 350° F. for 40 minutes. Let cool in pan 10 minutes before turning out on rack to cool completely.

★    *Cinnamon Carrot Cake*

| | |
|---|---|
| 1¼ cups oil (Wesson or peanut) | 2 tsps. baking powder |
| 2 cups sugar | 2 tsps. cinnamon |
| 4 eggs | 1 tsp. salt |
| 2 cups flour | 3 cups grated carrots |

Combine oil and sugar; cream together until smooth. Beat in the eggs, one at a time, beating well after each addition. Combine flour, baking powder, cinnamon and salt. Sift together three times. Add dry ingredients bit by bit to the egg mixture, beating until smooth after each addition. Stir in the carrots. Pour into 3 greased and floured 8-inch layer cake pans. Bake at 325° F. for 30 minutes. Turn layers out on rack to cool when done. Fill and frost as desired. My preference is a plain white icing.

Texas fruit cakes frequently include a wider variety of fruits than you find elsewhere—and more of each of them. Dates, of course, give a special richness.

# ★  Texas Fruit Cake

| | |
|---|---|
| 1 lb. butter | 3 lbs. raisins |
| 2 cups sugar | 1 lb. citron, slivered |
| 3 cups flour | 1 lb. pitted dates, cut up |
| 1 Tb. salt | 4 cups chopped pecans |
| 1 Tb. soda | Strained juice of 2 lemons |
| 2 Tbs. cinnamon | 1 cup molasses |
| 2 tsps. nutmeg | 12 eggs, beaten |
| 1 tsp. allspice | 4 ozs. rum or 2 ozs. bourbon |
| 1 tsp. cloves | whiskey |
| 2 lbs. currants | |

Cream butter and sugar until light and fluffy. Combine 2½ cups flour with other dry ingredients and sift together. Add remaining flour to combined fruits and pecans. Toss to dredge evenly. Add lemon juice and molasses to butter mixture. Blend. Work in the dry ingredients, then fruits and nuts with any excess flour. Stir in beaten eggs. Blend thoroughly. Butter two 9 x 5-inch loaf pans and line them with wax paper. Pour in batter. Tap the pans to settle the batter evenly. Bake at 275° F. for 2½ hours. When cakes are hot from the oven, pour 2 ounces rum or 1 ounce bourbon whiskey over each. Cool in pans. Store in tightly covered container with wax paper still on cakes. These cakes will be the better for storing several weeks before using.

Jam cakes of all kinds have always been rural favorites in this country. In Texas you find them everywhere.

---

## ★ Mrs. de Shaze's Jam Cake

| | |
|---|---|
| ¾ lb. butter | 1 tsp. ground allspice |
| 2 cups sugar | ½ tsp. salt |
| 2 cups blackberry jam | 1 tsp. soda |
| 4 cups flour | 6 Tbs. buttermilk |
| 1 tsp. ground cinnamon | 6 eggs, beaten |

Cream butter and sugar together until light and fluffy. Beat in jam. Combine flour, cinnamon, allspice and salt. Sift together. Dissolve soda in buttermilk. Add beaten eggs to milk and beat together. Add dry ingredients and the egg mixture alternately to the jam mixture. Beat after each addition. Pour into 4 buttered 9-inch layer cake pans. Bake at 350° F. until done, testing after 30 minutes (page 313). Turn cake out to cool on rack when done; let cool completely before filling and frosting with the Pecan Frosting (page 324). Finished 4-layer cake serves 12 at least.

## ★ Apple Butter Cake

| | |
|---|---|
| ¾ cup butter | ¼ tsp. ground cloves |
| 2 cups sugar | ½ tsp. ground nutmeg or mace |
| 2 eggs, beaten | 1 tsp. ground allspice |
| 2 cups apple butter (page 245) | 1 tsp. ground cinnamon |
| ½ cup hot water | 1 cup chopped pitted dates |
| 2 tsps. soda | 1 cup chopped pecans |
| 3 cups sifted flour | |

Cream butter and sugar together until light and fluffy. Add beaten eggs and beat together until very thick. Stir in apple butter. Add the hot water with soda dissolved in it. Combine 2¾ cups flour with spices and sift together. Dredge dates and pecans

**321**

with remaining ¼ cup flour. Add flour to apple butter mixture and blend. Stir in the dates and nuts. Pour into 3 buttered 9-inch layer cake pans. Bake at 350° F. for 30 to 35 minutes or until the cake tests done. Cool in pans 10 minutes, then turn out on rack to cool completely. When cold, fill and frost with Brown Sugar Pecan Frosting (page 324).

Despite their devotion to home-made cakes, Texas housewives are not averse to short cuts, provided the results are good. Here is an ingenious cake using a prepared pie filling and cake mix.

## ★ Cherry Pie Cake

| | |
|---|---|
| 1 can sour-cherry pie filling, #3 size | 1 cup finely chopped pecans |
| ½ pkg. white cake mix | 1½ cups heavy cream, whipped |
| ¼ lb. butter, melted | 2 Tbs. powdered sugar |
| | 1 to 2 Tbs. Kirsch |

Spread the cherry pie filling evenly over the bottom of a 9-inch square baking dish. Sprinkle the dry cake mix evenly over the cherries. Dribble the melted butter over the cake mix. Cover with pecans. Bake at 350° F. for 1 hour. Cover with foil loosely if the cake browns too quickly. While the cake is baking, whip cream and then whip in sugar and Kirsch. Serve cake, hot or cold, cut in squares with a generous topping of chilled cream. Serves 8 to 12.

No collection of American cakes would be complete without at least one upside-down cake.

## ★ Apple-Coconut Upside-down Cake

| | |
|---|---|
| 2 cups sliced, peeled, cored, tart apples | 2 Tbs. white vinegar |
| ¼ cup butter | ½ cup milk |
| 2 cups brown sugar, finely packed | ¼ cup butter |
| 1 tsp. grated lemon peel | ½ cup white sugar |
| 1 Tb. lemon juice | ⅓ cup flaked coconut (canned) |
| 1¼ cups sifted flour | ½ tsp. vanilla |
| ½ tsp. soda | 1 tsp. rum |
| ½ tsp. salt | 1 egg |
| | Sweetened whipped cream |

Place apple slices in a colander in a pan over hot water. Cover. Steam for 5 minutes. Set aside. Melt butter in a 9-inch tube pan. Tilt pan to coat it all over. Let stand until all the butter is on the bottom. Add brown sugar and blend. Add grated lemon peel and blend. Arrange apples in a layer on top of the sugar mixture. Sprinkle with lemon juice. Set aside.

Now combine flour, soda and salt and sift together. Combine the vinegar and milk. Cream second ¼ cup butter with white sugar; work in the coconut, vanilla and rum. Beat in the egg. Alternately add sifted dry ingredients and milk mixture to the egg batter, starting and ending with the flour mixture. Beat well after each addition. Pour the batter over the apples. Let stand 1 minute. Bake at 350° F. for 45 minutes or until the cake tests done (page 313). Let cool for 5 minutes in pan before turning out on a serving plate. Be sure that the plate is of ample proportions. Chill. Fill center of cake with lightly sweetened whipped cream before serving. Serves 8 to 12.

Among the favorite frostings and fillings for cakes in Texas are ones made with pecans.

## ★ Pecan Frosting

¾ lb. butter                    1½ tsps. vanilla
1 cup milk                      2 cups chopped pecàns
3 cups sugar

Combine butter, milk and sugar in a saucepan and boil slowly until the syrup forms a soft ball in cold water (240° F. on your candy thermometer). Remove from heat and beat until thick and creamy. Beat in vanilla. Beat in 1½ cups of the pecans. Fill and frost cooled layers of cake. Sprinkle the remaining ½ cup around the edge of the finished cake.

## ★ Brown Sugar Pecan Frosting

3 Tbs. melted butter            ½ cup very finely chopped pecans
1 cup milk                      ½ cup chopped pecans, medium
3 cups brown sugar                fine
¾ cup white granulated sugar    1 Tb. heavy cream
1 tsp. vanilla

Combine all ingredients *except* nuts and cream in a saucepan; bring to a boil and cook to the soft-ball stage (240° F. on your candy thermometer). Remove from heat and beat until creamy. Add nuts and beat until very thick. Then beat in the cream. Sufficient to fill and frost a 3-layer, 9-inch cake.

A recipe for a quick, easy and delicious cake frosting is always a handy thing to know. Here's one of lemon, sugar and sour cream.

---

## ★ Sour Cream Frosting

2½ cups confectioner's sugar     1 tsp. grated lemon rind
  2 Tbs. softened butter     2 Tbs. strained fresh lemon juice
  1 generous pinch salt     ⅓ cup sour cream

Cream sugar with butter. Beat in the remaining ingredients and continue beating until the frosting is light and fluffy. Frosts a 2-layer 8-inch cake.


## ★ Creamy Fudge Frosting

4½ squares (4 ozs.) unsweetened     4 egg yolks
   chocolate     ¼ cup butter or margarine
¼ cup hot water     1 tsp. vanilla
2¼ cups confectioner's sugar (sifted)

In a double boiler, melt chocolate over hot—not boiling—water; remove from heat. Add ¼ cup hot water and sugar. Add egg yolks, one at a time, beating after each. Add butter, 1 tablespoon at a time, still beating. Beat in vanilla. Makes enough to frost two 9-inch layers.

# TWENTY-FIVE

## COOKIES AND TEACAKES

IN the old days in Texas, the standard afternoon refreshments were Tea Cakes and home-made grape juice. Here are the Tea Cakes:

## ★ Old-fashioned Tea Cakes

| | |
|---|---|
| 1 cup butter | 1 tsp. cinnamon |
| 2 cups sugar | 1 tsp. allspice |
| 3 eggs, beaten | 1 pinch salt |
| 3½ cups sifted flour | ¼ cup sweet milk |
| 2 tsps. baking powder | Granulated sugar |

Cream butter with sugar, then add beaten eggs and beat together. Sift flour with baking powder, spices and salt. Add dry ingredients and milk alternately to egg batter, beating after each addition. When all has been thoroughly mixed, form dough into a roll. Wrap in wax paper. Refrigerate 24 hours. Slice crosswise and arrange slices on ungreased baking sheet. Bake at 350° F. for 10 minutes. Lift off baking sheet with a spatula when done and cool on rack. Sprinkle with granulated sugar while still warm. Makes about 6 dozen cookies.

Every ethnic group in Texas has contributed specialties to the state's roster of small cakes and cookies. You'll find Polish ones, Bohemian ones, German ones. Here is a Mexican favorite:

★ *Amarillo Orange Biscochitos*

1½ cups pure lard
1 cup sugar
6 egg yolks
½ cup undiluted frozen orange juice
3½ tsps. baking powder
2 tsps. anise seeds
5 to 5½ cups sifted flour
½ cup sugar (additional)
1½ tsps. ground cinnamon

Cream lard until very light and fluffy. Add sugar and cream again until blended. Add egg yolks and the orange juice (thawed). Beat thoroughly. Add baking powder, anise seeds and the flour. Knead to blend until smooth. Turn out on a lightly floured board and roll dough out to a rectangle, about ⅛ inch thick. Cut with a knife into strips about ¾ inch wide and 2 inches long. Twist into curlicues with the fingers. Combine extra sugar with cinnamon. Sprinkle curlicues with the mixture. Arrange on lightly greased baking sheet. Bake at 400° F. for about 10 minutes or until light brown. Cool thoroughly before storing. Makes about 6 dozen.

Mixed with the foreign cakes and cookies, you'll find such early American favorites as these:

★ *Grandmother Dennett's Lizzies*

4 whole eggs
½ cup sugar
2 cups dark molasses
4 cups flour
3 tsps. soda
3 tsps. milk
1½ lbs. pecans
1½ lbs. raisins
1 tsp. nutmeg
1 tsp. cloves
¾ cup bourbon whiskey

330

In a large bowl, combine all the ingredients in the order given. Blend thoroughly. Drop by rounded tablespoonfuls on greased baking sheet. Bake until golden brown at 350° F. Cool and store in stone crock for 2 weeks before eating. Makes about 8 dozen.

Why these should be called Ranger Cookies escapes me. They'd be good by any name.

## ★ *Ranger Cookies*

| | |
|---|---|
| 1 cup butter | 2 tsps. soda |
| 1 cup brown sugar | ½ tsp. salt |
| 1 cup white sugar | 2 cups crushed corn flakes |
| 2 eggs | 2 cups oatmeal |
| 2 cups flour | 1 cup chopped pecans |
| 1 tsp. baking powder | 1 cup coconut |

Cream butter with all the sugar until smooth. Beat in eggs one at a time. Combine flour, baking powder, soda and salt. Sift together and add to creamed mixture. One by one add and blend in the remaining ingredients. Drop by teaspoonfuls on ungreased cookie sheet. Bake at 400° F. for 15 minutes or until done. Lift off with spatula and cool on rack before storing. Makes about 10 dozen.

## ★  Oatmeal Macaroons

| | |
|---|---|
| 1 cup brown sugar | 1½ cups sifted flour |
| 1 cup white sugar | 1 tsp. soda |
| ¾ cup melted, cooled butter | 1 tsp. baking powder |
| 2 eggs, lightly beaten | ½ tsp. salt |
| 1 tsp. vanilla | 3 cups oatmeal |

In a mixing bowl, combine the sugars, butter, eggs and vanilla; blend. Combine all the dry ingredients (except oatmeal) and sift together. Add to egg mixture. Stir in the oatmeal. Drop by teaspoonfuls onto cookie sheet. Bake at 350° F. until a golden brown. Makes 10 dozen or more "macaroons," depending on what you consider a teaspoonful.

## ★  Old-fashioned Nutmeg Cookies

| | |
|---|---|
| 3 cups flour | 1 cup softened butter (*not* melted) |
| 1 cup sugar | 1 egg, slightly beaten |
| 1½ tsps. baking powder | 1 tsp. vanilla |
| ½ tsp. salt | 3 Tbs. heavy cream |
| ¾ tsp. nutmeg | Additional sugar |

Combine the dry ingredients and sift them together. Cut in the softened butter until the mixture has a pebbly consistency. Then one by one, and blending after each addition, add all the remaining ingredients except the extra sugar. Roll out to ⅛-inch thickness on a lightly floured board. Cut into shapes as desired. Sprinkle with extra sugar. Bake on a lightly greased cookie sheet at 400° F. for 5 to 8 minutes or until lightly browned. Lift off with a spatula when done and cool on a rack. Makes 6 to 7 dozen cookies.

---

★ *Old-fashioned Sorghum Cookies*

| | |
|---|---|
| 1½ cups lard | 2 Tbs. ground ginger |
| 1 cup sugar | 2 Tbs. ground cinnamon |
| 2 cups sorghum | 2 tsps. salt |
| 6 eggs, lightly beaten | 6 cups flour |
| 2 Tbs. baking soda | |

Combine lard, sugar and sorghum in saucepan; bring to a boil. Stir until sugar is dissolved. Remove from heat and cool. When cool, blend with beaten eggs. Combine dry ingredients and sift together. Add egg batter to dry ingredients and blend. If the dough is not stiff enough to roll out, add a little more flour. Turn dough out onto a lightly floured board. Roll out to ¼-inch thickness. Cut into shapes as desired. Arrange on lightly greased baking sheet and bake at 375° F. until brown. Lift off with spatula when done and cool on rack. When cold, pack in tin box with wax paper between layers. Cover tightly. The flavor improves if these are left several days before eating. Makes 8 to 9 dozen cookies.

From Valley Mills comes another Polish recipe:

★ *Krusczyki (Polish Pretzels)*

| | |
|---|---|
| ¾ cup butter | 4 to 4½ cups flour |
| 1 cup sugar | 1 tsp. baking powder |
| 5 eggs | 1 generous pinch salt |
| 1 tsp. vanilla | Powdered sugar |

Cream butter and sugar together until light and fluffy. Beat in the eggs, one at a time. Add vanilla. Sift together 4 cups of the flour, the baking powder and salt. Add this to the egg batter. If the dough seems too thin to roll, add what you need of the remaining ½ cup flour. Roll out on a lightly floured board to ¼-inch thickness. Cut into strips 1 inch wide and 4 inches long. Make a 3-inch long slit in the center of each strip, starting and stopping about ½ inch from either end. Take up each strip in your hands and carefully fold the ends down, then up through the center slit. Fry a few at a time in deep hot fat at 375° F. until a golden brown. Drain on paper and sprinkle with powdered sugar while still hot. Makes about 4½ dozen pretzels.

★ *Sliced Nut Cookies*

| | |
|---|---|
| 1½ cups melted butter | 4½ cups flour |
| 1 cup brown sugar | 2 tsps. soda |
| 1 cup white sugar | 1 tsp. ground cinnamon |
| 3 eggs, well beaten | ½ tsp. ground nutmeg |
| 1 cup chopped pecans | ½ tsp. ground cloves |

Cream butter with sugars. Slowly beat in the eggs. Add chopped pecans and blend. Combine all the dry ingredients and sift together twice. Add to egg mixture and work together thoroughly. Form into a roll about 2½ inches in diameter (or 2 rolls for easier handling); wrap in greased paper and refrigerate 24 hours. When ready to bake, slice the rolls crosswise thinly. Arrange cookies on baking sheet. Bake about 8 minutes at 375° F. Watch carefully. When done, lift off with spatula and cool on racks. Makes about 6 dozen cookies.

The spelling of the names of some Texas dishes seems to me a little freewheeling, but I have left them as they were given to me. Here is Blatterteich, a delicious sort of pastry roll, from Waco.

★ *Blatterteich*

| | |
|---|---|
| 1 cup butter | Jam or jelly as needed, or a mixture |
| 1 cup flour | of sugar, ground cinnamon and |
| 1 cup cottage cheese | finely chopped pecans |
| | Powdered sugar (optional) |

In a bowl cut butter into flour as you would for pastry. When mealy, cut in the cottage cheese. Press into a ball, roll in wax paper and refrigerate overnight.

Now roll out the dough to about ⅛-inch thickness on a lightly floured board. Cut into strips about 3 inches long and 2 inches wide. Spread each with a jam or jelly or the sugar-nut combination. Roll as you would a jelly roll. Seal ends and edges. Arrange on a lightly greased baking sheet and bake at 350° F. for 20 to 25 minutes. If desired, sprinkle with powdered sugar while still hot. Serve hot or cold. Makes about 3 dozen.

★ *Cinnamon Puffs*

| | |
|---|---|
| 2 cups sifted flour | ¾ cup rich sweet milk |
| ¼ cup sugar | 1 large egg |
| 1 Tb. baking powder | Corn oil for frying |
| 1 tsp. salt | 1 Tb. cinnamon |
| 1 tsp. nutmeg | ¼ cup granulated sugar |
| ¼ cup corn oil | |

Combine flour, sugar, baking powder, salt and nutmeg. Sift together into a bowl. Add ¼ cup oil, milk and egg. Beat to mix thoroughly. Drop by tablespoonfuls into corn oil heated to 360° F. Fry until golden brown on all sides. Lift out with perforated skimmer. Drain on paper towels. While hot, sprinkle with cinnamon and granulated sugar mixed together. Serve immediately. Makes about 3 dozen puffs.

*Kolaches* are filled pastries, popular everywhere in Central Europe and wherever Central Europeans have settled. Here are some from West, Texas.

## ★ *Mrs. Nemecek's Kolaches*

*Dough:*

| | |
|---|---|
| 2 envelopes active dry yeast | ½ cup sugar |
| ¼ cup lukewarm water | 2 tsps. salt |
| 1 Tb. sugar | 2 egg yolks, slightly beaten |
| 2 cups milk | 6¼ cups sifted flour |
| ½ cup plus 1 Tb. butter | Softened butter, as needed |

In a small bowl dissolve yeast in warm water. Sprinkle with 1 tablespoon sugar and let stand. Scald milk in saucepan. Remove from heat and stir in butter and ½ cup sugar. Cool to lukewarm. Add salt and egg yolks. Combine milk mixture and yeast in a large bowl. Bit by bit add the flour until all has been used. Knead dough on lightly floured board until glossy. Place in bowl, cover and let rise in warm place (80° F.) until doubled in bulk (about 1 hour). This dough will not be quite as stiff as a roll dough.

Now, using a tablespoon, take egg-size bits of the dough and

336

roll into balls on the floured board. Place on greased baking sheet about 1 inch apart. Brush each with softened butter. Let rise again, covered, until light.

Make an indentation in each large enough to hold 1 teaspoon of the fruit filling below. Sprinkle fruit in turn with some of the topping below. Bake at 425° F. for 15 minutes. Remove from oven. Brush again immediately with softened butter. Cool *kolaches* on a wire rack. Makes about 3½ dozen.

*Prune Filling:*

1 lb. prunes               ½ tsp. ground cinnamon
½ cup sugar

In a saucepan cook prunes in water just to cover until tender. Drain. (Reserve the liquid to mix with fruit juice if you like.) Discard pits. Mash pulp with sugar and cinnamon. Use as directed above. Enough for 3 dozen.

*Apricot Filling:*

1 pkg. dried apricots, 10-ozs.
1¼ cups sugar

Cook apricots in water just to cover until tender, at which time virtually all the water will have cooked away. Do not overcook or the fruit will darken. Mash apricots with sugar. Use as directed above. Fills about 3 dozen.

*Topping for Kolaches* (Posipka)

1 cup sugar               1 tsp. ground cinnamon
½ cup flour               2 Tbs. melted butter

337

Combine all ingredients and mix with fork until consistency of coarse meal. If any is left over, store in a covered glass jar in refrigerator until needed. It is good, too, on coffee cake.

Cheese *kolaches* are also popular, as are ones with a poppy-seed filling. These are made somewhat differently, however, though the dough is the same. After the first rising of the dough, take the egg-size spoonfuls of dough and roll each into a rectangle on the floured board. Place a teaspoonful of filling in the center of each, then fold the sides of the dough up over the filling and pinch them together to seal completely. Lay these seam-side down on baking sheet. Brush with butter, sprinkle with topping and let rise until light. Bake as above.

*Cheese Filling:*

½ lb. cottage cheese
½ tsp. salt
 1 egg yolk

½ cup sugar
1 tsp. grated lemon rind
1 Tb. lemon juice

Combine all ingredients and blend thoroughly. Fills 2 dozen *kolaches.*

*Poppy-Seed Filling:*

 2 cups poppy seeds
⅓ cup sugar

3 Tbs. white Karo syrup
2½ cups water

Grind the poppy seeds very fine. Combine all ingredients in a heavy saucepan. Simmer until very thick (about 1 hour). Remove from heat and cool. This thickens even more in cooling. Fills about 3 dozen *kolaches.*

338

## ★  *Mrs. Nemecek's Flaky Pastry*

| | |
|---|---|
| ¼ lb. sweet butter | 3 egg yolks |
| 1 cup flour | 1 pinch salt |

Cut butter into flour until mixture has a fine meal consistency. Stir in egg yolks and salt. Blend quickly, lightly and thoroughly. Refrigerate, covered, 24 hours or overnight before using. Excellent for pies, turnovers, etc., or *Maslove Tastecky* (below).

## ★  *Maslove Tastecky*

Roll Flaky Pastry dough (above) into walnut-size balls before refrigerating. When ready to use, roll out balls on a lightly floured board into circles about ⅛ to ¼ inch thick. Place spoonful of filling (below) in center of each; fold over and seal edges with tines of fork. Arrange on baking sheet and bake at 350° F. for 20 minutes, or until golden brown.

*For the Filling:*

| | |
|---|---|
| 2 egg whites | 1 tsp. grated lemon peel |
| ½ cup sugar | ½ cup chopped pecans |
| 1 Tb. fresh lemon juice | |

Beat egg whites until stiff; beat in sugar, lemon juice and peel in that order. Fold in pecans. Use as directed above.

# TWENTY-SIX
## *PIES*

# HOME-MADE pie is

one of the standard foods of virtually all Texas tables. Mention of pie in connection with Texas brings Pecan Pie instantly to mind; every Texas cook has her own special (and always the best) recipe for making it. But pie in Texas is not made only of pecans by any means; actually, it is more often of fruit than nuts—and more often of apples than anything else.

Pie pastry, like pie fillings, are made in scores of different ways. Many Texas housewives of European extraction have European recipes which suit their purposes best. The pastry on pages 308–309 is a good example. It is excellent. But others make pastry in the more ordinary way—flour, shortening and a bit of ice water. Here, for instance, is a typical recipe:

★ *Pie Crust Dough for a 2-Crust Pie or 12 Tart Shells*

| 2 cups sifted flour | ⅔ cup butter |
| ½ tsp. salt | 6 to 8 Tbs. ice water |

Sift flour and salt into a mixing bowl. Using 2 knives or a pastry blender, cut in the shortening until the mixture is of fine, meal-like consistency. Dribble in as much of the ice water as you

343

need to make the dough adhere in a ball. Turn out on a lightly floured board and roll to desired thickness. Wrap any unused dough in wax paper and refrigerate until needed. Handle the dough as little and as quickly as possible for best results.

To vary their pies, Texas housewives sometimes make fancy pie shells such as this:

## ★ *Coconut Pie Crust*

Spread the bottom and sides of a 9-inch pie pan with 2 to 3 tablespoons softened sweet butter. Sprinkle the pan evenly with 1½ cups shredded coconut. Press gently so it adheres to the butter. Bake in preheated oven at 350° F. for 10 minutes. Cool.

Apple Pies in Texas have been made and baked in every conceivable way.

## ★ *Paper-bag Apple Pie*

| | |
|---|---|
| 4 large cooking apples | 9-inch unbaked pastry shell |
| 1 cup sugar | 2 Tbs. strained fresh lemon juice |
| ½ cup flour plus 2 Tbs. | ½ cup butter |
| ½ tsp. cinnamon | |

Peel, core and slice apples. Combine ½ cup sugar with 2 tablespoons of the flour and cinnamon. Combine mixture with apple

344

slices. Toss to coat them evenly all over. Arrange floured slices in pie shell. Sprinkle with any excess mixture. Dribble the lemon juice over all. Combine remaining ½ cup sugar with ½ cup flour. Cut in the butter until mixture is mealy. Scatter this over the apples evenly. Place pie in a brown paper bag. Fold end over twice to seal. Fasten with 2 or 3 paper clips. Bake at 425° F. for 1 hour. Slit bag when done to remove the pie. Serve warm or cold, with or without heavy cream. Serves 6.

★  *Apple Cream Pie*

¾ cup sugar                    8-inch unbaked pie shell
2 Tbs. flour                   4 or 5 medium-size tart apples
¾ tsp. cinnamon                ½ cup heaviest cream
½ tsp. salt

Combine the sugar, flour, cinnamon and salt; blend thoroughly. Sprinkle half the mixture over the bottom of the unbaked pie shell. Pare, core and slice enough apples to fill shell with a slight mound at the center. Sprinkle apples with remaining sugar mixture. Pour cream gently over all. Bake at 450° F. for 15 minutes; reduce heat to 350° F. and bake until done (about 40 minutes longer). Serve hot or cold. Serves 6 to 8.

## ★  Mrs. Cheek's Crustless Apple Pie

6 medium-size tart apples
½ cup white sugar
½ cup brown sugar, packed
1 tsp. cinnamon
1 cup water

6 Tbs. butter
1 cup flour
1 tsp. baking powder
½ tsp. salt
Additional butter

Peel apples; core and slice. Place in pan with sugar, cinnamon and water. Cook 10 minutes. Turn into a Pyrex baking dish. Cream butter. Combine flour with baking powder and salt. Cut in the butter. When pebbly, sprinkle over apples. Dot with almost 2 tablespoons extra butter. Bake at 350° F. for 45 minutes. Serve with plain or whipped cream or vanilla ice cream. Serves 6.

Texas has many creations like the following which, you might say, are almost pies.

## ★  McGinties

1 lb. dried apples
1½ cups brown sugar
⅛ tsp. salt

1½ Tbs. ground cinnamon
1½ recipes for plain pie pastry
    (page 343)

Cover the apples with cold water and soak overnight. Using the same water (or with more added if necessary), cook apples until tender. Add sugar, salt and cinnamon. Continue to cook until *very* thick, stirring frequently to prevent burning. Remove from heat.

Line the bottom and halfway up the sides of a 9 x 13-inch

baking pan with pie crust dough rolled ⅛ inch thick. Fill with apple mixture. Cover with remaining dough. Seal edges. Gash the top to permit steam to escape and bake at 450° F. for 10 minutes; reduce heat to 350° F. Bake 20 minutes longer or until done to a golden brown. Cut into squares to serve either hot or cold. Heavy cream should be passed in a pitcher. Makes about 18 pieces.

Texans away from Texas talk more of Fried Pies than any other Texas dessert. These are favorites to serve after barbecue.

## ★   *Fried Pies*

| | |
|---|---|
| 3 cups diced fresh or well-drained canned fruit | 2 recipes plain pie-crust dough |
| 1 cup sugar | Lard or vegetable oil for frying |
| 1 Tb. flour | Additional sugar |

Place fruit in saucepan. Mix sugar and flour. Blend with fruit. Cook over medium flame (stirring frequently) until sugar has melted and syrup has thickened. Set aside.

On a lightly floured board roll pastry dough out to ⅛-inch thickness. Cut into 6-inch circles. Place 2 tablespoons fruit and thickened syrup in center of each circle, leaving a clear ½-inch border all the way round. Moisten border with cold water. Fold circles over in half. Seal edges by pressing with the tines of a floured fork. Prick top of pie with fork in several places. In a deep pot, heat lard or vegetable oil to 375° F. Fry a few pies at a time until golden brown on both sides (about 5 minutes). Drain on absorbent paper. Sprinkle with sugar while still hot. Serve hot or cold. If hot, serve with ice-cold heavy cream on the side. Makes about 2 dozen pies.

All through Texas, even in the sophisticated urban centers, early-day recipes turn up constantly such as this one for a Mock Mince Pie. Surprisingly it makes for a very good pie, indeed.

★ *Mock Mince Pie*

1 cup rolled soda crackers
1 cup molasses
1 cup sugar
1 cup chopped, pared, cored, tart apples
1 cup seedless raisins
1 cup boiling water
½ cup butter
1 tsp. *each* ground cloves and cinnamon
3 unbaked pie shells, 8 inches each
Brandy, rum, or bourbon (optional)

Combine all the filling ingredients in a mixing bowl and blend. Store covered in refrigerator until needed. Fill pie shells with the mixture. Brandy, rum or bourbon whiskey may be added to taste before baking. Bake at 450° F. until done (about 30 minutes). Tightly covered and chilled, the filling mixture will keep very well for several days. Makes 3 pies.

The only way I know of to discover what Pecan Pie you like best is to make several different kinds and taste them. Small variations in the quantities make very considerable difference in the finished pies. Here are three of them:

---

## ★ *Pecan Pie #1*

*Makes a crispy nut-brown top.*

3 eggs
1 cup sugar
1 cup Karo syrup (blue label)
1 tsp. vanilla

⅛ tsp. salt
2 Tbs. melted butter
1 cup pecan halves
1 unbaked 8-inch pie shell

Beat eggs until lemon-colored, then add sugar, Karo, vanilla, salt and melted butter. Spread pecan halves in unbaked pie shell. Pour egg mixture over nuts. Bake in hot oven (400° F.) 15 minutes; reduce heat to 350° F. and bake 30 or 35 minutes longer.

## ★ *Pecan Pie #2*

3 eggs
½ cup sugar
1 cup light Karo syrup
1 pinch salt

1 tsp. vanilla
1 cup broken pecan meats
1 unbaked 8-inch pie shell

Beat eggs slightly; add sugar and Karo and beat again. Stir in salt, vanilla and pecan meats. Bake pie shell for 10 minutes at 350° F. Do not brown. Beat filling once again and pour into partially baked pie shell. Bake pie at 350° F. for about 45 minutes. Serve hot or cold. Serves 6 to 8.

★ *Pecan Pie #3*

3 slightly beaten eggs          1 tsp. vanilla
1 cup sugar                     1 cup broken pecan meats
½ cup light corn syrup          1 unbaked 9-inch pie shell
3 Tbs. butter, melted and cooled

In a mixing bowl, combine eggs, sugar, syrup, butter and vanilla. Blend thoroughly. Add nuts. Pour into pie shell. Bake at 450° F. for 10 minutes; reduce heat to 350° F. and bake 30 minutes longer. Serve at room temperature. Serves 6 to 8.

Though not as well known outside of Texas as Pecan Pie, the richer Osgood Pie, with its pecans, dates and raisins, seems to be a fixture in every *real* Texas household.

★ *Osgood Pie*

½ cup butter                    1 cup pitted, cut-up dates
1 cup sugar                     ½ cup white raisins
3 eggs, separated               1 pinch salt
1 cup pecan meats               1 unbaked 9-inch pie shell

Cream butter and sugar and beat in the egg yolks. Fold in nuts, dates, raisins and salt. Beat egg whites until stiff and fold into the mixture. Turn into pie shell and bake at 325° F. until done (about 45 minutes). Serve hot or cold. Serves 6 or 8.

Though less common in Texas than in New England, Pumpkin Pies are still thought of as special for Thanksgiving. Often mashed sweet potatoes or yams are used instead of pumpkin (as in the rest of the South), but the effect is much the same.

## ★ *Pumpkin Custard Pie*

1 cup brown sugar, firmly packed
3 Tbs. butter, softened
2 cups mashed, cooked pumpkin
½ tsp. ground ginger
¾ tsp. ground allspice
¼ tsp. ground nutmeg
¼ tsp. ground cinnamon
½ tsp. salt
3 slightly beaten eggs
2 cups half-and-half (or light cream)
1 unbaked 9-inch pie shell
Sweetened whipped cream

In a mixing bowl, combine the sugar, butter and mashed pumpkin. Blend. Add all the spices and salt; blend. Combine eggs and half-and-half and beat into pumpkin mixture. Pour into unbaked pie shell. Bake at 450° F. for 10 minutes; reduce heat to 325° F. and bake 35 minutes longer. Serve cold with a border of sweetened whipped cream piped around top of pie. Or serve hot or warm with ice-cold heavy cream on the side. Serves 8.

Old-fashioned pies are as popular in Texas as any others.

## ★ *Old-fashioned Egg Pie*

3 eggs
2 cups sugar
½ cup butter, softened
½ cup flour
1½ cups milk
1 tsp. vanilla
2 unbaked 8-inch pie shells

Beat eggs until thick and lemon-colored. One by one, beat in sugar, butter and flour. Add milk and vanilla. Blend. Pour into 2 unbaked pie shells. Bake at 425° F. for 10 minutes; reduce heat to 350° F. and bake 20 minutes longer. When done, the top of the pies should be crusted a golden brown. Have one pie today, hot, and the other one tomorrow, cold. Each one serves 6.

It has been said that Vinegar Pie was originated in the Texas Panhandle in imitation of lemon pie, lemons being hard, if not impossible, to come by in the old days five hundred miles from nowhere. But I rather suspect that settlers carried the recipe for Vinegar Pie with them from either New England or the South, it having always been a country favorite in both regions. Anyway, Vinegar Pie was justifiably popular in nineteenth-century Western Texas—and still is where home-baked pies appear at all.

★ *Vinegar Pie*

Pastry for a 9-inch pie with lattice top
1 cup cider vinegar
2 cups water
1 cup brown sugar
2 Tbs. butter
½ cup flour

Line a 9-inch pie plate with pastry dough. Chill while preparing the filling. Combine vinegar, water and sugar in a saucepan. Bring to boil and cook 3 minutes. Add butter and stir until melted. Mix flour with just enough cold water to make a smooth paste. Stir slowly into the hot butter-syrup. Cook, stirring constantly, until thickened and smooth. Pour filling into pie shell. Crimp edges of shell. Lay on the lattice strips. Press ends of strips securely to edge of crust. Bake at 450° F. for 10 minutes; reduce

heat to 350° F. and bake 25 minutes longer. Serve hot or cold.
Serves 6 to 8.

NOTE: If desired, spices may be added to the hot syrup—cinnamon, nutmeg, mace or allspice—singly or in combination.

## ★ *Lemon Chess Pie*

4 eggs
2 cups sugar
1 Tb. flour
1 Tb. cornmeal
¼ cup half-and-half

¼ cup butter, melted and cooled
¼ cup strained fresh lemon juice
1 Tb. grated lemon rind
1 unbaked 8-inch pie shell

Beat eggs until thick and lemon-colored. Combine sugar, flour and cornmeal. Mix thoroughly. Add dry ingredients to the eggs a bit at a time. Add butter and lemon juice in the order given, beating after each addition. Stir in the grated lemon rind. Pour into unbaked pie shell and bake at 375° F. for 40 minutes. Serve hot or cold. Serves 6.

Sweetened condensed milk is used in many Texas desserts and it gives a rather special richness and consistency.

## ★ *Lemon Meringue Pie*

1 crumb crust for 8-inch pie
½ cup strained fresh lemon juice
1 tsp. grated lemon peel
15-oz. can Eagle Brand Sweetened
   Condensed milk

3 eggs, separated
¼ tsp. cream of tartar
¼ cup sugar

Prepare crumb crust, press into 8-inch pie plate and chill. Combine lemon juice with grated rind and gradually stir it into the condensed milk. Beat the egg yolks slightly, add to milk mixture and beat again. Pour into chilled pie shell. Beat egg whites until stiff but not dry with cream of tartar. Beat in the sugar gradually. When glossy, pile meringue in ring around edge of pie. Bake at 325° F. for 15 minutes or until lightly browned. Serve cold. Serves 6.

This is a very typical Texas household specialty—and a good one, too.

## ★ Oatmeal Pie

| | |
|---|---|
| 4 eggs | ½ cup oatmeal |
| ⅔ cup white sugar | ½ cup shredded coconut |
| 1 cup brown sugar | ½ cup chopped pecans |
| 2 Tbs. butter, softened | 1 unbaked 8-inch pie shell |
| 1 tsp. vanilla | |

Beat eggs and then beat in the sugars bit by bit. Beat in butter and vanilla. Stir in oatmeal, coconut and pecans. Pour into unbaked pie shell. Bake at 375° F. for 35 minutes. Serves 6.

Sour milk has always been widely used in rural cookery—not only because of its cooking qualities (which are excellent), but its flavor as well. In addition, there was always an economic factor in its use; nothing was wasted. Today, commercial buttermilk takes the place of sour milk; the dishes made with it are quite as delicious.

## ★ Buttermilk Pie

| | |
|---|---|
| ½ cup buttermilk | 1 tsp. vanilla |
| 2 cups sugar | ¼ tsp. cinnamon |
| ⅛ lb. butter (½ stick), melted | 1 pinch nutmeg |
| 3 eggs, beaten | 1 unbaked 8-inch pie shell |

In a mixing bowl, combine buttermilk with sugar and butter. Add eggs and beat together thoroughly. Stir in vanilla and seasonings. Pour into unbaked pie shell. Bake at 350° F. for 45 minutes or until golden brown. Serve warm or ice cold. Serves 6.

A favorite pie everywhere in Texas is this super-rich Banana Cream Pie.

## ★ Banana Cream Pie

| | |
|---|---|
| ⅔ cup sugar | 1 tsp. lemon juice |
| 3½ Tbs. cornstarch | ½ tsp. vanilla |
| ½ tsp. salt | 1 tsp. rum |
| 2½ cups milk | 2 ripe bananas, sliced |
| 1 Tb. butter | 1 baked 9-inch pie shell |
| 3 eggs, separated | 3 Tbs. confectioner's sugar |
| 1 ripe banana, mashed | |

Combine sugar, cornstarch, salt and milk in top of double boiler; blend. Place over hot water. Cook, stirring constantly, until thickened. Stir in butter and cook over lowest heat, stirring occasionally, 15 minutes longer. Beat egg yolks until thick and lemon-colored. *Slowly* pour the hot milk mixture into the yolks, beating as you do so. Mix mashed banana with lemon juice, vanilla and rum. Stir into egg yolk custard. Arrange sliced bananas over bottom of unbaked pie shell. Cover with custard. Let stand at room temperature until cool and firm, then chill. Before serving, whip egg whites until stiff but not dry, then beat in sugar. Make circle of meringue around top of pie. If desired, brown meringue quickly and lightly under broiler before serving. Serves 8 or 10.

# TWENTY-SEVEN

## *CANDY*

N O T infrequently you will find that dessert is omitted from an informal-party dinner menu and, instead, pralines may be served or some other similar sweet, which outside of Texas would be thought of as simply a candy. Here are some Buttermilk Pralines:

★  *Buttermilk Pralines*

2 cups sugar
1 cup buttermilk
1 tsp. soda
1 Tb. light corn syrup (Karo)

1½ cups chopped pecans
1 Tb. vanilla
¼ cup butter

Combine sugar, buttermilk, soda and syrup in a saucepan. Over moderate heat, cook to soft ball stage (234° to 240° F. on your candy thermometer). Remove from heat. Add pecans, vanilla and butter. Stir until butter has melted. Cool until mixture begins to thicken. Drop by spoonfuls onto sheets of waxed paper.

NOTE: Watch this closely once it has been taken from the stove and has had the butter stirred in. It thickens very fast as a rule. If desired, use rum and vanilla, half and half, for your flavoring. Makes 6 to 7 dozen pralines.

*Leche Quemada* is a Mexican sweet often served in Texas in lieu of dessert at the close of a Texas-Mexican meal and sometimes even at the close of buffets.


★ *Leche Quemada*


2 qts. milk
1 lb. sugar

Combine the milk and sugar in your heaviest saucepan and cook over moderate heat until the syrup shows signs of boiling. Reduce heat then to a slow-bubbling simmer and cook for about 2 hours or until the mixture leaves the sides of the pan. It should be a beautiful golden-brown color and very smooth. Stir almost constantly—or should I say at constant, frequent intervals. When done, pour into a greased pan and cool. When cold, cut into squares. A pecan half may be placed on each square. The candy is delectable just as it is, however.


★ *Marshmallow-Pecan Fudge*


¼ lb. sweet butter
1 can evaporated milk, 14-oz. size
1 pinch salt
5 cups sugar
1½ cups semi-sweet chocolate bits
2 cups small marshmallows
1 tsp. vanilla
1½ cups chopped pecans

Combine butter, milk, salt and sugar in a stainless steel or enamel saucepan and cook over low heat, stirring constantly, until sugar is dissolved and butter melted. Increase heat and boil 8 minutes without stirring. Meanwhile combine chocolate bits and marshmallows in a greased bowl. When the syrup is done, pour it immediately over the chocolate mixture. Do not scrape the pan. Stir until chocolate is dissolved. Add vanilla and pecans. Whip until fudge has a thick satiny consistency. Spread on a buttered platter and let cool completely. Cut into squares as desired.

## ★  *Date-Nut Roll*

2 cups sugar
1 can condensed milk, 14-oz. size
2 Tbs. butter

1½ cups pitted dates, cut fine
1 cup chopped pecans

Combine sugar, condensed milk and butter. Cook over low heat, stirring constantly, until the mixture reaches a boil. Continue cooking until your candy thermometer registers 240° F. Remove from heat. Add dates and nuts. Stir until mixture thickens. Form into 2 rolls, 1½ inches in diameter. Wrap each in a damp cloth. Chill until firm; or, store in cool, dry place at least 24 to 48 hours before slicing. Cut into ¼-inch slices and store in tin box with wax paper between layers. Makes about 3 dozen.

And that brings us to the close of this particular tour through the wide world of Texas cooking. That there are other tours to take, rest assured; but this is enough for one trip. I trust you have enjoyed it as much as I have.

# Index